PEARSON

Dawn Parrish Wood • Mary E. Pascarella

Essentials of Microsoft® Office Project 2007

Custom Edition

With Contributions by David Foley

Taken from:
Essentials Microsoft® Office Project 2003
by Dawn Parrish Wood and Mary E. Pascarella

ISBN 10: 1-256-67157-6
ISBN 13: 978-1-256-67157-2

Dedications

Dawn Parrish Wood

I would like to dedicate this series of books to my supportive and loving family. I especially want to thank my husband, Kenneth, who encourages me to achieve the highest level of success to which I am able, and helps me to be the best person I can be. To my girls, Micaela and Kendra, who allow me to write while being "Mommy." To my parents, Norman and Wilma, for teaching me that integrity and hard work are not an option in life. To my sister, Mara Thibodeau, for being my best friend and for being proud of me. To my niece, Abby, for just being the miracle that she is and loving her Aunt Dawn.

A hearty thank you to Mary Pascarella too, without whom I couldn't have tackled this project; who keeps me sane in times of confusion; and who is almost as big a perfectionist as I am. It is a pleasure and an honor to work with someone with so much integrity and knowledge. Thanks, Mary, for everything.

Mary E. Pascarella

I would like to dedicate this book to my dear son, Jack.

Acknowledgments

Dawn Parrish Wood

I would like to thank all the staff members involved with the series for their extremely hard work and timeliness in the project, including series authors, editors, production, and marketing staff. Thanks to Jodi McPherson for allowing me the opportunity to work on such a fine series. Thanks to our technical editor, Donna Clements, for using an extra fine-tooth comb to review the book so we could produce the highest quality product for the students and instructors. Another thanks to Anne Garcia, Alana Meyers, Melissa Sabella, and Trisha O'Shea for coordinating efforts and managing the development process of the books and supplements. A very special thanks to the series editors, Marianne Fox Metzelaar and Larry Metzelaar, whose comments, suggestions, experience, and assistance were most helpful.

Mary E. Pascarella

This book would not have happened without the expertise and friendship of my colleague Dawn Wood, who made working on this book a pleasure. Her knowledge, professionalism, and sense of humor are invaluable. Thanks to Jodi McPherson, who provided me with the opportunity to write this book. I'd also like to thank our series editors, Larry C. Metzelaar and Marianne Fox, for their guidance. Finally, I'd like to thank the entire *Essentials* team: Alana Meyers, Melissa Sabella, Trisha O'Shea, April Montana, Angela Urquhart, and Donna Clements for their dedication in creating such a fine series.

About the Authors

Dawn Parrish Wood—Dawn Wood provides software training and freelance writing through her own business, Technically Speaking Consultants. She teaches customized courses to local businesses and individuals to upgrade employee skills and knowledge of computers. She also teaches at Valdosta Technical College in Valdosta, Georgia, as an adjunct instructor. She also earned MOS Excel XP Expert certification. In the past, she worked for Valdosta Technical College as the computer coordinator/lead instructor for the Continuing Education department. Prior to teaching, she worked as a technical support representative and technical writer for a software firm. She lives in Valdosta, Georgia, with her husband, Kenneth, and their two daughters, Micaela (8 years) and Kendra (6 years).

Mary E. Pascarella—Mary Pascarella specializes in project management, database design and development, and computer training and support through her company, JMP Consulting, Inc. She has worked in many different types of industries providing training and end-user support. She has done extensive contract work for Lucent Technologies on several training implementation and Web portal projects.

Prior to owning JMP Consulting, Mary began work as a corporate computer training specialist providing classroom-based, instructor-led training and end-user support at several large corporations in the South Florida area. Upon moving to Valdosta, Georgia, she became the computer coordinator for the Business and Industry Services department at Valdosta Technical Institute. She later joined Ambling Companies as their software implementation specialist, where she managed the rollout of a suite of property management software.

Mary is a graduate of the University of Kansas with a degree in English, and lives in South Georgia with her husband John and daughter Grace.

David Foley is the Director of Project Management for LHP Software, Inc. where he manages a staff of project managers for the entire company. He has worked for more than 25 years in the automotive and aerospace industries where he has managed and delivered complex embedded software systems. Prior to joining LHP Software, he worked for Cummins Engine Company and McDonnell-Douglas. He is an expert in the management and development of software systems and also has applied experience in quality assurance and process improvement. He is a graduate of Rose Hullman Institute of Technology where he received a B.S. in Electrical Engineering. He resides in Columbus, Indiana where he lives with his wife, Nancy, and their two children, Patrick (16), and Rachel (14).

Contents at a Glance

Table of Contents

PROJECT 4   SCHEDULING RESOURCES AND ASSIGNING COSTS   99

PROJECT 5   MODIFYING TASK INFORMATION   135

PROJECT 6   MODIFYING TASKS USING THE GANTT CHART   171

PROJECT 7   CUSTOMIZING MICROSOFT PROJECT AND SHARING INFORMATION   205

PROJECT 8   INTEGRATING PROJECT DATA   243

Introduction

Essentials courseware from Prentice Hall Information Technology is anchored in the practical and professional needs of all types of students.

The *Essentials* series is conceived around a learning-by-doing approach that encourages you to grasp application-related concepts as you expand your skills through hands-on tutorials. As such, it consists of modular lessons that are built around a series of numbered, step-by-step procedures that are clear, concise, and easy to review.

The end-of-project exercises have likewise been carefully constructed, from the routine Checking Concepts and Terms to creative tasks in the Discovery Zone that prod you into extending what you've learned into areas beyond the explicit scope of the lessons proper.

How to Use This Book

Typically, each *Essentials* book is divided into eight projects. A project covers one area (or a few closely related areas) of application functionality. Each project consists of six to nine lessons that are related to that topic. Each lesson presents a specific task or closely related set of tasks in a manageable chunk that is easy to assimilate and retain.

Each element in the *Essentials* book is designed to maximize your learning experience. A list of the *Essentials* project elements and a description of how each element can help you follows. To find out more about the rationale behind each book element and how to use each to your maximum benefit, take the following walk-through.

Typeface Conventions Used in This Book

Essentials Microsoft Office 2007 uses the following typeface conventions to make it easier for you to understand the material.

Key terms appear in ***italic and bold*** the first time they are defined in a project.

Monospace type appears frequently and `looks like this`. It is used to indicate text that you are instructed to key in.

Italic text indicates text that appears onscreen as (1) warnings, confirmation, or general information; (2) the name of a file to be used in a lesson or exercise; and (3) text from a menu or dialog box that is referenced within a sentence, when that sentence might appear awkward if it were not set off.

Hotkeys are indicated by underline. Hotkeys are the underlined letters in menus, toolbars, and dialog boxes that activate commands and options, and are a quick way to choose frequently used commands and options. Hotkeys look like this: <u>F</u>ile, <u>S</u>ave.

TAKING A TOUR OF PROJECT 2007

OBJECTIVES

IN THIS PROJECT, YOU LEARN HOW TO

- **Start Microsoft Project, open a project, and save a project**

- **Explore the Project window**

- **Understand the task table**

- **Understand the timeline in Gantt Chart view**

- **Preview and print a standard report**

- **Get Help**

- **Close a project and exit Microsoft Project**

WHY WOULD I DO THIS?

Microsoft Project is a project management program used by project and resource managers to collaborate, administer, track, and analyze project information. Managers use projects primarily for organizing and analyzing the details involved with achieving a specific goal or objective. With little effort, you can manage an advertising campaign, introduce a new inventory system in a production plant, balance caseloads in a law firm, and much more.

A *project* is a self-contained group of tasks performed to achieve a specific objective. Projects are temporary, lasting only until a specific goal is met. Some projects, such as planning a birthday party, are simple and require only a few tasks. Some projects are complex, such as building a house, preparing a legal case, or creating a new software application. Simple projects may require only one person, while projects that are more complex require a team of people or even several departments or companies. Regardless of the complexity, every project has a definite start and finish date. Although few businesspersons would classify themselves as project managers, in reality many professionals are informal project managers. A *project manager* is simply one who oversees all stages of a project plan. Many professions—such as construction, engineering, architecture, and law—are project-based.

A project is comprised of a series of *tasks*—specific activities that have a start date, duration, and completion time. Time, resources, and cost usually limit each project. A *resource* is anything needed to complete the task, and each task has at least one resource. For example, a resource may be an employee, a vendor, a conference room, a building, or equipment. Finally, the project manager must consider the overall expenditure of a project.

Microsoft Project is a powerful organizing tool for project management. Microsoft Project stores the details of the project plan in its database. Then, it uses the information you provide to calculate and maintain the project plan's schedule and costs. As you make changes to individual tasks, Microsoft Project adjusts the schedule, resources, and costs accordingly. There are two versions of Microsoft Project: Project Standard and Project Professional. This book and its figures are based on Microsoft Project 2007 Standard. Microsoft templates are the basis for some of the project plans used in this book. A *template* is a model providing generic tasks and resources, which you can then modify to suit your individual project plan specifications. The lesson files used in this book are designed to be fun and smaller in scale, outlining projects the average person might encounter so as to demonstrate the usefulness, benefits, and features of Microsoft Project.

This initial project in your text illustrates how Microsoft Project organizes and assists the user in managing a project. After you start Microsoft Project and open a sample project—the development of a marketing brochure—you explore the elements that comprise the project environment as well as the main features of the program. You view the tasks involved in the brochure project, view the schedule, and print a report. You also learn how to use Help to access more information about Microsoft Project.

V I S U A L   S U M M A R Y

Unless you change the original settings, a project file displays in Gantt Chart view when you open it in Microsoft Project. **Gantt Chart view** contains the task table and the Gantt chart for a project file. A **Gantt chart** is a project management tool that can be used to represent the timing of tasks required to finish a project and to measure the progress toward completing the tasks. Gantt charts were developed by Henry Laurence Gantt (1861–1919), a mechanical engineer, as a visual tool to show scheduled and actual progress of large-scale engineering projects.

In Microsoft Project, the Gantt Chart view has two main areas. A list of tasks, called the **task table,** displays on the left side of the window. Each column of data in the task table represents a **field** of data for each task in the project, such as task name, start date, and finish date. The Gantt chart displays on the right side of the window and has two parts: the timeline and timescale (see Figure 1.1). The **timescale,** which in the sample is the calendar month and day, appears across the top of the Gantt chart. The **timeline** is the horizontal bar graph.

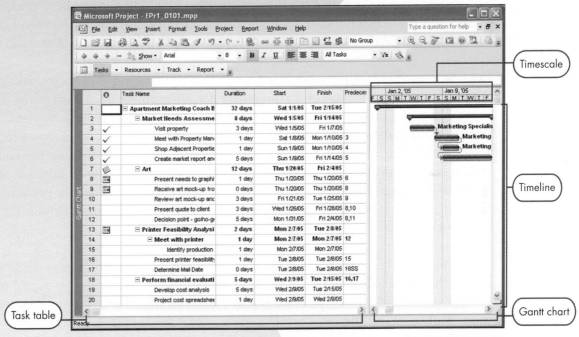

FIGURE 1.1

In this initial text project, you open the brochure project shown in Figure 1.1. You glimpse the power of the Microsoft Project program as you explore this predesigned project. You view the schedule, the timeline, and a sample report. You also print the report and use Help.

LESSON 1:   Starting Microsoft Project, Opening a Project, and Saving a Project

To understand the planning phase of a project, you must first grasp the fundamentals of a simple project plan. Project plans must clearly state a specific and measurable goal. Generally, project plans are measured in time and money. How long will it take, and how much will it cost? Once a project is defined, the planning stage ensues. The planning stage involves laying the groundwork for the project. Usually a project manager is put in place; a project manager oversees all aspects of a project, including the assignment of tasks, resources, and budgeting. During the planning stage of a project, the project manager and/or project team lay out an approximation of the costs, identify ***stakeholders*** (key players), and state the project deliverables. Planning is crucial so that stakeholders do not make unrealistic assumptions or assign unavailable resources. A ***constraint*** is a condition that you cannot overlook or ignore for a task's completion. If the project manager identifies all constraints and potential obstacles from the outset, the project has a greater chance of finishing on time and within budget.

The project manager is responsible for coordinating tasks and resources and must manage the budget and time constraints. The project manager must also communicate all deliverables, inform project stakeholders of the overall progress, and coordinate any changes to the plan.

Once you complete the planning phase, you can begin creating your project file in Microsoft Project. It contains the tools and utilities to track and manage all aspects of the three critical components of a project plan: budget, time, and scope. Project managers refer to these constraints as the ***constraint triangle.*** The ***budget*** is the amount of money slated to finance the project. It is what the business unit deems the project plan's result is worth. The ***time constraint*** refers to the deadline of the overall project plan as well as how much time each individual task requires. Finally, the ***scope*** of the project plan encompasses the performance expectations (quality). It defines the minimum quality level that is acceptable and is the product of how much time and money is spent.

Once you create a project file by using Microsoft Project, you should save it so you can later reopen the project file and resume working with its data. You can also open and use a project file that someone else developed by using Microsoft Project. If you want to keep revisions, you must save the project file.

Microsoft Project provides a variety of ways to open a file. You can start the process by clicking the Open button on the Standard toolbar, or selecting File, Open on the menu bar (see Figure 1.2). Those actions open the Open dialog box, in which you specify the name and location of the file you want to use.

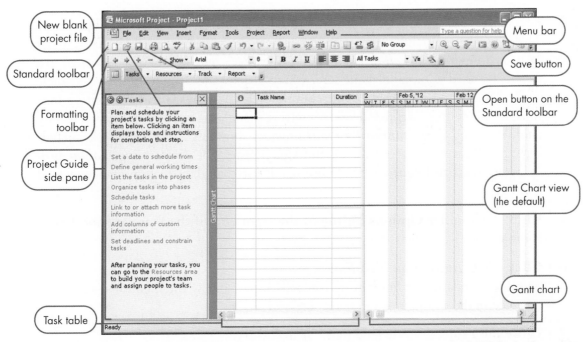

FIGURE 1.2

You save a previously named file under the same name by clicking the Save button on the Standard toolbar or by selecting File, Save on the menu bar. If you are saving a project for the first time, or if you want to save an existing project under a new name and/or location, choose the File, Save As command sequence. The Save As dialog box has the same layout as the Open dialog box.

In this lesson, you open the student data file shown in the Visual Summary (refer to Figure 1.1). You then save the file under another name, thus creating a copy of the original. Throughout this book, you work on copies of original data files so that you can restart any lesson or exercise if desired.

To Start Project 2007 and Open a Project

1 **Move the mouse pointer to the Start button; then click the left mouse button.**
The Start button's popup menu displays.

2 **Move the mouse pointer to the *All Programs* menu item.**
You see a listing of available programs on your system.

3 **Move the mouse pointer to the Microsoft Office folder and then to Microsoft Office Project 2007; then click the left mouse button.**
Microsoft Project loads into the computer's memory and a blank project displays (refer to Figure 1.2).

4 **Locate the toolbar area below the menu bar on your screen (refer to Figure 1.2).**
The *menu bar* contains common menu names that, when activated, display a list of related commands. A *toolbar* is a set of buttons. Each button provides a shortcut to a frequently used command. Your screen may display the default setting of a single toolbar comprised of only the most commonly used Standard and Formatting buttons. In this context, *default* refers to a setting that a program uses unless you specify another setting. The *Standard toolbar* provides shortcuts to common tasks including Save, Print, Cut/Paste (Move), and Copy/Paste. The *Formatting toolbar* provides shortcuts to frequently used commands for changing the appearance of field contents.

5 **Click the Toolbar Options button at the right end of the Standard toolbar.**
A drop-down list opens.

6 **Click *Show Buttons on Two Rows*.**
Separate Standard and Formatting toolbars display below the menu bar—the view reflected in the text figures and hands-on instructions.

7 **Close the Project Guide side pane, if necessary.**

8 **Choose File on the menu bar.**
The File menu opens to display a number of commands.

9 **Choose the Open command.**
The Open dialog box opens.

10 **Click the drop-down arrow at the right end of the *Look in* box, and select the drive and folder containing the student files for this text (see the sample location in Figure 1.3).**

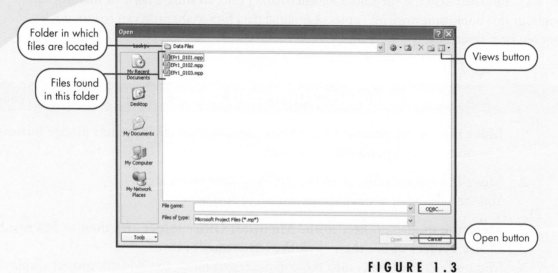

FIGURE 1.3

The *Look in* drop-down list reflects the drives, folders, or files on a specific computer. The drives, folders, and files on your system may be different, depending on the software and hardware on the computer.

If you have problems . . .

Do not be concerned if you see a different arrangement of information from that shown in Figure 1.3. Figures in this text display file extensions, such as .mpp (which indicates a Microsoft Project project). The presence or absence of extensions is a function of a Windows setting specified from the Control Panel. You can use the Views button in either the Open or the Save As dialog box to select one of eight file displays. The icon for the current view displays with a color background and border. Selecting a view is a matter of personal preference; you can apply each option one at a time to see which view you prefer. The figures in this book reflect List view.

11 Click the *EPr1_0101* filename or its icon within the list of files.
EPr1_0101 displays with blue highlighting.

12 Click the **Open** button in the lower-right corner of the Open dialog box.
The apartment brochure project shown in Figure 1.4 opens, and *EPr1_0101* displays in the title bar. The **title bar** displays the name of the software and the name of the active project—either a default name, such as Project1, or a user-determined filename. It also includes buttons at the right end of the bar that you can click to change window size or close the window.

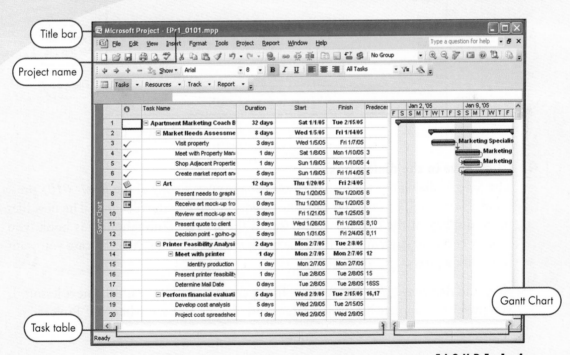

FIGURE 1.4

When you name a file, the filename that you specify must comply with the Windows file-naming rules. You can include numbers, upper- and lowercase letters, spaces, and selected characters such as dashes and underscores. Microsoft Project automatically stores the file in the default file format, adding the .mpp (Microsoft Project project) file extension.

To Save a Copy of a Project

1 **Choose the <u>F</u>ile menu again; then choose the Save <u>A</u>s command.**
The Save As dialog box opens.

2 **In the *File <u>n</u>ame* text box, type `Apartment_Brochure` to replace *EPr1_0101*.**

3 **From the *Save <u>i</u>n* drop-down list, select the appropriate drive and folder for saving the new file (see the sample location in Figure 1.5).**

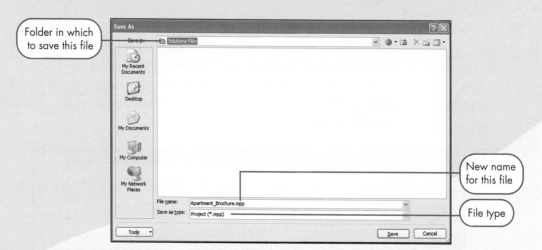

FIGURE 1.5

4 **Click <u>S</u>ave in the dialog box.**
The Save As dialog box closes. Microsoft Project saves a copy of the *EPr1_0101* project as *Apartment_Brochure* and adds the extension *.mpp* to the filename. The new filename displays in the title bar at the top of the screen. Throughout this book, you modify copies of student data files. Each original file remains intact in case you want to rework a project.

Keep the *Apartment_Brochure* project file open and continue with the next lesson. If you prefer to complete the project later, close the file and exit Microsoft Project.

TO EXTEND YOUR KNOWLEDGE . . .

OPENING A FILE
To open a file quickly from the Open dialog box, double-click the file's name, or the icon that precedes its name, in the list of files. You can also display the Open dialog box by clicking the Open button on the Standard toolbar (refer to Figure 1.2).

LESSON 2:   Exploring the Project Window

The project window consists of a title bar and six additional sections: the menu bar, one or more toolbars, the Project Guide (or one of five task panes), the entry bar, task table, and Gantt chart. At times a task pane, rather than the Project Guide, displays at the left side of the screen. These elements form the Project work environment (see Figure 1.6).

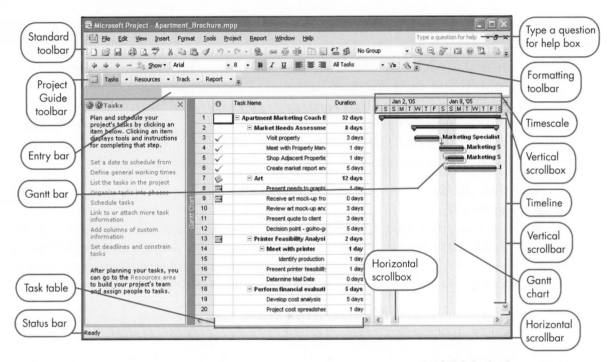

FIGURE 1.6

Table 1.1 explains other elements shown in Figure 1.6 that relate specifically to Microsoft Project.

TABLE 1.1 SELECTED PROJECT-RELATED ELEMENTS

SCREEN ELEMENT	DESCRIPTION
Entry bar	A bar that displays the contents of the current field.
Project Guide toolbar	A toolbar that provides access to step-by-step instructions and wizards in four different goal areas: task creation, resource assignment, task tracking, and project reporting.
Timescale	The time period legend appearing across the top of the Gantt chart.
Timeline	The graph area of a Gantt chart.
Gantt bar	A horizontal bar within a Gantt chart showing task information, due date, and task dependencies.

Microsoft Project features easy access to onscreen Help. For example, the *Type a question for help box* near the right end of the menu bar enables you to specify a new Help topic or redisplay a previous Help topic. You learn how to access Help in a variety of ways in Lesson 6.

For a quick start to learning the power of Microsoft Project, launch the program and explore the work environment. The following steps guide you through the process.

To Identify Parts of a Project

1 | **Open the *Apartment_Brochure* file, if necessary; then locate the Project Guide toolbar and the entry bar (refer to Figure 1.6).**
The Project Guide toolbar helps you learn, explore, and use features as you work through the project management process. The entry bar displays the contents of the current (active) field. If the Project Guide toolbar is not onscreen, choose <u>V</u>iew, <u>T</u>oolbars, Project Guide.

2 | **Click the Tasks button on the Project Guide toolbar (refer to Figure 1.6).**
The Tasks side pane opens. A *side pane* is an overall project guide that appears to the left side of the Microsoft Project window when you click the corresponding button on the Project Guide toolbar. It provides links to topics that guide you through the steps of creating a basic project. The Tasks side pane provides assistance with task-related steps.

3 | **Click the *List the tasks in the project* link.**
The List Tasks content displays. There are several methods for entering tasks in a project.

4 | **Position the mouse pointer on the Show/Hide Project Guide button on the Project Guide toolbar.**
The name of the button displays in a ScreenTip (see Figure 1.7).

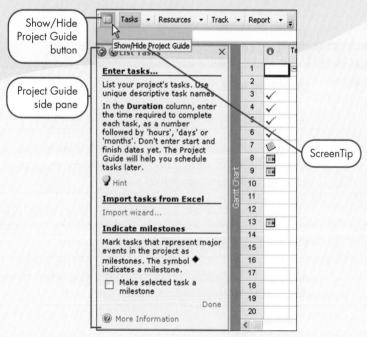

FIGURE 1.7

5 | **Click the Show/Hide Project Guide button.**

The side pane closes. The project window extends to both sides of the screen.

6 | **Locate the status bar near the bottom of the screen (refer to Figure 1.6).**

The *status bar* provides information about the current actions or settings.

7 | **Move to various project locations of your choice, using scrollbar features.**

The *scrollbar* enables you to move the project window vertically and horizontally so that you can see other parts of the work area. Notice that there are two horizontal scrollbars—one for the task table area and one for the Gantt chart. However, there is only one vertical scrollbar, which controls the task table and the Gantt chart movements simultaneously. A *scrollbox* is an object within a horizontal or vertical scrollbar that you can drag. Dragging the scrollbox quickly shifts the display within a window in the direction that you drag the scrollbox. You can also scroll by clicking and holding down the arrow at either end of a scrollbar or by clicking once either above or below the scrollbox to move a page at a time.

8 | **Press** Ctrl + Home **.**

Pressing Home while holding down Ctrl moves you quickly to the beginning of the task table.

Keep the *Apartment_Brochure* project file open and continue with the next lesson. If you prefer to complete the project later, close the file and exit Microsoft Project.

TO EXTEND YOUR KNOWLEDGE . . .

DISPLAYING THE PROJECT GUIDE OPTIONS WITHOUT DISPLAYING THE SIDE PANE

You can display the list of options for the Project Guide without displaying the Project Guide side pane by clicking the arrows on the Project Guide toolbar buttons (Tasks, Resources, Track, Report) rather than the buttons themselves.

LESSON 3:   Understanding the Task Table

Individual tasks are listed in the task table, one component of the Gantt Chart view. A *task table* is a table containing fields that relate to tasks. Microsoft Project contains many predefined tables and also allows the creation of custom tables. The default task table is the *entry table,* which is used to enter and edit tasks. The task table resembles an Excel worksheet, arranging data in a row and column format. Each row is numbered and that number comprises the *Task ID.* Columns represent a category of information called a *field.* By default, the entry table contains the following fields: Indicator, Task Name, Duration, Start Date, Finish Date, Predecessors, and Resource Names. Rows contain one complete record of information, in this case a task.

In this lesson, you explore the *Apartment_Brochure* project. This project file is comprised of many levels of tasks needed to create a marketing brochure for an apartment complex. Several tasks belong to more than one resource. Some tasks are partially completed while others are complete.

To View Individual Tasks

1 **Open the *Apartment_Brochure* file, if necessary; then in the task table area of the Gantt Chart view, point the mouse pointer to the first column of Task 3 (*Visit property*).**

The first column in the Gantt chart task table has a letter *i* within a blue circle as the column header. This column is the **indicator column,** which displays icons, where appropriate, to provide general information about a task. When you point to an icon next to a particular task, a ScreenTip appears with information about task completion (see Figure 1.8). Task 3 is complete.

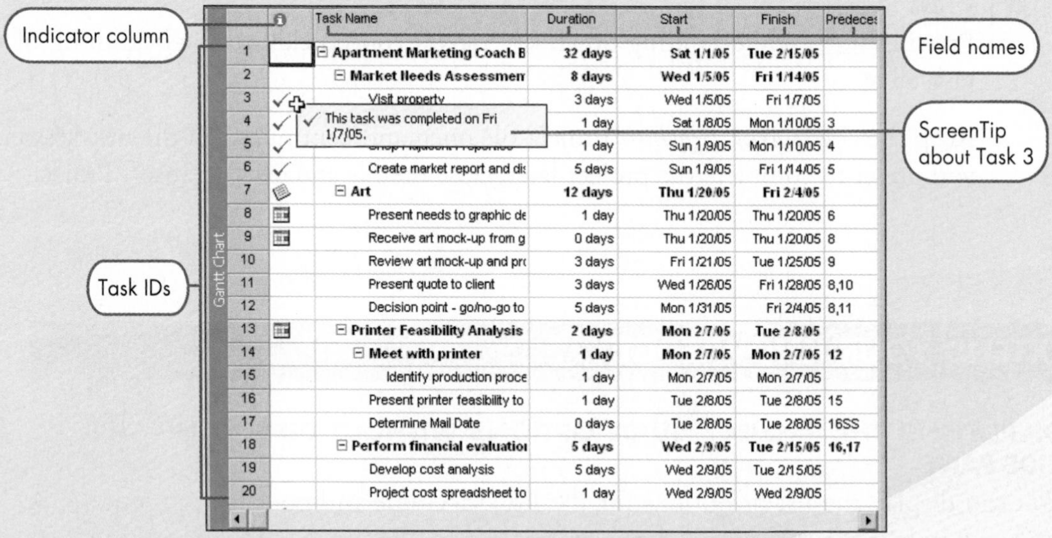

		Task Name	Duration	Start	Finish	Predece:
1		⊟ Apartment Marketing Coach B	32 days	Sat 1/1/05	Tue 2/15/05	
2		⊟ Market Needs Assessmen	8 days	Wed 1/5/05	Fri 1/14/05	
3	✓	Visit property	3 days	Wed 1/5/05	Fri 1/7/05	
4	✓	This task was completed on Fri 1/7/05.	1 day	Sat 1/8/05	Mon 1/10/05	3
5	✓		1 day	Sun 1/9/05	Mon 1/10/05	4
6	✓	Create market report and di:	5 days	Sun 1/9/05	Fri 1/14/05	5
7	📋	⊟ Art	12 days	Thu 1/20/05	Fri 2/4/05	
8	🔲	Present needs to graphic de	1 day	Thu 1/20/05	Thu 1/20/05	6
9	🔲	Receive art mock-up from g	0 days	Thu 1/20/05	Thu 1/20/05	8
10		Review art mock-up and pro	3 days	Fri 1/21/05	Tue 1/25/05	9
11		Present quote to client	3 days	Wed 1/26/05	Fri 1/28/05	8,10
12		Decision point - go/no-go to	5 days	Mon 1/31/05	Fri 2/4/05	8,11
13	🔲	⊟ Printer Feasibility Analysis	2 days	Mon 2/7/05	Tue 2/8/05	
14		⊟ Meet with printer	1 day	Mon 2/7/05	Mon 2/7/05	12
15		Identify production proce	1 day	Mon 2/7/05	Mon 2/7/05	
16		Present printer feasibility to	1 day	Tue 2/8/05	Tue 2/8/05	15
17		Determine Mail Date	0 days	Tue 2/8/05	Tue 2/8/05	16SS
18		⊟ Perform financial evaluatior	5 days	Wed 2/9/05	Tue 2/15/05	16,17
19		Develop cost analysis	5 days	Wed 2/9/05	Tue 2/15/05	
20		Project cost spreadsheet to	1 day	Wed 2/9/05	Wed 2/9/05	

Labels: Indicator column; Field names; ScreenTip about Task 3; Task IDs; Gantt Chart

FIGURE 1.8

If you have problems . . .

ScreenTips appear for only a short time. If the ScreenTip disappears and you want to redisplay it, move the mouse pointer away and then back again, and the ScreenTip reappears.

2 **Move your mouse pointer to the Task Name field for Task 8 (*Present needs to graphic designer*).**

A ScreenTip displays the entire task name. Because of the width of the column, the task name is not fully visible.

3 **Point the mouse pointer to the indicator column for Task 7 (*Art*) and pause on the icon.**

A ScreenTip appears with a note (see Figure 1.9).

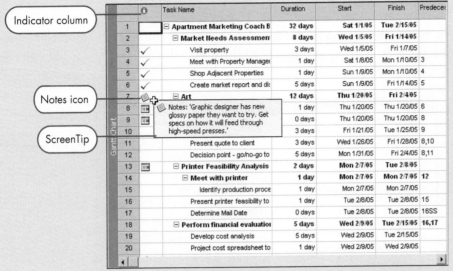

FIGURE 1.9

4 | **Click the right-pointing arrow on the horizontal scrollbar of the task table until the last column displays.**

The Resource Names column displays. Notice the various departments that are responsible for various tasks within this project.

5 | **Scroll back to the left and position the mouse pointer in the indicator column for Task 9 (*Receive art mock-up from graphic team*).**

The ScreenTip indicates that this task has a constraint—there is a certain condition that cannot be ignored for this task's completion. Also, notice that the duration for this task is zero days. This task is a *milestone* task, meaning that it marks the completion of one or more tasks yet has no duration of its own. *Duration* is the length of time needed for task completion as well as the completion of the overall project.

6 | **Double-click anywhere in the Task 9 row.**

The Task Information dialog box opens (see Figure 1.10). This dialog box shows detailed information about a task, and you can use it to alter the properties of a task.

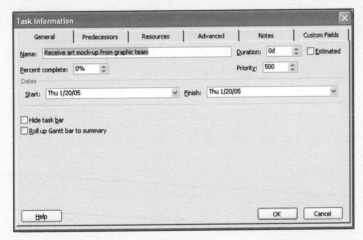

FIGURE 1.10

7 **Click the Advanced tab.**

Notice the details of the task (see Figure 1.11). The Advanced tab shows supplemental data about a task, such as any constraints (deadlines) or any special calendar applied to that task.

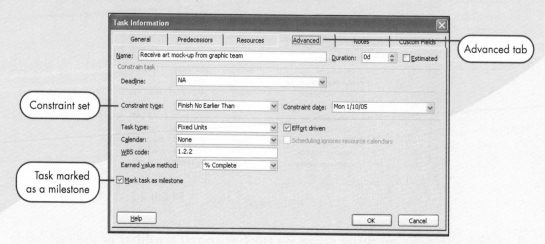

FIGURE 1.11

8 **Click Cancel and then press** Ctrl + Home.

Keep the *Apartment_Brochure* project file open and continue with the next lesson. If you prefer to complete the project later, close the file and exit Microsoft Project.

TO EXTEND YOUR KNOWLEDGE . . .

HIDING A COLUMN IN THE TASK TABLE

At some time, you may need to hide a column in the task table. For example, you may want to print a copy of the task table, but you do not need the predecessor column. To hide a column, right-click within that column and select *Hide Column*. To unhide the column, right-click within the task table headings and select *Insert Column*. Then choose the column name from the drop-down list and click *Best fit* to ensure the column width is readable. The new column is inserted to the left of the selected column.

LESSON 4: Understanding the Timeline in Gantt Chart View

The default view for Microsoft project is Gantt Chart view, which includes the task table and the Gantt chart. A Gantt bar represents the duration for each task in the timeline of the Gantt chart.. Gantt charts also display *task links* (or *task dependencies*), indicating when the start or finish of one task depends upon the start or completion of another task.

The Gantt chart includes a timescale in the top portion of the chart. The timescale includes dates and the days of the week. Gantt bars represent each task in the timeline. Gantt bars are shown in the appropriate time window for the task duration. The Gantt bar style indicates the task type of the task.

In this lesson, you explore the timeline and identify a task type by its Gantt bar.

To Use the Gantt Chart

1 **Open the Apartment_Brochure file, if necessary; then move the mouse pointer to the split bar separating the task table and the Gantt chart.**
The mouse changes to a resizing shape (see Figure 1.12).

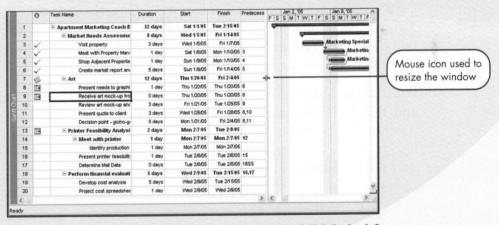

Mouse icon used to resize the window

FIGURE 1.12

2 **Drag the border to the left until the Gantt chart takes up about ⅔ of the window.**
Now you can see more of the Gantt chart and less of the task table.

3 **Use the horizontal scrollbar in the Gantt chart to display Tasks 3–6 and point to the second summary task bar above them, if necessary (see Figure 1.13).**

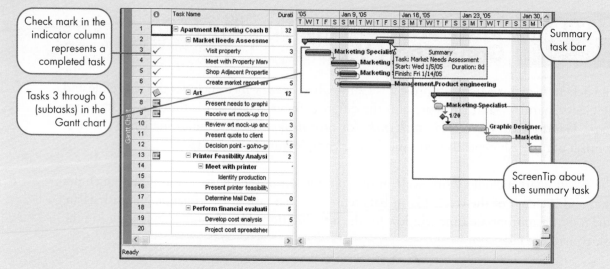

Check mark in the indicator column represents a completed task

Tasks 3 through 6 (subtasks) in the Gantt chart

Summary task bar

ScreenTip about the summary task

FIGURE 1.13

A ScreenTip with the task name, task type, start date, finish date, and duration appears (refer to Figure 1.13). A *summary task* is a task that consists of additional tasks called *subtasks* (mini-tasks) indented and listed below it.

Summary tasks appear bold in the task table. Each summary task can be expanded to view the subtasks below it or collapsed so that the subtasks are not visible. You expand or collapse a summary task by clicking on the plus or minus sign that appears to the left of the task name in the task table. To complete a summary task, you must complete all subtasks. A summary task is represented by a solid black Gantt bar expanding across all subtask Gantt bars in the Gantt chart. Notice that Gantt bars for Tasks 3–6 have black lines through them. The black line indicates the percent of completion of a task. When the black line is the length of the Gantt bar, it indicates a completed task, just like a check mark in the indicator column in the task table.

4   **Point to the blue line between Task 6 (*Create market report and distribute*) and Task 8 (*Present needs to graphic designer*).**
A ScreenTip about the task relationship appears (see Figure 1.14). The blue arrow linking Tasks 6 and 8 designates a task link, which defines a dependency between the start and finish dates of two tasks. In other words, Task 8 cannot begin until Task 6 is complete.

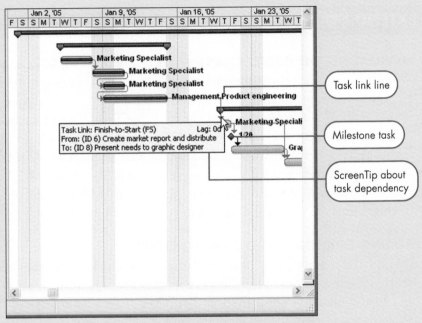

FIGURE 1.14

5 | **Point to the black diamond beside Task 9 (*Receive art mock-up from graphic team*).**

A ScreenTip about the task appears (see Figure 1.15). The black diamond beside Task 9 indicates that this task is a milestone. Remember, a milestone task is a task that has no duration but is essential for project completion.

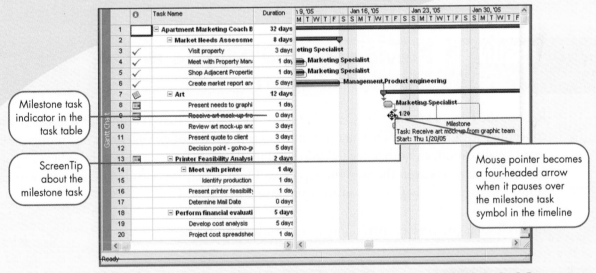

FIGURE 1.15

6 | **Scroll through the rest of the chart to view other tasks and Gantt bars. When finished, return to the top-left position on the timeline.**

Keep the *Apartment_Brochure* project file open and continue with the next lesson. If you prefer to complete the project later, close the file and exit Microsoft Project.

TO EXTEND YOUR KNOWLEDGE . . .

NAVIGATING THE GANTT CHART WITH THE VERTICAL SCROLLBAR

When working with the Gantt chart, it can be a bit confusing to find the specific Gantt bar you want to view. You can click and hold down your mouse on the vertical scrollbox to display a ScreenTip with the Task ID and Task Name of the Gantt bar that is currently in view. To move to a particular Task ID, you can scroll vertically and both the Task table and the Gantt chart move simultaneously. Pointing the mouse and pausing on a Gantt bar displays the Task ID and the Task Name as well and can help you orient yourself. In addition, clicking on a Gantt bar highlights the task in the task table.

ADDING GRIDLINES TO THE GANTT CHART

If you have trouble seeing the correlation between the task table and the Gantt chart, adding gridlines in the Gantt chart may prove helpful. To do so, right-click within the Gantt chart and select *Gridlines*. Select *Gantt Rows* in the *Line to change* list and select the gridline type and color you desire.

USING THE VIEW BAR IN MICROSOFT PROJECT

Gantt Chart view is the default view in Microsoft Project, but there are many other helpful views. You can change the view using the View Bar. To utilize the View Bar, choose <u>V</u>iew, <u>V</u>iew Bar. A task pane displays that lists all the view types available, and the current view has a yellow square behind it. Click the name of the view you wish to see.

LESSON 5:   Previewing and Printing a Standard Report

Reports are essential to the effective use of Microsoft Project. Reports summarize the activities concerned with a project. They are useful for keeping track of completions, upcoming tasks, resource allocation, and other needed information. Before printing a report, it is always a good idea to preview onscreen the way the report will look when it is printed. That way, you can adjust the page setup before you print—and save a tree as well.

In this lesson, you preview two standard reports and print one.

To Use Buttons to Preview and Print

1 **Open the *Apartment_Brochure* file, if necessary; then select <u>R</u>eport and then <u>R</u>eports from the menu.**
The Reports dialog box opens (see Figure 1.16). There are six report categories: Overview, Current Activities, Costs, Assignments, Workload, and Custom. Within each category are more specific report types.

FIGURE 1.16

2 Click the <u>A</u>ssignments button and then click <u>S</u>elect.
The Assignment Reports dialog box opens. More specific report options are now available.

3 Click <u>W</u>ho Does What, if necessary, and then click <u>S</u>elect.
A preview of the report displays (see Figure 1.17).

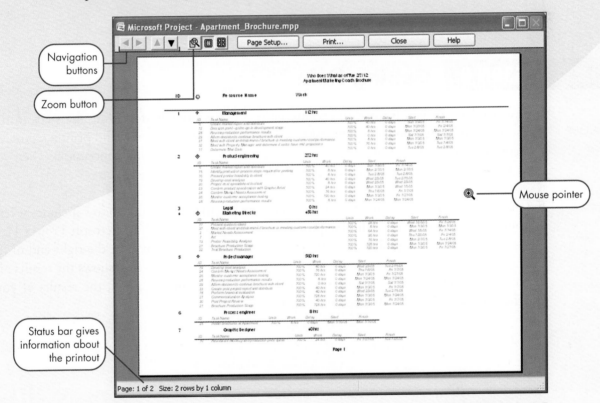

FIGURE 1.17

4 Click the Zoom button; then scroll through the window to view the report.

5 Click inside the report preview area.
The report returns to full screen view.

6 Click <u>P</u>rint on the toolbar.
The Print dialog box opens.

7 | **Click OK (or click Cancel if you do not want to print at this time).**
Microsoft Project sends the report to the default printer (or cancels printing).

8 | **Click Close and then click Close again.**
The Reports dialog box closes.

Keep the *Apartment_Brochure* project file open and continue with the next lesson. If you prefer to complete the project later, close the file and exit Microsoft Project.

TO EXTEND YOUR KNOWLEDGE . . .

PRINTING THE INFORMATION IN THE GANTT CHART VIEW
You can print a copy of the project window by simply choosing File, Print or by clicking the Print button on the Standard toolbar.

LESSON 6: Getting Help

In just five lessons, you learned to execute quite a few actions by following the steps in this text—open and save a project, view tasks, use the Gantt Chart, preview and print a report. As you continue to use the program on your own, there likely will be many occasions when you don't know the steps to produce a desired result.

Extensive help is built into all Office programs. The Microsoft Project window includes several methods for accessing Help: the Help option on the menu bar, the Microsoft Project Help button on the Standard toolbar, and the *Type a question for help* box near the right end of the menu bar (see Figure 1.18). Figure 1.19, in the exercise steps that follow, shows the results of a Help topic search. Because Microsoft continually updates online Help, the results of your searches may vary from the figures in this book.

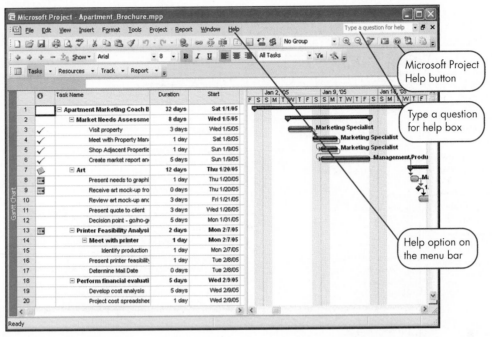

FIGURE 1.18

To get information quickly about a specific topic, you can type a descriptive word or phrase in the *Type a question for help* box and press ⏎Enter. You do not have to type your request in the form of a question.

The *Type a question for help* box and the Project Help window are likely to be your primary means to get information. You use both of these resources in the following steps. Opportunities to use these and other Help features are also provided throughout the text.

Microsoft's Help support is so extensive that some of its content can be accessed only if you have an Internet connection. The following steps are written as though your Internet connection is active. Additional steps on your part might be necessary to activate a connection as needed.

To Get Help

1 Type `project guide` in the *Type a question for help* box (refer to Figure 1.18); then press ⏎Enter.

After the search is complete, the Project Help window opens and displays the Search results. (see Figure 1.19).

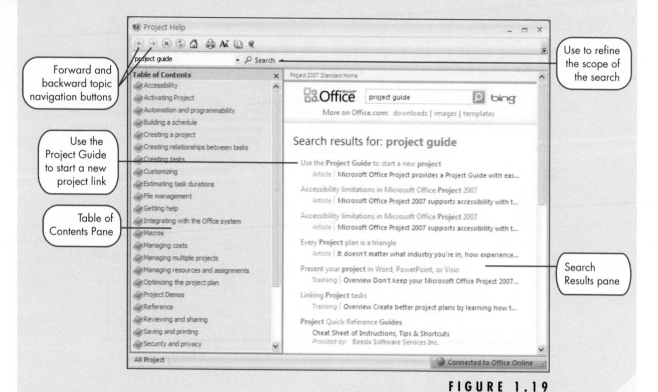

FIGURE 1.19

2	**Click *Use the Project Guide to start a new project* in the Search Results list.**

The selected Help topic appears in the Project Help window (see Figure 1.20). If the Table of Contents pane is open, the selected Help topic is highlighted.

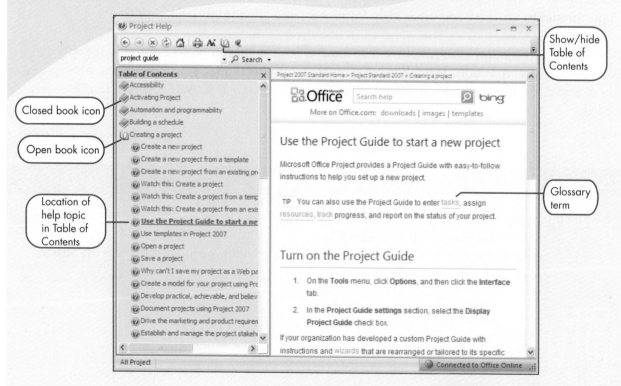

FIGURE 1.20

3 | **Close the Microsoft Project Help window; then close the Search Results task pane.**

4 | **Click Microsoft Project Help on the Standard toolbar.**
The Project Help window displays. You can also press F1 or choose <u>H</u>elp from the menu bar to display the Project Help window.

5 | **Click the *Show Table of Contents* button on the Project Help toolbar.**
The Table of Contents displays (see Figure 1.20). Topics display with closed or open book icons, depending on which topics were recently reviewed. Clicking a closed book icon expands the level of detail in the table of contents. Clicking an open book icon collapses the level of detail. The Table of Contents is available both online and offline.

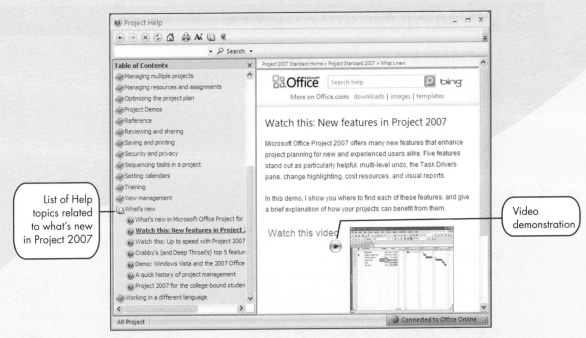

List of Help topics related to what's new in Project 2007

Video demonstration

FIGURE 1.21

6 **Click the *What's new* help topic.**
The What's new book expands into a list of topics. Click on the topic Watch this: New features in Project 2007 (see Figure 1.21). A video demonstration of new features may be viewed as desired.

7 **Close the Project Help window and return to the Project 2007 application window.**
Continue to the last lesson, in which you close the file and exit Microsoft Project.

TO EXTEND YOUR KNOWLEDGE . . .

DISPLAYING THE VERSION OF PROJECT

To display the version number of the Project software you are using, choose Help, About Microsoft Office Project.

USING WEB-BASED HELP

If you have an online connection, Microsoft Project provides access to broad Web-based support for all Office applications by clicking Help, Microsoft Office Online. For example, you can click *support, Office Training* in the browser window to access a *Training* area and select among 30- to 60-minute interactive tutorials on selected features in products such as Word, Excel, Access, Visio, Outlook, Publisher, PowerPoint.

LESSON 7: Closing a Project and Exiting Microsoft Project

The steps you take to close a project depend on whether you also plan to exit Project. If you have finished working in Project, use an Exit command. If you want to close the current project but continue working in Project, use a Close command.

You can perform Close and Exit operations by using buttons or menu options (see Figure 1.22). Whichever command you choose, Project provides a warning if changes to a project have not been saved.

Also access Close and Exit here

Close (exit) Microsoft Project button

Close current project button

FIGURE 1.22

In the following steps, you close the project, saving your changes. If you do not plan to continue with end-of-project exercises, you can complete an optional step to exit Project.

To Close a File and Exit Project

1   **Click the Close button for the *Apartment_Brochure* window.**
This action closes the open project and leaves you with the main Project window open. If you made changes to the file but did not save them, Microsoft Project warns you of unsaved changes. To save those changes, click Yes. To close the file without saving changes, click No. To cancel the close and leave the project file open, click Cancel.

2   **Click Yes, if necessary.**
If you want to continue exploring Microsoft Project, you can work through one or more exercises at the end of this project, or begin a new project in this text. If you want to exit Microsoft Project, complete the next step.

3   **Click the Close Microsoft Project button.**
Microsoft Project closes.

SUMMARY

In this initial project in your text, you first learned definitions related to project management in general and the Microsoft Project software. You then explored the Microsoft Project work environment by opening an .mpp extension file for a project that tracks the steps for creating a marketing brochure for an apartment complex. Navigation in the project file and recognition of the various components in the Microsoft Project window are essential, as you learned through practice. After you looked at the individual tasks both in the task table and in the Gantt chart, you viewed a standard report and printed it. Assistance is sometimes necessary when learning a new program, so you accessed Microsoft Help button on the Standard toolbar. Finally, you closed and saved the project and exited Microsoft Project.

You can extend your learning by reviewing concepts and terms and by practicing variations of skills presented in the lessons. Use the following table as a guide to the numbered questions and exercises in the end-of-project learning opportunities.

LESSON	MULTIPLE CHOICE	DISCUSSION	SKILL DRILL	CHALLENGE	DISCOVERY ZONE
Starting Microsoft Project, Opening a Project, and Saving a Project	5	1, 3	1	1, 4	2
Exploring the Project Window	10		2	2, 3	
Understanding the Task Table	2, 4, 6	2	2	2	
Understanding the Timeline in Gantt Chart View	1, 7		3	2	
Previewing and Printing a Standard Report	9		4	4	
Getting Help	3		5	2	1, 2
Closing a Project and Exiting Microsoft Project	8		4	3, 4	

KEY TERMS

budget	entry table	indicator column
constraint	field	menu bar
constraint triangle	Formatting toolbar	milestone
default	Gantt bar	project
duration	Gantt chart	Project Guide
entry bar	Gantt Chart view	project manager

resource	subtask	template
scope	summary task	time constraint
scrollbar	Task ID	timeline
scrollbox	task links (task dependencies)	timescale
side pane		title bar
stakeholders	task pane	toolbar
Standard toolbar	task table	*Type a question for help* box
status bar	tasks	

CHECKING CONCEPTS AND TERMS

SCREEN ID

Label each element of the project window shown in Figure 1.23. [L2]

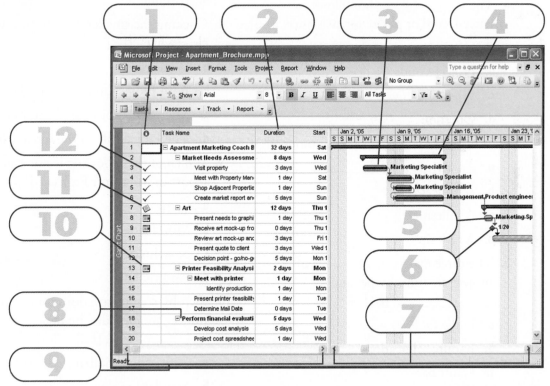

FIGURE 1.23

A. Gantt bar

B. Completed task

C. Summary task Gantt bar

D. Summary task

E. Time needed to complete a task

F. Note about the task

G. Task table

H. Indicator column

I. Task with a constraint

J. Task dependency (link line)

K. Gantt chart

L. Milestone task

MULTIPLE CHOICE

Circle the letter of the correct answer for each of the following.

1. A graphical illustration of a project is called a _____. [L4]

   a. bar chart

   b. Gantt chart

   c. task pane

   d. scrollbar

2. What is a single activity or action that has a duration? [L3]

   a. Task

   b. Project

   c. Gantt chart

   d. Gantt bar

3. The _____ box allows you to enter a word or phrase for assistance. [L6]

   a. Office Assistant

   b. Project Guide

   c. *Type a question for help*

   d. Question

4. Which type of task has no duration? [L3]

   a. An activity

   b. A project

   c. A milestone

   d. A task tip

5. The three main considerations of a project are time, scope, and _____. [L1]

   a. budget

   b. resource allocation

   c. Gantt bar

   d. task duration

6. A(n) _____ could be a person, group of people, piece of equipment, or even a building. [L3]

   a. task

   b. activity

   c. project manager

   d. resource

7. What is the term for the amount of time it takes to complete a task? [L4]

   a. Gantt bar

   b. Duration

   c. Cost

   d. Baseline

8. Clicking the smaller close button will close what? [L7]

   a. Windows

   b. Both Project and all open files

   c. Microsoft Project application

   d. The Project file in the active window

9. Which of the following is not a standard report in Microsoft Project? [L5]

   a. Costs

   b. Workload

   c. Stakeholders

   d. Assignments

10. Step-by-step instructions for creating a project are provided by the _____. [L2]

    a. Formatting toolbar

    b. Standard toolbar

    c. Task pane

    d. Project Guide toolbar

DISCUSSION

1. Imagine that you are responsible for planning a surprise party. According to project management fundamentals, there are three main constraints when completing tasks in a project: time, budget, and scope. What happens to the other constraints when one of them changes? For example, suppose you decide to have a formal party rather than a luau (change in scope). How does this affect time and budget? Consider changing the time and the budget as well, and discuss the implications for the project. [L1]

2. Suppose you are the editor of the school newspaper. When publishing any newspaper, what resources would you need to utilize (consider both persons and equipment)? Which resources would be used with every paper, and which ones would be used only occasionally? [L3, Why Would I?]

3. Make a list of potential responsibilities for a project manager. Consider various types of projects when compiling the list. [L1]

SKILL DRILL

Skill Drill exercises reinforce project skills. Each skill reinforced is the same, or nearly the same, as a skill presented in the project. Detailed instructions are provided in a step-by-step format.

You should complete exercises 1–4 in sequence. Skill Drill exercise 5 is independent of the others and can be worked at any time.

1. Open a Project and Save It with a New Name

You are the project manager for the development and implementation of a new software package. The project includes planning, designing, testing, documenting, training, piloting, implementing, and reviewing the software. Every phase is your responsibility, although you have assigned various resources to complete each phase and task. To manage this project as effectively as possible, you are using Microsoft Project. Your assistant has entered the information into a file and has given it to you for review.

To open a project and save it with a new name, follow these steps:

1. From the File menu, select Open.
2. Click the drop-down arrow at the right end of the *Look in* box, and select the drive and folder containing the student files for this project.
3. Select *EPr1_0102* and then click Open.
4. Choose the File menu, and select Save As.
5. Select the folder in which you are storing your solutions.
6. Type **Software_Deployment** in the *File name* box.
7. Click Save and leave *Software_Deployment* open for the next exercise.

2. View the Tasks and Project Information

Now that you have the project open, you want to take a few minutes to orient yourself with the various tasks and the layout. There are 12 summary tasks in this project, including 86 tasks. You look at the tasks to make sure they are correct and inclusive for this project.

To view several tasks in the task table, follow these steps:

1. Open *Software_Deployment*, if necessary; select <u>P</u>roject and then <u>P</u>roject Information from the menu.

   The Project Information dialog box opens.

2. Read the general project parameters and then click <u>C</u>ancel.

3. Drag the split line between the task table and the timeline to the right to widen the task table as shown in Figure 1.24.

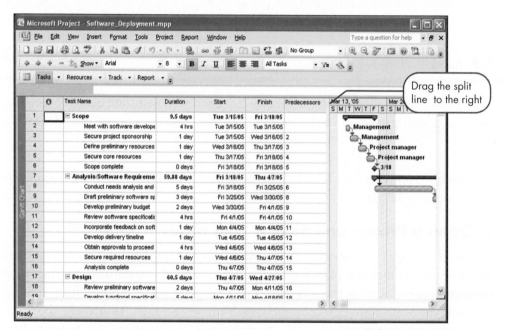

FIGURE 1.24

4. Locate Task 8 (*Conduct needs analysis and . . .*) and pause your mouse pointer on it.
   Read the ScreenTip to see the complete task name.

5. Point to the vertical column header border between Task Name and Duration; then drag to widen the column enough to see the complete task name.

6. Locate Task 33 (*Develop unit test plans using product specifications*).
   Notice that the predecessor for this task is Task 24 (*Design complete*).

7. Double-click the task and preview each tab in the dialog box; click <u>C</u>ancel when finished.

8. Save *Software_Deployment* and leave it open for the next exercise.

3. Explore the Gantt Chart

Now you need to familiarize yourself with the timeline. This visual representation of the tasks shows you the time period in which the project and each task must be accomplished as well as how tasks link to one another.

To view the Gantt chart, follow these steps:

1. Open *Software_Deployment*, if necessary, and drag the split line between the task table and the timeline to the left to widen the timeline.

2. Press Ctrl+Home, and then point to Task 1 (*Scope*) in the Gantt chart.

   Task 1 is a summary task for Tasks 2–6.

3. Point to Task 6 (*Scope complete*) in the Gantt chart area.

   Task 6 is a milestone task. If you have difficulty locating Task 6 in the Gantt chart, hover the mouse over the bar to read the task information. You can also turn on the gridlines.

4. Scroll to Task 78 (*Train Support Staff*) in the Gantt chart and hover the mouse over the bar to read the task information.

5. Point to the line linking Task 78 to Task 77.

   Task 77 must be complete in order to begin Task 78.

6. Navigate back to Task 1 (*Scope*) in the task table and in the Gantt chart.

7. Save *Software_Deployment* and leave it open for the next exercise.

4. Print a Report

The project is finally under way. Microsoft Project is proving to be a useful tool. Just to make sure that you stay on task, you would like a list of the tasks that are specifically your responsibility. Luckily, there is a standard report to do just that.

To print a report, follow these steps:

1. Open *Software_Deployment*, if necessary, and choose Report, Reports.

2. Select *Assignments* and then click Select.

3. Select *To-do List* and then click Select.

4. From the drop-down list in the Using Resource dialog box, select *Project manager* and then click OK.

   A To Do List report displays in Print Preview.

5. Click the Page Setup button.

6. Click the *Adjust to* down spinner until the number is 80 (otherwise the report prints on two pages). Click OK.

7. Click Print and then click OK.

8. Click Close on the Reports dialog box; then save and close *Software_ Deployment*.

5. Use Help to Learn About Templates

Before creating a project from scratch, it may be useful to preview the templates that come packaged with Microsoft Project. Help is a great place to start, and the quickest and easiest form of Help is the *Type a question for help* box. Use it now to learn about templates and how to use them. (Note: You need an Internet connection to complete this exercise.)

To learn about templates, follow these steps:

1. Click in the *Type a question for help* box and type **template**. Press ↵Enter.

2. Click the *Use templates in Project 2007* link in the *Search Results* pane of the Project Help window.

3. Read the information; then click the *What's the function of templates in Project 2007?* link.

4. Read this information. Also read the *What types of templates does Project 2007 provide?* and *How do I use a template file?* topics. Click the Back button until the Search Results are again displayed.

5. Click the *Microsoft Project Templates* link in the Search Results pane. Your Web browser opens and the Microsoft Online Help window displays.

6. Click several template names to display information about those particular templates. Read the information, close the Help window in the Web browser, and then close the Project Help window.

CHALLENGE

Challenge exercises expand on or are somewhat related to skills presented in the lessons. Each exercise provides a brief narrative introduction, followed by instructions in a numbered-step format that are not as detailed as those in the Skill Drill section.

Exercises 1–3 should be worked in order. Challenge exercise 4 is independent of the others and can be worked at any time.

1. Use a Template to Create a Project

You have decided to start your own business and you want to use Microsoft Project to track the tasks involved in preparing a business plan. Before you take the time to create the project, you want to look at the templates provided by Microsoft Project to see if one fits your needs, such as the New Business template.

To preview several templates and save the New Business template as the starting point for a project, complete the following steps:

1. Take a look at several of the templates located on your computer under *Project templates* in the New Project task pane.

2. Select the New Business template located on your computer under *Project templates.*

3. Scroll through the task table and Gantt chart to learn about the tasks and durations.

4. Click the collapse button (minus sign) beside the first summary task (Task 1); then collapse all other summary tasks.

5. Compare the Predecessor column information with the link lines in the Gantt chart.

6. Save the template as a project named `New_Business`, and leave it open for the next exercise.

2. View Project Information and Tasks in a Project Gantt Chart

Now you need to review the template so that you can later customize it to fit your schedule. To do so, you need to know what tasks are included, their durations, and overall project information. For starters, the dates given for the project and all tasks are old dates. You need to identify the tasks that you do not need, as well as areas where you will need to add new tasks.

1. Open *New_Business*, if necessary, and drag the split line between the task table and the timeline to the left.

2. View Task 8 (*Interview owners of similar businesses*).

   Notice that Task 7 must be complete before starting Task 8.

3. In the task table, double-click Task 8.

   Notice that the Task Information window appears; read through the options in this window.

4. Locate the Resources tab in the Task Information window, click on it, and read through the options. Click Cancel.

5. In the timeline, locate the first milestone (Task 25) and click on it. Notice that the task is highlighted in the task table as well. See if you can locate an additional three milestone tasks in this project file.

6. Move to Task 1 (*Phase 1 - Strategic Plan*).

7. Save *New_Business* and leave it open for the next exercise.

3. Preview Various Views in a Project

Gantt Chart view is just one of many views you can use in Project. Other views are helpful in different circumstances. Take a few minutes now to look at the other views in Project.

1. Open *New_Business*, if necessary, and then select View, View Bar.

2. Click the Calendar button and then click the Print Preview button to see how many months are necessary to complete this project. Then, close the preview.

3. Scroll down the list, select the Resource Sheet button, and review the various resources assigned in this project as well as the types of resources.

4. Preview other views.

5. Return to Gantt Chart view and turn off the View Bar.

6. Save and close *New_Business*.

4. Preview a Costs Report

As a manager of a software company, you handle many new software developments. You are beginning a new project that is very similar to a project you did in the past. To plan better, you want to look at the cost information from that project to predict more accurately the budget for this project. You print a report to do so.

1. Open the *EPr1_0103* file and save it as **Software**.

2. Open the Reports dialog box and select *Costs Report*. Then select *Budget*.

3. Zoom in on Task 39 (*Conduct marketing/technical review*). The total cost of this task was $34,592.

4. Before printing, access Page Setup and modify the header and footer. The header should be **Budget Report for 2012 Project** on the top line and *your name* on the second line.

5. Modify the footer to include the page number printed on the right side.

6. Change the page setup so that the report fits on two pages. Print it.

7. Save and close *Software*.

DISCOVERY ZONE

Discovery Zone exercises require advanced knowledge of topics presented in *Essentials* lessons, application of skills from multiple lessons, or self-directed learning of new skills. Each exercise is independent of the others, so you may complete them in any order.

1. Using Interactive Help

It is always important to fully understand the scope of a venture before beginning. In this case, you should have a basic understanding of projects and how to effectively plan and manage one. Microsoft Project 2007 provides several options for learning through interactive means, including the tutorials. The Project Map walks the user through building a project plan, tracking the project's progress, and communicating project information with others.

Access the Project Map (refer to online Help if necessary) and read as much information about the building process as possible. Keep notes on what you learn for future reference. Create an outline of steps. Then, go online to find additional information about three of the topics on which you took notes.

2. Researching Project Management

To better understand the role of a project manager, it would be useful to research some of the responsibilities, expectations, and lingo of project management. Project management differs from typical management in that it is shorter-lived by comparison. In other words, management in a company is required as long as there is a company, but project management is necessary only as long as there is a project—whether the duration of the project is 2 weeks or 20 years.

Visit the Project Management Institute Web site (www.pmi.org). PMI is the leading authority on project management. Using this Web site, research the overall project management role and its responsibilities. Be sure to learn about the profession as well as project management standards in particular. Use links listed on the Web site to learn about project management from other sources as well. Write a short paper about what you discover. Be sure to cite your sources.

SPECIFYING OVERALL PROJECT SETTINGS

OBJECTIVES

IN THIS PROJECT, YOU LEARN HOW TO

- Create a new project and assign the start date

- Create a project calendar

- View and modify project options

- Modify calendar working time options

- Print the Working Days calendar

- Create a project from a template

WHY WOULD I DO THIS?

After you complete the initial project planning phase, you create your project file in Microsoft Project. You may either use an existing template or create one from a blank file. One of the many benefits of using Microsoft templates is that you can start with a model project, with tasks and resources already entered, and then you modify those tasks and resources to suit your individual project plan. Upon first creating a project file, you must enter the preliminary data, including the start and finish dates of the project. Most projects are created from the ***project start date,*** with the finish date automatically calculated as you enter tasks and their durations.

You also create the overall project calendar. The ***project calendar*** includes the working days and hours, the number of hours in a given week, and any ***nonworking time*** such as holidays or vacation time. Besides maintaining the working times and days off for the entire project, the project calendar dictates when tasks are scheduled and when resources are scheduled to work on assigned tasks. The project calendar forms the basis for the overall project.

 VISUAL SUMMARY

In Lessons 1–4, you create a project file by using a new blank file. You specify the start date, create a project calendar, modify project options, and modify working times. Tasks are scheduled based on the default working times created in the project calendar, and resources are assigned individual calendars based on the project calendar. In Lesson 5 you print a calendar that shows the working and nonworking days (see Figure 2.1).

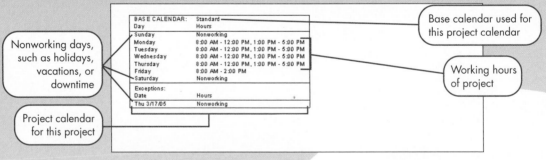

FIGURE 2.1

Lesson 6 provides an alternative method of creating a project file. You create a project file by using a template. Creating a project by using both methods allows you to compare the two processes and determine which method is best for a given situation.

The instructions in this project reflect entering or revising project dates in March 2005, which will be in the past when you work through this text. You should follow the directions given so that dates associated with tasks are consistent with those shown in the figures. For your own projects, of course, the dates that you view and enter will be current or in the future.

LESSON 1: Creating a New Project and Assigning the Start Date

After you define the project objectives, scope, and constraints, it is time to create your project file. You can create a new project in several ways: from another project file saved with a new name, from a template located on your computer or from Microsoft Online, or from a blank template. The first step, after creating the project file, is setting the start date. Later, as you develop the project plan, Microsoft Project uses this start date to compute the finish date based on the task deadlines you assign. The finish date of a project is equal to the finish date of the last task in the project plan and is fluid so it continually changes as you add tasks and modify durations.

In Project 2, you and a coworker create a project file for tracking the orientation process for new employees. In this lesson, you use the Project Guide to create a project file named *New_Hires* and provide the start date for the orientation. The Project Guide provides instructions and wizards to guide you through the process of creating and managing a project. A ***wizard*** is a feature of Microsoft Office programs that walks you step-by-step through an activity.

To Create a New Project and Assign a Start Date

1 **Start Microsoft Office Project 2007.**

The Tasks side pane displays (see Figure 2.2).

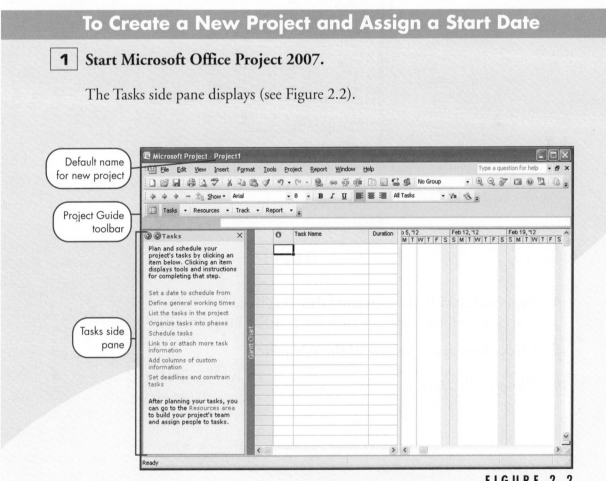

FIGURE 2.2

If you have problems . . .

If you do not see the Project Guide toolbar, choose <u>V</u>iew, <u>T</u>oolbars, Project Guide. If you accidentally close the Project Guide side pane, reopen it by clicking Tasks on the Project Guide toolbar.

2 | **Click the *Set a date to schedule from* link.**
The *Set a date to schedule from* wizard displays.

3 | **Click the drop-down arrow next to the estimated date text box in the side pane.**
A calendar displays (see Figure 2.3). You may select the date from this calendar, or you may type the date into the text box.

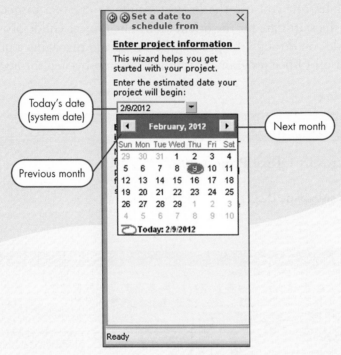

FIGURE 2.3

4 | **Type 3/1/2005 in the estimated date text box.**
Once the start date is set, you are ready to define the project base calendar.

5 | **Click Done at the bottom of the side pane.**

6 | **Choose <u>F</u>ile, Save <u>A</u>s.**

7 From the *Save in* drop-down list, select the appropriate drive and folder for saving the file.

8 In the *File name* text box, type New_Hires, and then click *Save*.

9 Close the *New_Hires* project file.
You have created a new project file and assigned a start date for the project plan. If you prefer to complete the project later, exit Microsoft Project.

TO EXTEND YOUR KNOWLEDGE . . .

USING THE PROJECT INFORMATION DIALOG BOX
You can also set the *S*tart date by using the Project Information window. Choose *P*roject, *P*roject Information. Enter the start date by using the drop-down calendar or type in the date manually.

LESSON 2:   Creating a Project Calendar

After you set the start date, you need to define the working days and times for the project. The *working times* may be the typical 8:00 A.M. to 5:00 P.M. time frame, but it can also include holidays and other nonworking times, such as evenings and weekends.

Microsoft Project provides three default base calendars: Standard, 24 Hours, and Night Shift. A *base calendar* is a project and task calendar that specifies default working and nonworking times. These times are used for task and resources scheduling. You can modify a base calendar to create your own unique project calendar. The Standard base calendar defines a work day as 8:00 A.M. to 5:00 P.M., Monday through Friday, with a one-hour lunch from noon to 1:00 P.M. The 24 Hours base calendar has no nonworking hours. The Night Shift base calendar defines a work day as midnight to 8:00 A.M., Tuesday through Saturday, with a one-hour lunch.

In this lesson, you create a project calendar to schedule task constraints. Your coworker has already added some tasks for the project but you must alter the project calendar to avoid having task deadlines falling on a nonworking day. While working through this project, the start date of the tasks changes as the project calendar changes.

To Create a Project Calendar

1 Open the *EPr1_0201* file.

2 Save the file as `New_Hire_Orientation`.

3 View Task 7 (*COBRA*) and notice that the start date is listed as *Thu 3/17/05*.

4 Click Tasks on the Project Guide toolbar, if necessary, and then click the *Define general working times* link in the Tasks side pane.

The *Project Working Times – Define the project's general working hours* wizard displays in a side pane on the left, and the Preview Working Time window displays on the right (see Figure 2.4).

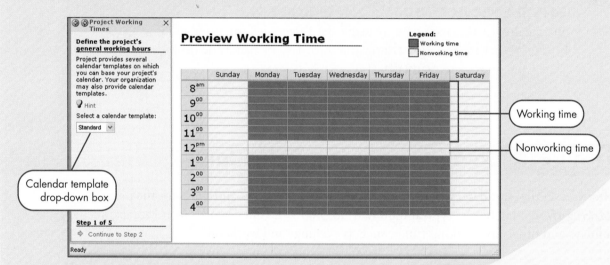

FIGURE 2.4

5 Click the drop-down arrow in the *Select a calendar template* box.

There are three base calendars to choose from: Standard, 24 Hours, and Night Shift (see Figure 2.5). For this project, the Standard calendar template is most appropriate.

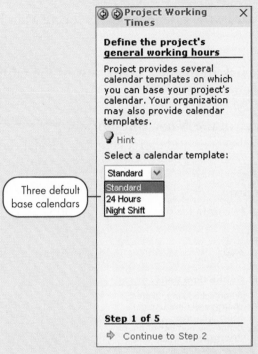

FIGURE 2.5

6 | Select the Standard calendar template, if necessary; then click *Continue to Step 2*.

The *Define the work week* side pane displays. The *I'll use the hours shown in the preview on the right* option is the default option, which you accept.

7 | Click *Continue to Step 3*.

The *Set Holidays and Days Off* side pane displays.

8 | Click *Change Working Time*.

The Change Working Time dialog box opens (see Figure 2.6).

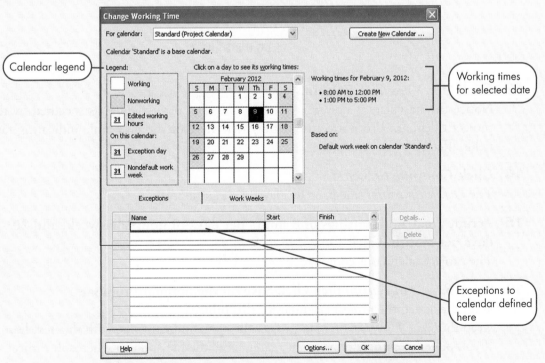

FIGURE 2.6

9 Use the vertical scrollbar in the calendar box to locate March 2005; then click *17*.

10 In the *Exceptions* tab, click in the first blank row of the table in the *Name* column.

11 Type "Company Picnic" in the *Name* column.

March 17, 2005, has just been set aside for a company picnic; thus it is a nonworking day.

12 Click in the *Start* column.

Notice that the *Start* and *Finish* fields are set to 3/17/2005.

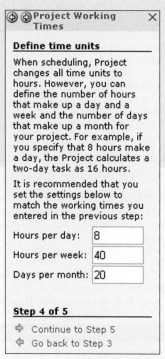

FIGURE 2.7

13 Click OK. View Task 7 again.

Notice the start date is now *Fri 3/18/05*. The start date changes as specified by the project calendar. Also notice the highlighted areas of the task table indicating task fields affected by the change.

14 Click *Continue to Step 4*.

The *Define time units* side pane displays (see Figure 2.7).

15 Accept the default settings of 8 hours per day, 40 hours per week, and 20 days per month. Click *Continue to Step 5*.

The project calendar is complete.

16 Click *Save and Finish*; then click Save on the Standard toolbar.

You have added the project calendar for this project.

Keep the *New_Hire_Orientation* project file open and continue with the next lesson. If you prefer to complete the project later, close the file and exit Microsoft Project.

TO EXTEND YOUR KNOWLEDGE . . .

CREATING A NEW BASE CALENDAR

If you use the same modified calendar on a regular basis, you can create a custom calendar so you do not have to re-create it with each new project. To do so, choose <u>T</u>ools, <u>C</u>hange Working Time. Click the Create <u>New Calendar</u> button. Type a calendar name in the <u>Na</u>me box. Select the <u>Make a copy of (base) calendar</u> arrow and select the base calendar you need. Click OK and set the working times as necessary. The calendar that you create becomes a calendar template that you can then choose when setting project working times.

LESSON 3:   Viewing and Modifying Project Options

The Project Information dialog box contains the basic properties of a project at a glance. It contains the start, finish, current, and status dates as well as the base calendar on which the project calendar was created. The ***current date*** is the system date, the date provided by your computer. It can be used as an optional start date for new tasks rather than the project start date, which is the default setting.

The ***status date*** is used when both recording and reporting progress information for individual tasks as well as the entire project plan. The status date is also used for calculating earned value totals. ***Earned value*** is the cost of work up to the status date. The status date can also be modified if you are reporting actual work remaining. For example, if you receive actual data on a Friday but do not enter the data until the following week, the status date would be incorrect. By modifying the status date you can avoid this pitfall. You may also set the status date to *NA*. If you do, Microsoft Project uses the current date as the status date.

In the following steps, you open the Project Information dialog box. You also change the settings for the current date and the status date.

To View and Modify Project Options

1 Open the *New_Hire_Orientation* file, if necessary; then choose <u>P</u>roject, **Project Information.**

The Project Information for 'New_Hire_Orientation.mpp' dialog box opens (see Figure 2.8).

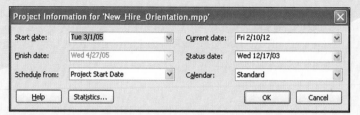

Project Information for 'New_Hire_Orientation.mpp'

Start <u>d</u>ate:	Tue 3/1/05	C<u>u</u>rrent date:	Fri 2/10/12
<u>F</u>inish date:	Wed 4/27/05	Status date:	Wed 12/17/03
Schedu<u>l</u>e from:	Project Start Date	Calendar:	Standard

Help   Statistics...   OK   Cancel

FIGURE 2.8

2 Click the *C<u>u</u>rrent date* **drop-down arrow.**

A calendar displays. You need to change the current date to March 2, 2005, which falls within the begin and end dates of the project.

3 Use the arrows in the calendar toolbar to locate March 2005; then click *2.*

In the *C<u>u</u>rrent date* text box, *Wed 3/2/05* displays.

4 Click the *Status date* **down arrow and change it to** *Thu 3/17/05.*

All dates are now set (see Figure 2.9).

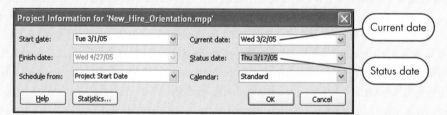

Project Information for 'New_Hire_Orientation.mpp'

Start <u>d</u>ate:	Tue 3/1/05	C<u>u</u>rrent date:	Wed 3/2/05
<u>F</u>inish date:	Wed 4/27/05	Status date:	Thu 3/17/05
Schedu<u>l</u>e from:	Project Start Date	Calendar:	Standard

Help   Statistics...   OK   Cancel

Current date

Status date

FIGURE 2.9

5 Click OK; then click Save on the Standard toolbar.

Keep the *New_Hire_Orientation* project file open and continue with the next lesson. If you prefer to complete the project later, close the file and exit Microsoft Project.

TO EXTEND YOUR KNOWLEDGE . . .

SCHEDULING FROM THE PROJECT FINISH DATE

The Project Guide provides the option to create a schedule from a known starting date. This option provides the greatest flexibility. However, you can also create a schedule from a finish date by applying the ***project finish date*** setting. To do so, select Project, Project Information. Change the *Schedule from* option to *Project Finish Date*. Select the finish date.

If you define a project plan based on the finish date, Microsoft Project calculates the start date rather than the finish date and assigns the default constraint of *As Late As Possible (ALAP)* to existing tasks.

CHANGING THE DEFAULT START DATE FOR NEW TASKS

For projects scheduled from a finish date, it may make more sense that any new tasks you enter into the project plan use the current date as their default start date, rather than the project's finish date. To change this option, select Tools, Options and click the Schedule tab. Click the *New Tasks* drop-down arrow and choose *Start on Current Date*.

LESSON 4:   Modifying Calendar Working Time Options

Generally speaking, the base calendar templates provide the dates and times necessary to create a project calendar. However, at times there are exceptions to the "normal" working times.

The ***default working time*** reflects the hours the team works on a project. For example, office hours may be 9:00 A.M. to 5:00 P.M. ***Nondefault working time*** refers to the work day hours that are not available for the project. Use this option when you need to change a day or a selection of days to nonworking time (such as Thanksgiving Day) or to change the working hours (such as closing early on Christmas Eve). You can also designate a particular time as nonworking time, such as a lunch hour from noon to 1:00 P.M.

In this lesson, you change March 17 back to a working day. The company has rescheduled the picnic, but the new date is not known yet. You also change the working times for Fridays.

To Modify Calendar Working Time Options

1 **Open the *New_Hire_Orientation* file, if necessary; then select Tools, Change Working Time.**
The Change Working Time dialog box opens.

2 **Scroll to March 2005 in the calendar.**
Notice that the date of March 17, 2005, is bold and underlined (see Figure 2.10). This date is set in the project calendar as a nonworking day for a company picnic. However, the company has changed the date of the picnic.

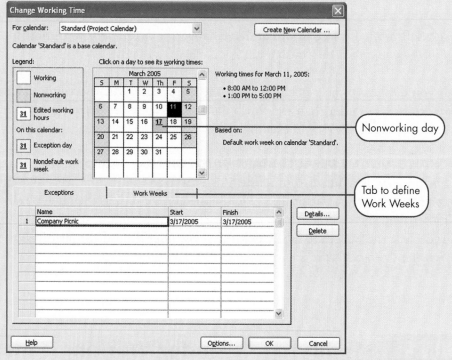

FIGURE 2.10

3   **Select March 17, 2005; then click the *Delete* button next to the *Exceptions* table containing the Company Picnic entry.**

March 17 is now a working day again.

4   **Click *Work Weeks* tab (refer to Figure 2.10), click in the first row of the *Work Weeks* table containing the [*Default*] entry, and then click the *Details* button.**

On Fridays, this office is open only from 8:00 A.M. to 2:00 P.M.

5   **Select Friday from the *Select day(s):* list, select *Select day(s) to these specific working times:*, click in the first *To* text box (*12:00 PM*), delete the current text, and then type 2:00 PM.**

Now the working time is six hours without a break (see Figure 2.11).

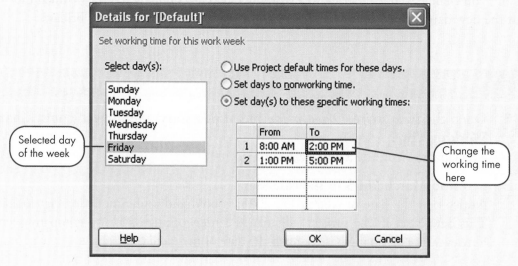

FIGURE 2.11

6   **Click in the second *From* text box.**

7 Press Del to delete *1:00 PM;* click OK, and then click OK again.

You updated the project calendar for the current project file and adjusted the working time for Fridays. You have also adjusted the overall hours for a work week from 40 to 38.

If you have problems . . .

A warning box appears if you did not delete the second *From* and *To* hours. One period must end before another begins. If the starting time for the next period is earlier than the end of the previous period, you cannot save the change. Make the correction, and then click OK.

---

8 Look at Task 7 (*COBRA*).

Notice the start date for this task is March 17, 2005. You just found out that the human resource technician assigned to this task is taking vacation time that day, so you need to change March 17 to a nonworking day.

9 Choose <u>T</u>ools, <u>C</u>hange Working Time.

10 Scroll to March 2005 in the *Sele<u>c</u>t Date(s)* calendar, and then select *17*.

The calendar shows which dates are typical working hours, and which are nonworking days (see Figure 2.12).

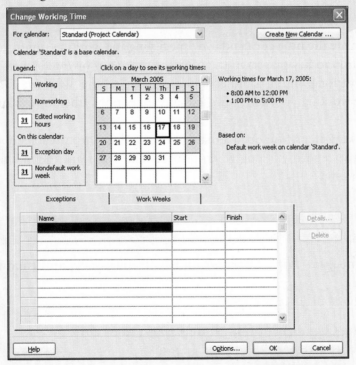

FIGURE 2.12

11 In the *Exceptions* tab, click in the first blank row of the table in the *Name* column, type "Human Resource Tech Vacation", click in the Start column and click OK.

12 | **Look at Task 7 again.**
The start date for the task is now March 18.

13 | **Save *New_Hire_Orientation*.**
Keep the *New_Hire_Orientation* project file open and continue with the next lesson. If you prefer to complete the project later, close the file and exit Microsoft Project.

TO EXTEND YOUR KNOWLEDGE . . .

RESOLVING WORK WEEK CONFLICTS

If you adjust the overall hours on the base calendar (as in this lesson) from a 40-hour work week to a 38-hour work week, scheduling a task over a week assigns a 40-hour work week when in reality it is a 38-hour work week. To resolve this problem, adjust the formula that Microsoft Project uses to convert task duration into time amounts. Choose Tools, Options, and then click the Calendar Tab. Change the *Hours per week* option to **38**.

LESSON 5:   Printing the Working Days Calendar

After you create the project calendar by specifying the working times, you may need to print it for distribution to key players in the project or for your own reference. Microsoft Project provides a report for printing a project's calendar, called the ***Working Days report.*** This report displays the working days and times and any exceptions (the nonworking days).

In the following steps, you open a dialog box that lists the available reports. You view how the Working Days report will look when printed, and you learn the methods to print or to close without printing.

To Preview a Report and View Print Options

1 | **Open the *New_Hire_Orientation* file, if necessary; and then select Report, Reports.**
The Reports dialog box opens.

2 | **Click the *Overview* option, if necessary; then click *Select*.**
The Overview Reports dialog box opens.

3 | **Click the *Working Days* option and click *Select;* then click within the top of the report to zoom it.**
You see an onscreen display of the Working Days report, showing which base calendar was used to create it (see Figure 2.13). This is a preview of what the printed output would look like.

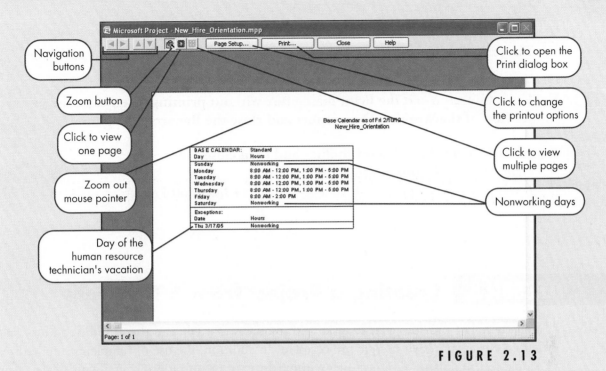

FIGURE 2.13

4 **Click the Page Setup button from the Print Preview toolbar (refer to Figure 2.13).**

The Page Setup – Base Calendar dialog box opens.

5 **Click the Header tab, and then click the Right tab in the *Alignment* area.**

There are three sections in the header: left, center, and right (see Figure 2.14). You want to add your name to the right side of the header.

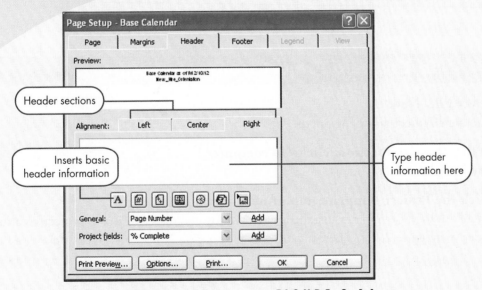

FIGURE 2.14

6 **Click in the white text box and type your first and last name; then click OK.**

Your name now appears in the header of the report.

7 | **Click Print from the Print Preview toolbar.**
The Print dialog box opens. Selecting OK at this point would send the output to the specified printer. For now, forego printing to conserve paper.

8 | **Click Cancel to exit the Print dialog box without printing; then close the preview of the Working Days report and close the Reports dialog box.**

9 | **Click Save on the Standard toolbar and then close the New_Hire_Orientation project file.**
If you prefer to complete the final lesson later, exit Microsoft Project.

LESSON 6: Creating a Project from a Template

Using a template provides generic tasks and resources that you can then modify, add to, and delete to create your own unique project plan. In addition, the use of templates standardizes the look, feel, and usage of project files within a team or organization. Even if you create a new blank project, a global template named *global.mpt* is invoked. The **global template** is a collection of default settings controlling everything from startup view options to how Microsoft Project calculates formulas. When you use a template, you can still modify the project file options such as the working time, as discussed in previous lessons.

Microsoft Project installs some templates on your computer and makes others available online. In the following steps, you open one of the templates on your computer, save it under its default name, and explore its contents.

To Create a Project from a Template

1 | **Select File, New.**
The New Project task pane opens.

2 | **In the *Templates* section, click *On computer*.**
The Templates dialog opens.

3 | **Click the Project Templates tab, if necessary.**
There are many templates installed with Microsoft Project to make project creation easier (see Figure 2.15). There are also many more on Microsoft's Web site.

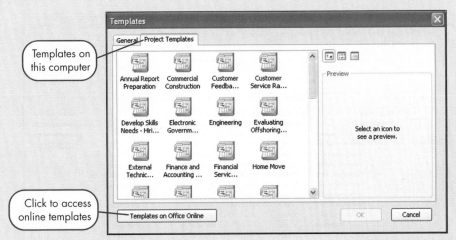

FIGURE 2.15

4 **Select the *Office Move* template; then click OK.**

A copy of the template loads and the Tasks side pane displays (see Figure 2.16).

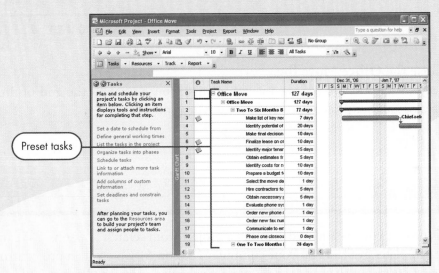

FIGURE 2.16

5 **Select File, Save As.**

6 **From the *Save in* drop-down list, select the appropriate drive and folder for saving the file.**

7 **Accept the default filename of Office Move, and click Save.**

8 **Click the Close button on the Tasks side pane and navigate through the Office Move project file.**

Notice that preset tasks are in the file along with resource allocations (see Figure 2.17). In later lessons, you learn how to modify these preset entries.

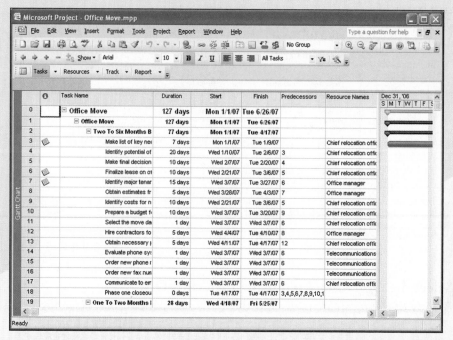

FIGURE 2.17

9 **Close the Office Move file.**

Leave Microsoft Project open if you plan to continue with the end-of-project exercises or another project; otherwise, exit Microsoft Project.

SUMMARY

In this project you experienced creating a project from scratch (Lessons 1–5) and by using one of the templates available on your computer (Lesson 6). To create a project from scratch, you must first create a new project and a project calendar, using the Project Guide toolbar and the step-by-step wizards to set the working times. You also modified the working times, start date, and current date from the Tools menu and set up printing for the Working Days report. Finally, you created a project from the *Office Move* template and viewed the default entries.

You can extend your learning by reviewing concepts and terms and by practicing variations of skills presented in the lessons. Use the following table as a guide to the numbered questions and exercises in the end-of-project learning opportunities.

LESSON	MULTIPLE CHOICE	DISCUSSION	SKILL DRILL	CHALLENGE	DISCOVERY ZONE
Creating a New Project and Assigning the Start Date	1, 3	1	1	1, 4	
Creating a Project Calendar	2, 5	2	2	2, 4	1
Viewing and Modifying Project Options	6, 9, 10	1		1, 4	
Modifying Calendar Working Time Options	4	2	3, 4	3	
Printing the Working Days Calendar	7			4	2
Creating a Project from a Template	8	3		4	2

KEY TERMS

base calendar

current date

default working time

earned value

global template

nondefault working time

nonworking time

project calendar

project finish date

project start date

status date

wizard

Working Days report

working time

CHECKING CONCEPTS AND TERMS

MULTIPLE CHOICE

Circle the letter of the correct answer for each of the following.

1. The pane shown below the Standard and Formatting toolbars that displays step-by-step instructions on how to create a new project file is the
_____. [L1]

   a. task pane

   b. guide bar

   c. Project Guide

   d. wizard

2. Which of the following is provided as a guide to help you create a project calendar? [L2]

   a. Base calendars

   b. Tasks lists

   c. Project information

   d. Standard templates

3. What is the date you enter to designate when the project starts? [L1]

a. Begin date

b. Start From date

c. Working date

d. Schedule From date

4. Which option in the Details dialog box (selected from the Change Working Time dialog box) modifies the working times in the project calendar for a selected day of the week? [L4]

a. Use Project default times for these days.

b. Begin and end time

c. Set days to nonworking time.

d. Set day(s) to these specific working times:

5. When using the Standard base calendar, what are the default work day times? [L2]

a. 9:00 A.M. to 5:00 P.M.

b. Work day times are not set. You specify them.

c. 8:30 A.M. to 5:30 P.M., Sunday through Friday, with a one-hour lunch break

d. Monday through Friday, 8:00 A.M. to 5:00 P.M., with noon to 1:00 P.M. for lunch

6. What does the earned value calculation indicate? [L3]

a. The current cost of work, up to the status date

b. How much time it will take to complete the project

c. How much money you will earn while working on the project

d. How much extra time you will earn

7. To print the project calendar, you would choose which report category? [L5]

a. Reports

b. Current Activities

c. Overview

d. Page Setup

8. Which of the following is a generic project plan that you can modify to your own specifications? [L6]

a. Project plan

b. File

c. Template

d. Office Online

9. Which date, by default, reflects the date and time set by your computer but can be modified to match your project plan? [L3]

a. Start date

b. Finish date

c. Earned value

d. Current date

10. Which date is used to report earned value? [L3]

a. Start date

b. Status date

c. Current date

d. Finish date

DISCUSSION

1. Imagine that you are assigned to manage a project. Your supervisor does not know when the actual work will come in but does know that the project must be completed before the end of the current business quarter. You are provided a basic set of tasks and resources and told to start creating the project even though you don't know when you will actually begin work on it. With this agenda, would you schedule your project with a begin date or an end date? Discuss which option you would choose and why. [L1, L3]

2. You create the project calendar by specifying the begin and end dates of the work week and the begin and end times of each work day. This project calendar then makes up the calendar that each resource uses when working on the project. You can create additional project calendars and utilize multiple calendars in one project file. Discuss some reasons why you would do this and how it would be useful. [L2, L4]

3. Take a look at some of the templates available for use in Microsoft Project, both on your computer and online. Which template or templates could you use if you were going to upgrade the software used in your office to a new version? [L6]

SKILL DRILL

Skill Drill exercises reinforce project skills. Each skill reinforced is the same, or nearly the same, as a skill presented in the project. Detailed instructions are provided in a step-by-step format.

You should complete exercises 1 and 2 in sequence. Skill Drill exercises 3 and 4 are independent of the others and can be worked at any time.

1. Creating a New Blank Project for New Member Orientation

You are the office manager for a large real estate board. Many real estate agents who are new to the area join this nonprofit association. Bylaws require the board to provide each new member with a very specific orientation, including the services offered and the rules and regulations of the governing body. To ensure that you do not forget a piece of information and possibly jeopardize the nonprofit status of the board, you decide to create a simple project plan to help you with this new member orientation.

To create a new project plan, follow these steps:

1. Choose File, New; then click the *Blank Project* link in the New Project task pane.
2. Click the *Set a date to schedule from* link in the Tasks side pane.
3. Click in the *Project will begin* text box and type **7/1/2012**.
4. Click Done.
5. Choose File, Save As.
6. Select the appropriate drive and folder for saving the file.
7. In the *File name* text box, type **Board_New_Member.**
8. Then click Save; and leave *Board_New_Member* open for the next exercise.

2. Modifying the Working Times in the New Member Orientation Project

Now that you have created the *Board_New_Member* project plan file, you need to specify the *Schedule from* date and the project working times to coincide with the time frame of your project.

To create the project calendar, follow these steps:

1. Open *Board_New_Member* , if necessary, and in the Tasks side pane, click *Define general working times*.

2. Select the Standard calendar template, if necessary, and then click *Continue to Step 2*.

3. Click the *I'll use the hours shown in the preview on the right* option, if necessary; then click *Continue to Step 3*.

4. Click *Continue to Step 4*.

5. Click in the *Hours per day* text box and type **7**. Press Tab⇆ to move to the *Hours per week* text box and type **35**. Click *Continue to Step 5*.

6. Click *Save and Finish;* then click Save on the Standard toolbar.

7. Close the *Board_New_Member* project file.

3. Modifying Project Working Times in a Forms Project

Another responsibility of the real estate board is processing forms. You have a project file that assists you in completing this portion of the orientation. To customize an existing project plan, you modify the project calendar working times.

To modify working time, follow these steps:

1. Start Microsoft Project, if necessary, and open the *EPr1_0202* project file; then save it as `Forms_Procedures`.

2. Click Tasks on the Project Guide toolbar, if necessary; then click *Define general working times* in the Tasks side pane.

3. Click *Continue to Step 2*.

4. Click the *I want to adjust the working hours shown for one or more days of the week* option.

5. Scroll down in the task pane so you can view the *Hours for, From,* and *To* text boxes.

6. Click the first *From* drop-down arrow and select *8:30 AM*.

7. Click the last *To* drop-down arrow and select *5:30 PM*.

8. Click *Apply to All Days* and then click *Continue to Step 3*.

9. Click *Continue to Step 4*. Click *Continue to Step 5*.

10. Click *Save and Finish;* then click Save on the Standard toolbar.

11. Close the *Forms_Procedures* project file.

4. Scheduling Holiday Time in a Purchase Order Processing Project

As the accounts payable manager for a college, you keep track of all purchase orders used in the school. The college is being audited and you are required to track and take notes of all the things you do when purchase orders are processed. You decide to create a project file to ensure that you document each step of the process. Now, you need to mark nonworking days in the project calendar.

To schedule nonworking times, follow these steps:

1. Start Microsoft Project, if necessary; and open *EPr1_0203* and save it as **PO_Routing**.

2. Close the Tasks side pane, if necessary. Notice that the start date for Task 3 (*Review inbox*) is *Tue 7/4/06*.

3. Choose Tools, Change Working Time.

4. Scroll to July 2006.

5. Click the calendar square for July 4, 2006; then click the first entry in the Name column of the Exceptions tab. Type **4th of July Holiday**, click in the Start column of the same entry, verify the populated Start and Finish dates, and click OK. Notice that the start date for Task 3 (*Review inbox*) is now *Wed 7/5/06*, rather than *Tues 7/4/06*.

6. Click Save on the Standard toolbar.

7. Save and close *PO_Routing*.

CHALLENGE

Challenge exercises expand on or are somewhat related to skills presented in the lessons. Each exercise provides a brief narrative introduction, followed by instructions in a numbered-step format that are not as detailed as those in the Skill Drill section.

Exercises 1–2 should be worked in order. Challenge exercises 3–4 are independent of the others and can be worked at any time.

1. Scheduling a Project from the Finish Date

You are a technical writer for a small software company. You work in a team of four writers and an editor. For every new software program created or current software updated, you write and format the software documentation. You use the same procedures for creating each manual. The project completion date is the key to scheduling; the company predicts the software distribution date, and the software manual must be ready to accompany it. So you take the distribution deadline and set your schedule accordingly.

To set your schedule, follow these steps:

1. Open *EPr1_0204* and save it as **Manual_Schedule**.

2. Close the Tasks side pane if necessary; and then review the tasks in this project.

   This project takes 30 days to complete.

3. Open the Project Information dialog box; then set the current date to April 6, 2005.

4. Change the *Schedule from* option to *Project Finish Date*.

5. Change the finish date to December 1, 2005, and click OK. Close the Project Information dialog box.

6. Scroll through the Gantt chart and see when the project must begin in order to be completed on schedule.

7. Save *Manual_Schedule* and leave it open for the next exercise.

2. Creating a Custom Base Calendar

The software company has two shifts of technical support representatives, so your working hours differ from the typical 8-to-5 work day. In the three-week period prior to software release, the company requires all employees involved in software testing, programming, and documentation to work two Saturdays. To project the schedule correctly, you need to create a custom base calendar. Your calendar must account for legal holidays as well as those two working Saturdays.

To create a custom base calendar that accounts for legal holidays as well as the two working Saturdays, follow these steps:

1. Open *Manual_Schedule*, if necessary, and then open the Change Working Time dialog box.

2. Create a new calendar called **Writers** based on the Standard base calendar.

3. Change the Monday through Thursday working times of the new *Writers* calendar you created to 9:00 A.M. to 6:00 P.M., with an hour for lunch.

4. Change Friday's *Start* and *From* schedule to 9:00 A.M. to 1:00 P.M. removing any other times.

5. Change November 12 and 19, 2005, to working days, 9:00 A.M. to 4:00 P.M., with one hour for lunch.

6. Mark all legal holidays on the calendar, such as Columbus Day, Veterans Day, and Thanksgiving.

7. Apply the Writers calendar to the entire project.

8. Save and close *Manual_Schedule*.

3. Resolving a Work Week Conflict

Your work week is only 36 hours rather than the typical 40 hours. However, the base calendar is for a 40-hour week. You need to resolve the conflict so that any tasks that span more than 40 hours have correctly calculated finish dates.

To resolve the calendar conflict by correcting the number of hours in the work week, follow these steps:

1. Open *EPr1_0205* and save it as **Magazine_Article**.

2. Open the Change Working Time dialog box and view the nondefault working time options.

   Notice that for this project, the working day begins at 8:00 A.M. and ends at 2:30 P.M., with a 30-minute lunch. It is a 6-hour working day.

3. Look through this project file and notice that the summary tasks (tasks in bold) are calculated in days while the subtasks are calculated in hours.

   Notice also that the summary task calculations are incorrect and do not reflect a 6-hour work day.

4. In the Change Working Time dialog box, use the Options button to change the hours per day to 6 and the work week to 30 hours.

5. Review the project file again and notice that for the entire project plan, the summary tasks now calculate correctly with the adjustment of the hours per day and per week.

6. Save and close *Magazine_Article*.

4. Modifying a Template's Calendar and Working Times

You are an assistant to a general contractor for residential housing. The stages of building a house are constant for all jobs. You need to create a project file, and Microsoft Project provides a template that you decide to use. The template contains the basic tasks you need as well as a few custom project calendars.

To create a project file for your firm that reflects the stages of building a house, follow these steps:

1. Open a new project file, access the templates on your computer, and click the Project Templates tab.

2. Open the *Residential Construction* template and save it as **Building_Plan**.

3. Set June 1, 2006, as the start date for the project.

   Notice the finish date for the project. You may need to move the split bar between the task table and the Gantt chart.

4. Access the Change Working Times dialog box and look at all the available calendars.

5. Change the working times for the general contractor as follows: Monday through Friday, 7:00 A.M. to 7:00 P.M., with a one-hour lunch. Make sure this change is applied to all days.

6. Mark all major holidays for the 2006 year.

7. Save and close the *Building_Plan* project.

DISCOVERY ZONE

Discovery Zone exercises require advanced knowledge of topics presented in *Essentials* lessons, application of skills from multiple lessons, or self-directed learning of new skills. Each exercise is independent of the others, so you may complete them in any order.

1. Creating a Project with Multiple Calendars

You are the production manager for a chocolate factory. One of the year's busiest production times is Valentine's Day, when the company generally produces 100% more than during the rest of the year. You hire two temporary crews in addition to your usual employees to meet this demand. Your employees will work a total of three shifts during the month of January to ensure that your company produces enough chocolate to fulfill future orders. This will include weekend shifts as well.

Create a new project and save it as **Production**. Set the *Schedule from* date for January 3, 2005. Create three project calendars for this time period. First shift works 7:00 A.M. to 3:00 P.M., second shift works 3:00 P.M. to 11:00 P.M., and third shift works 11:00 P.M. to 7:00 A.M. Each shift has a one-hour break to eat. You can base the first shift calendar on the Standard calendar and the third shift on the Night Shift base calendar. Also create a project calendar for management personnel, who work 8:00 A.M. to 5:00 P.M.

Use the Tasks side pane to view the new calendars in the *Calendars* drop-down list.

Note: When creating the third shift calendar, remember that the finish time of the shift must be later than the start time. See the If You Have Problems feature in Lesson 4. Also, note that you cannot use the 24 Hours calendar when creating a three-shift work day.

2. Creating a Template

Microsoft Project provides many useful templates, but at times you need a unique template. You can create a template of your own. Use Help to learn how to create a template and have it display on the Project Templates tab in the Templates dialog box. Use one of the project files in this project to create a template. Close the file; then open the template from the New Project task pane.

ENTERING TASKS AND CREATING A PROJECT SCHEDULE

OBJECTIVES

IN THIS PROJECT, YOU LEARN HOW TO

- Enter tasks and specify duration

- Organize tasks

- Create milestone and recurring tasks

- Link tasks by specifying task predecessors

- Use outline features and view Work Breakdown Structure (WBS) codes

- Apply a calendar to a task

- Set constraints

WHY WOULD I DO THIS?

One of the difficult aspects of creating a project plan is finding the right words to convey your thoughts about all of the work that needs to be completed. There are several actions you can take to help ensure that tasks are not overlooked. Collaborate with team members and ask them for their "to-do" lists on similar projects they have worked on in the past. Research related projects, both within your organization and on the Internet. Remember to consult with the stakeholders involved with the project plan—the ones who are not directly associated with working on the project but are affected by its outcome. Chances are they may have some insight into the proposed project. If there is a written document describing the scope of the project plan, it too can be a source of valuable information. Finally, as you identify the tasks to include in the project plan, you may find it helpful to create a large list of tasks in a word-processed document, not worrying about anything but entering the names of the tasks. Then you can further refine this list—combining, deleting, and reorganizing the tasks until you form a cohesive project plan.

Once the project planning phase is complete and the project calendar is in place, you should launch Microsoft Project and begin entering the tasks necessary to complete the project plan. If you are working with a template or a copy of another project plan, you can modify the tasks already in place and add to the plan as needed.

Besides entering tasks, you also create phases by using the outline features. A *phase* is a major step, or a group of related tasks, in a project plan and phases are present throughout the project life cycle, much like the beginning, middle, and end of a story. You also enter *deliverables,* which are the tangible and measurable results you get from completing a task or series of tasks.

 VISUAL SUMMARY

You are one of many key people working on a large regional sales conference. Now that the tasks involved in planning this event have been identified, it is your responsibility to begin setting up the overall project file by using Microsoft Project.

Your efforts include entering tasks and their duration, organizing those tasks into a logical order, creating milestones and recurring tasks, applying a calendar to certain tasks, and setting constraints. The Gantt chart in Figure 3.1 illustrates the results of those efforts.

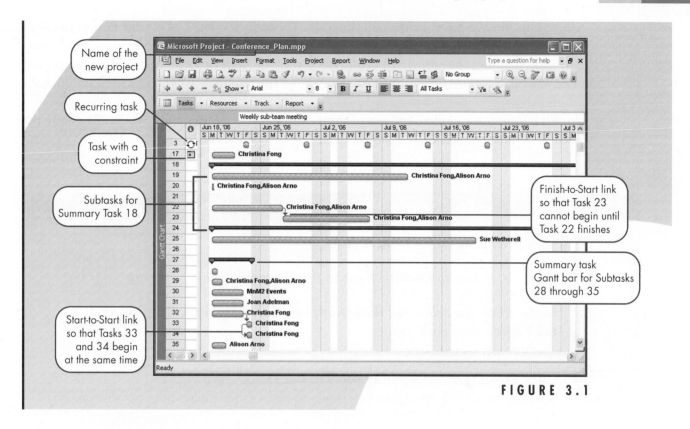

FIGURE 3.1

Entering Tasks and Specifying Duration

A project file is comprised of tasks. Each task is one piece of the project puzzle. Each task has a start date, duration, and finish date. Most tasks are assigned to a resource. Once the project calendar is in place, it is time to enter tasks.

There are several ways to enter a task. You can enter them by using the Gantt chart, by using the task table, or by importing data. Microsoft Project allows up to 1 million tasks in a single project file, far more than a personal computer can hold or an individual can manage.

Before entering tasks, an understanding of the fields in the task table is essential. The task table, by default, contains eight fields: ID, Indicator, Task Name, Duration, Start, Finish, Predecessors, and Resource Names. The *ID field* is a number automatically assigned by Microsoft Project that is used as a unique identifier for each task. You cannot input this ID or edit it, and it is automatically updated when a task moves to another location.

The Indicator field is used to display icons that signal there is additional information about a task—such as notes, constraints, and finish status. The *Task Name field* describes the task and can contain up to 255 characters. Unlike the Task ID, the Task Name does not have to be unique.

The Duration field is perhaps the most important field in the task table, because it specifies how long it takes to complete a task. In many cases, the duration is an estimate that can be entered in increments of months, weeks, days, or hours, with the default duration being days. The *Start field* and the *Finish field* show the calendar date of when the task starts and when the task finishes, as based on the task duration. Typically, you want Microsoft Project to calculate these dates to allow for the most flexibility in the schedule. The *Predecessors field* shows any tasks that must be considered before calculating the start or finish date of the current task. The *Resource Names field* in the task table shows the resources assigned to work on the task.

In this lesson, you complete two sets of steps. You begin by creating the project calendar. In the second set of steps, you enter 11 tasks, including their durations.

To Create the Project Calendar

1 Start Microsoft Office Project 2007.

2 Click *Set a date to schedule from* in the Tasks side pane.

3 In the *Enter the estimated date your project will begin* text box, select *6/19/2006;* then click Done.
The start date is now set.

4 Click *Define general working times* in the Tasks side pane.
A wizard opens to help you set up the working times for the resources of this project plan.

5 In the *Define the project's general working hours* side pane, click *Continue to Step 2.*
This action accepts the default Standard calendar template.

6 Click *I want to adjust the working hours shown for one or more days of the week;* then change the working hours to 9:00 A.M.–12:30 P.M. and 1:30 P.M.–6:00 P.M.

7 Click *Apply to All Days;* then click *Continue to Step 3.*
This modifies the working hours of the project calendar.

8 Click *Change Working Time* in the Set Holidays and Days Off side pane.

9 Add July 4 and September 4, 2006, to the list of Exceptions and click OK; then click *Continue to Step 4.*

10 Click *Continue to Step 5;* then click *Save and Finish.*
The working times and nonworking times for this calendar are set.

11 Drag the border of the task table to display the Start column.

You completed defining the project base calendar. The next set of steps involves entering tasks and specifying the associated durations for those tasks.

To Enter Tasks and Specify Durations

1 Click *List the tasks in the project* in the Tasks side pane.
The List Tasks side pane displays.

2 Click in the Task Name box of Row 1, type `Planning meetings and con-ference calls`, and press `↵Enter`.
Notice that a start date for Task 1 automatically displays in the Start column as *Mon 6/19/06,* and a default duration of *1 day?* appears in the Duration column (see Figure 3.2). The question mark indicates that the duration is an estimate.

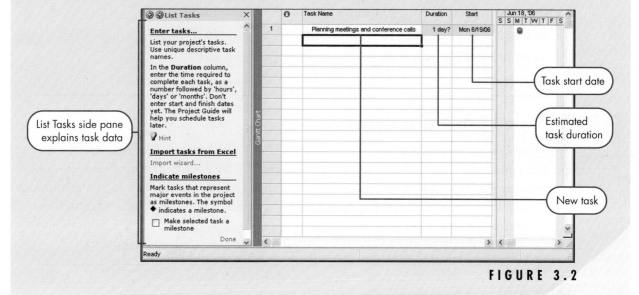

FIGURE 3.2

? If you have problems . . .

The entire task name may not appear after you enter it. To widen the Task Name column to show more of the contents, point to the right border of the column header and drag it to the right, or double-click the right border of the column header to AutoFit the contents of the Task Name column.

3 Type `Schedule bi-weekly status meetings` in the Task Name box in Row 2.

4 Press `Tab⇥` to move to the Duration column; type `2?`; and then press `↵Enter`.
2? expands to *2days* because "days" is the default duration type.

5   **Enter the remaining tasks and durations as shown in the table below.**

Task Name	Duration
Arrange core-team site visit	3d?
Budget funding and tuition	1d?
Develop budget	16d?
Determine tuition	0.5d?
Review status with sub-team leaders	1d?
Network group management review	1.5d?
Determine billing process	6.5d?
Budget reconciliation process	7d?
Identify all vendors	22d?

If you have problems . . .

Overflow markers are crosshatch characters (###) that indicate the entry in a field is too wide to fit within the column. These markers may appear in your Duration column as you enter tasks. To resolve this problem, move your mouse to the gridline between the Duration and Start column headers, and drag the gridline to the right to increase the width of the Duration column. You can also double-click the column border in the column header to allow AutoFit to resize the column to fit the data.

6   **Click Done in the List Tasks side pane.**

7   **Click Save on the Standard toolbar, and then save the file as** `Conference_Preplanning`.

8   **Close the file.**
You have added the project calendar for this project and entered tasks. If you prefer to complete the project later, exit Microsoft Project.

TO EXTEND YOUR KNOWLEDGE . . .

SETTING TASK DURATIONS
The default duration type is days (d), and it is an estimated time as indicated by the question mark that appears next to it. You can also specify durations as minutes (m), hours (h), weeks (w), or months (mo). Likewise, you do not have to use estimated time. To change the duration type, type in the duration, using the correct ending. For example, if a task will take 2 hours, type **2h**.

CHANGING THE DEFAULT DURATION

You can modify the default duration type by selecting Tools, Options and clicking the Schedule tab. Click the *Duration is Entered in* list box and choose the desired duration type.

EDITING A TASK

You can edit a task in the task table by selecting the task and pressing F2 or clicking in the entry bar, then making corrections. Alternatively, you can simply click twice in the field that needs to be changed and make your corrections.

USING UNDO

In Microsoft Project 2007, you can make changes and then revert back to the state before you made the changes. To undo the most recent action, click the Undo button on the Standard toolbar or press Ctrl+Z. To undo additional changes, click the arrow next to the Undo button and click the action you want to undo in the list. When you undo a change, you also undo all changes you made after it. Project also provides the ability to redo the changes by clicking the Redo button normally located to the right of the Undo button.

LESSON 2: Organizing Tasks

In a perfect world, you would enter tasks in the correct order as you type them the first time. However, that is not usually the case. If you are creating a project from scratch, you may need to combine, delete, and reorganize the master list of tasks you created to form a cohesive project plan. If you are using a template or an existing spreadsheet or project file, you may need to add and/or delete tasks so that the project plan reflects the current work at hand. Once you have created a basic project plan, you need to group the tasks into phases and organize the project tasks into a more logical order.

In this lesson, you use cut-and-paste method to reorganize tasks in a project to plan a conference.

To Organize Tasks

1 Start Microsoft Project and then close any open side panes, if necessary.

2 Open *EPr1_0301* and save it as `Conference_Plan`.
This file is the same as the one you created in the previous lesson. However, there are 32 additional tasks added at the end of the file.

3 Click within Task 11 (*Identify all vendors*).
You need to insert an additional task above row 11.

4 Choose Insert, New task; add the task name `Vendor support`; and then press ↵Enter.
Microsoft Project automatically adds an estimated duration of *1 day?* (see Figure 3.3).

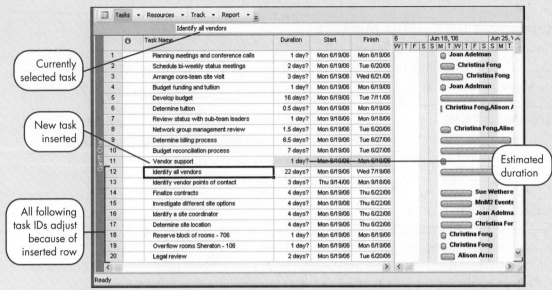

Currently selected task

New task inserted

All following task IDs adjust because of inserted row

Estimated duration

FIGURE 3.3

5 **Click within Task 15 (*Investigate different site options*); then press Insert.**
Insert also inserts a new row above the selected task. All of the subsequent task IDs adjust when the new task is inserted.

6 **Type Site/hotel as the task name, and then press ↵Enter.**

7 **Insert a row above Task 24 (*Make arrangements for receipt and storage of shipments*), type General issues as the task name, and then press ↵Enter.**

8 **Click the ID field for Task 8 (*Network group management review*), and then choose Edit, Cut Task.**
The previous Task 9 becomes Task 8 when the task is cut (see Figure 3.4).

		Develop budget	16 days?	Mon 6/19/06	Tue 7/11/06	
6		Determine tuition	0.5 days?	Mon 6/19/06	Mon 6/19/06	Christina Fong,Alison A
7		Review status with sub-team leaders	1 day?	Mon 9/18/06	Mon 9/18/06	
8		Determine billing process	6.5 days?	Mon 6/19/06	Tue 6/27/06	
9		Budget reconciliation process	7 days?	Mon 6/19/06	Tue 6/27/06	
10		Vendor support	1 day?	Mon 6/19/06	Mon 6/19/06	
11		Identify all vendors	22 days?	Mon 6/19/06	Wed 7/19/06	
12		Identify vendor points of contact	3 days?	Thu 9/14/06	Mon 9/18/06	
13		Finalize contracts	4 days?	Mon 6/19/06	Thu 6/22/06	Sue Wethere

Selected row

Row heading and ID field

Tasks move up when task is cut

FIGURE 3.4

9 **Now click the row heading for Task 15 (*Investigate different site options*); then choose Edit, Paste.**
The previous Task 8 (*Network group management review*) is pasted above the original Task 15 and becomes the new Task 15. All tasks following have new task IDs.

If you have problems . . .

Note that there are two *Network group management review* tasks; one is in row 15 and the other in row 23. For this project, that particular task must be duplicated.

10 **Scroll down and select Tasks 24 (*General issues*) through 33 (*Presenter check-in*) by clicking Task 24's ID field and dragging to Task 33's ID field.**

All 10 tasks are selected (see Figure 3.5). Any action taken affects all selected tasks.

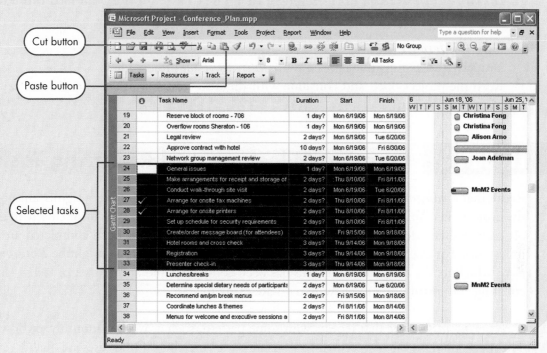

FIGURE 3.5

If you have problems . . .

If not all tasks in the group are visible before selecting, dragging the pointer toward the bottom of the screen as you are selecting may cause the tasks to scroll on the screen too quickly. To avoid this problem, scroll down to display all tasks to be selected before selecting them.

When dragging to select, be careful not to move the tasks. If you select the wrong task, click within any task to deselect and try again.

---

 11 **Choose Cut on the Standard toolbar.**

A warning box opens (see Figure 3.6). The message appears because several of the tasks have a value entered in the % Complete field.

FIGURE 3.6

12 **Click Yes.**

 13 **Click anywhere in the first blank row after Task 36 (*Provide information to communications team for web page*); then click Paste on the Standard toolbar.**
The tasks are moved to the new location.

14 **Save *Conference_Plan*.**
You have successfully reorganized the *Conference_Plan* project file.
Keep the project open and continue with the next lesson, or close the file and exit Microsoft Project.

LESSON 3: Creating Milestone and Recurring Tasks

Recall that a *milestone task* is one that has no duration but instead marks a significant point in the project plan. You should create milestones for stages you want to monitor closely in a project plan. Specific deliverables that occur after a group of tasks has been completed are often milestones. For example, if you were printing a newsletter, a milestone might be *Printing complete,* which marks that one set of tasks has been completed and another set of tasks—such as collating and distributing the newsletter—are ready to start.

A *recurring task* is one that repeats with some pattern, such as weekly, monthly, or bi-weekly. The most common use of a recurring task is for status meetings. Other uses are quality reviews, risk assessments, and weekly/monthly workers' meetings. The effort toward the project plan is captured, but there are no real work-related tasks involved. A recurring task is placed in the task list as a summary task, with each occurrence as a subtask. A summary task is a task that appears in bold type with several related tasks indented and listed below it. Microsoft Project calculates the duration of the recurring task by using the start of the first subtask and the finish of the last subtask. The summary task uses roll-up formatting; in the Gantt chart, each subtask shows short segments for the scheduled times rather than one large Gantt bar. If you have a task that recurs but has no pattern, schedule it as several individual tasks instead.

In this lesson, you create a recurring task for the weekly sub-team meeting for the conference. You also change Task 60 (*Conference begins*) and Task 49 (*Approve transportation plan*) to milestones because they mark the completion of a set of tasks.

To Create a Recurring Task and a Milestone Task

1 **Open the *Conference_Plan* project file, if necessary, and then click Task 3 (*Arrange core-team site visit*).**

2 **Choose Insert, Recurring Task.**
The Recurring Task Information dialog box opens (see Figure 3.7).

FIGURE 3.7

3 Type `Weekly sub-team meeting` in the *Task Name* text box.

4 Select *Weekly* under *Recurrence pattern,* if necessary; then check *Friday* and click OK.

A warning box appears (see Figure 3.8). Because you are inserting a new recurring task into a Microsoft Project file with existing tasks, there are start date conflicts that need to be resolved.

FIGURE 3.8

5 Click Yes to allow Microsoft Project to reschedule the conflicts.

A new recurring task is entered into row 3 with an icon in the Indicator column signifying that it repeats (see Figure 3.9). This recurring meeting must occur on a scheduled day each week. Each occurrence automatically has a ***Start No Earlier Than*** constraint applied to it, which means that the task must start on or after the specified date for each meeting occurrence.

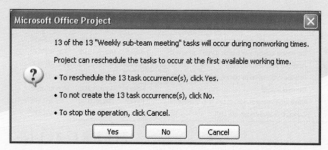

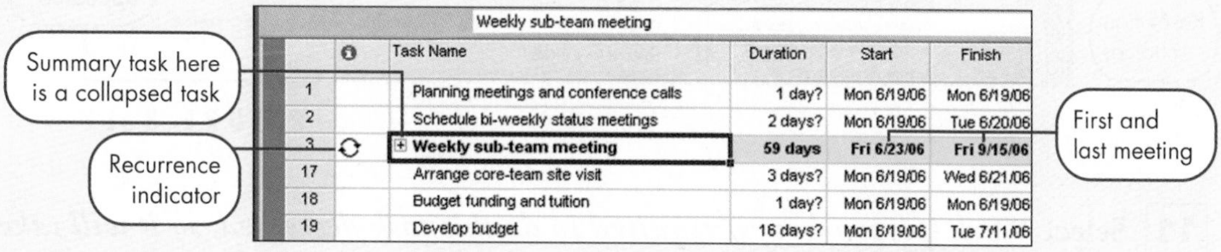

FIGURE 3.9

6 **Click in the first blank row after Task 60 (*Presenter check-in*), and then type Conference begins.**

7 **Press `Tab⇄` to move to the Duration field, type 0, and then press `↵Enter`.**
Entering a zero duration marks a task as a milestone, as indicated by the symbol on the Gantt chart (see Figure 3.10).

	ⓘ	Task Name	Duration	Start	Finish	8 ... Jun 18, '06 ... Jun 25, '
54	✓	Arrange for onsite fax machines	2 days?	Thu 8/10/06	Fri 8/11/06	
55	✓	Arrange for onsite printers	2 days?	Thu 8/10/06	Fri 8/11/06	
56		Set up schedule for security requirements	2 days?	Thu 8/10/06	Fri 8/11/06	
57		Create/order message board (for attendees)	2 days?	Fri 9/15/06	Mon 9/18/06	
58		Hotel rooms and cross check	3 days?	Thu 9/14/06	Mon 9/18/06	
59		Registration	3 days?	Thu 9/14/06	Mon 9/18/06	
60		Presenter check-in	3 days?	Thu 9/14/06	Mon 9/18/06	
61		Conference begins	0 days	Mon 6/19/06	Mon 6/19/06	◆ 6/19

Duration of 0 signifies a milestone

Milestone symbol

FIGURE 3.10

8 **Click in the Duration column of Task 49 (*Approve transportation plan*), type 0, and then press `↵Enter`.**
A small green flag appears in the upper-left corner of the cell, indicating a note (see Figure 3.11). Microsoft Project requires additional information about this duration change for Task 49.

47	Determine shuttle services to/from airport	2 days?	Mon 6/19/06	Tue 6/20/06	
48	Determine any special needs given conference	2 days?	Mon 6/19/06	Tue 6/20/06	
49	Approve transportation plan	0 days	Mon 6/19/06	Mon 6/19/06	
50	Provide information to communications team fo	2 days?	Mon 6/19/06	Tue 6/20/06	
51	General issues	1 day?	Mon 6/19/06	Mon 6/19/06	
52	Make arrangements for receipt and storage of	2 days?	Thu 8/10/06	Fri 8/11/06	
53	Conduct walk-through site visit	2 days?	Mon 6/19/06	Tue 6/20/06	

Green flag

FIGURE 3.11

9 **Move the mouse to the green flag and pause.**
A smart tag appears. Smart tags appear whenever a change is made that requires additional information.

10 **Point to the smart tag, and then click the down arrow when it appears.**
A list of choices displays (see Figure 3.12).

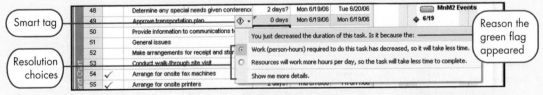

Smart tag

Resolution choices

Reason the green flag appeared

FIGURE 3.12

11 **Select *Work (person-hours) required to do this task decreased, so it will take less time.***
The first option is the default action Microsoft Project uses if no action is taken with the smart tag.

12 **Save *Conference_Plan*.**

You have successfully created a recurring task and specified milestones in the *Conference_Plan* project file.

Keep it open and continue with the next lesson, or close the file and exit Microsoft Project.

LESSON 4: Linking Tasks by Specifying Task Predecessors

Some tasks work hand-in-hand with other tasks in the project file. For example, Task 1 may need to be completed before you start Task 2. When you link a task, you specify a ***predecessor task*** (the first task in the link) and a ***successor task*** (the dependent or linked task). A task link—also referred to as task dependency—sets the field for working with lag and lead time. ***Lead time*** is an overlap of time between two dependent tasks, while ***lag time*** is a delay between two tasks. The advantage to using links in a task list is clear when changes in scheduling become necessary. If the schedule for the predecessor task changes, Microsoft Project automatically reschedules the dependent tasks and recalculates the schedule for you.

When referring to a task dependency, you name the linked date of the predecessor task first and then the linked date of the successor task. The most common and default type of task dependency is ***Finish-to-Start (FS).*** An FS link means that the successor task cannot begin until the previous task, or predecessor, is complete.

You can also create a ***Finish-to-Finish (FF)*** dependency, which mandates that when a predecessor task finishes, the successor task also finishes. A ***Start-to-Start (SS)*** dependency means that both the predecessor and successor tasks start at the same time. This type of link is employed when several related tasks must begin at the same time. There is also a ***Start-to-Finish (SF)*** dependency in which, as soon as a predecessor task starts, the successor task can finish. This type of relationship is used less frequently than the other types.

In this lesson, you create a variety of task links by specifying task predecessors. You begin by creating multiple FS (Finish-to-Start) task links. You also create FF (Finish-to-Finish) and SS (Start-to-Start) task links.

To Link Tasks by Specifying Task Predecessors

1 **Open the *Conference_Plan* file, if necessary; then drag the split bar between the Task table and the Gantt chart to the right until you can see some of the Predecessors column.**

The mouse pointer becomes a resizing pointer when positioned on the split bar (see Figure 3.13). The task table now occupies approximately ¾ of the screen.

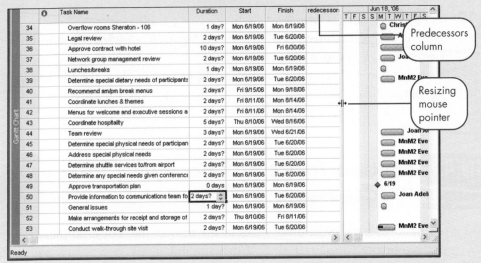

FIGURE 3.13

2 | **Click in Task 19 (*Develop budget*).**

Notice that the task has a start date of *Mon 6/19/06* and a finish date of *Tue 7/11/06*. This task cannot begin until you identify the source for the budget funding and tuition monies specified in Task 18.

3 | **Click in the Predecessors column for Task 19, type 18, and press ⏎Enter.**

A Finish-to-Start link between Tasks 18 and 19 appears on the Gantt chart (see Figure 3.14). The link line begins at the end of the first task's Gantt bar and ends at the start of the second task's Gantt bar. Notice that both the start and finish dates for Task 19 have been increased by one day—the duration it will take to complete Task 18.

FIGURE 3.14

4 | **Select Tasks 22 (*Determine billing process*) and 23 (*Budget reconciliation process*).**

 If you have problems . . .

To select adjacent tasks, click the first task's ID field and drag to the last task's ID field. To select two or more nonadjacent tasks, click the first task's ID field, press Ctrl, and click the other tasks' ID fields.

5 **Click Link Tasks.**

The number *22* is inserted in the Predecessors column in Task 23, creating an FS link, and the start and finish dates for Task 23 adjust (see Figure 3.15).

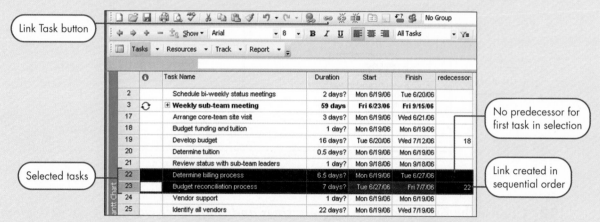

FIGURE 3.15

6 **Select Tasks 47 (*Determine shuttle services to/from airport*) through 50 (*Provide information to communications team for web page*), and then click Link Tasks.**

Each successor has the previous task as the predecessor. Microsoft Project assigns predecessors for a group of tasks in sequential order.

7 **Select Tasks 53 (*Conduct walk through site visit*) through 61 (*Conference begins*), and then click Link Tasks.**

8 **Click in the Predecessors column for Task 42 (*Menus for welcome and executive sessions and special evening event*), type 40, and then press ⏎Enter.**

A *noncontiguous link* joins tasks that are not directly adjacent. In this case, a default FS link between Task 42 and Task 40 (*Recommend am/pm break menus*) is created because both tasks deal with the selection of menus for breaks and special sessions.

9 **Press Ctrl+Home.**

Tasks 1 and 2 are so closely linked that both must be completed at the same time.

10 **Click anywhere in Task 2 (*Schedule bi-weekly status meetings*).**

11 **Choose Project, Task Information; and then click the Predecessors tab.**

12 **Click in the Task Name column, and then click the drop-down arrow.**

A list of all tasks entered into the Project plan, except the selected task, appears (see Figure 3.16).

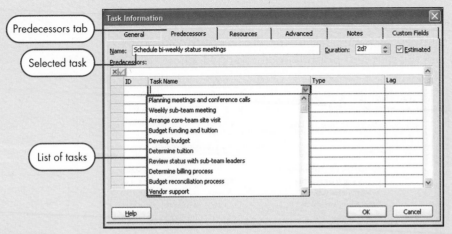

FIGURE 3.16

13 Choose the first task (*Planning meetings and conference calls*).

14 Click in the Type column, click the drop-down arrow, choose *Finish-to-Finish (FF),* and then click OK.

The Predecessors column shows *1FF,* indicating the Finish-to-Finish link with Task 1. A join line has been added from the end of the Task 1 Gantt bar to the end of the Task 2 Gantt bar (see Figure 3.17). Notice also that this type of relationship does not affect the finish date for Task 2.

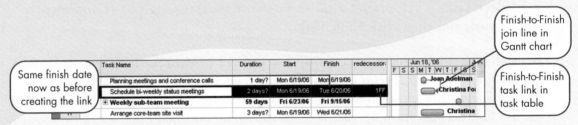

FIGURE 3.17

15 Locate Task 33 (*Reserve block of rooms - 706*); then click in the Predecessors column, type **32**, and press ⏎Enter.

A default FS link to Task 32 (*Determine site location*) is created, adjusting the start date from *Mon 6/19/06* to *Fri 6/23/06.*

16 Double-click Task 34 (*Overflow rooms Sheraton - 106*), and then click the Predecessors tab, if necessary.

17 In the Task Name column, type **Res**; then click the drop-down arrow and choose *Reserve block of rooms - 706.*

As you type letters in the *Task Name* text box, Microsoft Project automatically searches in the task names for a match. When you click the drop-down arrow, the list displays the first match as the selected task name.

18 **Choose *Start-to-Start (SS)* in the Type column and click OK.**

The Predecessors column shows *33SS,* indicating the Start-to-Start link with Task 33. A join line has been added from the beginning of the Task 33 Gantt bar to the beginning of the Task 34 Gantt bar (see Figure 3.18). In addition, the start date is adjusted to match that of Task 33.

	32	Determine site location	4 days?	Mon 6/19/06	Thu 6/22/06			Christi
	33	Reserve block of rooms - 706	1 day?	Fri 6/23/06	Fri 6/23/06	32		Chr
	34	Overflow rooms Sheraton - 106	1 day?	Fri 6/23/06	Fri 6/23/06	33SS		Chr
	35	Legal review	2 days?	Mon 6/19/06	Tue 6/20/06			Alison Arno
	36	Approve contract with hotel	10 days?	Mon 6/19/06	Fri 6/30/06			

Start-to-Start task link in task table

Start-to-Start join line in Gantt chart

FIGURE 3.18

19 **Save *Conference_Plan.***

You created links between the various tasks in your project plan and specified dependencies and predecessors. Keep the *Conference_Plan* file open and continue with the next lesson, or close the file and exit Microsoft Project.

TO EXTEND YOUR KNOWLEDGE . . .

CHOOSING THE DEPENDENT TASK

If you have equal scheduling control over two related tasks, make the task that must be completed first the predecessor and the later task the successor. If you do not have control, make the more flexible task the successor, regardless of which task actually comes first.

LESSON 5: Using Outline Features and Viewing Work Breakdown Structure (WBS) Codes

The outline features provided with Microsoft Project enable you to visually identify the phases of a project and to group related tasks. When you use outlining, major topics are called summary tasks, which appear in bold type in the task table, and subordinate tasks that represent the details of a summary task are called subtasks. Subtasks are indented below the corresponding summary task. The duration of a summary task is the combined durations of the subtasks below it.

To make a task a subtask, you demote the task by using the Indent button on the Formatting toolbar. The summary task occurs as a result of having tasks demoted below it. When you create a summary task, Microsoft Project calculates the duration, using the start date of the first subtask and the finish date of the last subtask. You cannot edit the duration of a summary task.

When you utilize the outline features, Microsoft Project automatically assigns **Work Breakdown Structure (WBS) codes.** These codes are the default outline numbers automatically assigned to each task that identify its hierarchical position within your project plan.

Once a project plan has been outlined, you can use the Show features—the plus (+) or minus (–) symbol—to collapse and expand the tasks that you want to view. This feature can be especially handy for creating a quick report for a stakeholder or manager who is not interested in the fine details of a project.

In this lesson, you create summary tasks in the Conference_Plan project file by utilizing outlining techniques. You also view the WBS codes of several tasks that have been assigned by Microsoft Project.

To Use Outline Features

1 Open *Conference_Plan,* if necessary; then select Tasks 2 (*Schedule bi-weekly status meetings*) through 17 (*Arrange core-team site visit*).

2 Click Indent on the Formatting toolbar.
Task 1 (*Planning meetings and conference calls*) becomes a summary task, while Tasks 2 through 17 become subtasks (see Figure 3.19).

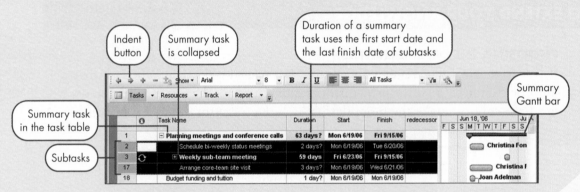

FIGURE 3.19

3 Select Tasks 19 (*Develop budget*) through 23 (*Budget reconciliation process*); and then click Indent.

4 Select Tasks 25 (*Identify all vendors*) through 27 (*Finalize contracts*) and indent these tasks as well.

5 Select Tasks 28 (*Site/hotel*) through 35 (*Legal review*) and then click Indent two times.
Task 27 (*Finalize contracts*) becomes a summary task for Tasks 28 through 35, while it also remains a subtask of Task 24 *Vendor support* (see Figure 3.20). Task 24 starts a phase within a phase.

First summary task in phase

Second summary task in same phase

23	Budget reconciliation process	7 days?	Tue 6/27/06	Fri 7/7/06	22
24	⊟ **Vendor support**	**65.7 days?**	**Mon 6/19/06**	**Wed 9/20/06**	
25	Identify all vendors	22 days?	Mon 6/19/06	Wed 7/19/06	
26	Identify vendor points of contact	3 days?	Fri 9/15/06	Wed 9/20/06	
27	⊟ **Finalize contracts**	**5 days?**	**Mon 6/19/06**	**Fri 6/23/06**	
28	Site/hotel	1 day?	Mon 6/19/06	Mon 6/19/06	
29	Network group management review	1.5 days?	Mon 6/19/06	Tue 6/20/06	
30	Investigate different site options	4 days?	Mon 6/19/06	Thu 6/22/06	
31	Identify a site coordinator	4 days?	Mon 6/19/06	Thu 6/22/06	
32	Determine site location	4 days?	Mon 6/19/06	Thu 6/22/06	
33	Reserve block of rooms - 706	1 day?	Fri 6/23/06	Fri 6/23/06	32
34	Overflow rooms Sheraton - 106	1 day?	Fri 6/23/06	Fri 6/23/06	33SS
35	Legal review	2 days?	Mon 6/19/06	Tue 6/20/06	
36	Approve contract with hotel	10 days?	Mon 6/19/06	Fri 6/30/06	

FIGURE 3.20

6 | Select Tasks 36 (*Approve contract with hotel*) and 37 (*Network group management review*), and then click Indent.

7 | Finish outlining the project plan, beginning with Task 39 (*Determine special dietary needs of participants*), as shown in the table below.

Tasks	Indentation
Tasks 39–42	Indent once
Tasks 44–58	Indent once
Tasks 59–60	Indent twice

The outlining of the project is complete. There are now eight summary tasks. Recurring tasks are displayed as summary tasks, but in the Gantt chart, individual Gantt bars are displayed rather than one summary task.

8 | Press Ctrl+Home, click **S**how on the Formatting Toolbar, and then choose *Outline Level 1*.

This view displays only the level 1 summary tasks you created (see Figure 3.21). Note that Task 81 (*Conference begins*) is not a summary task; however, it is a level 1 task thus it is included in this view.

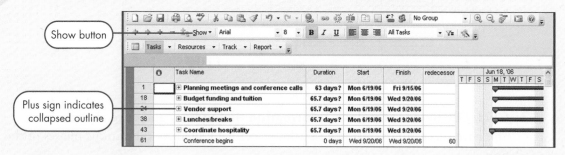

Show button

Plus sign indicates collapsed outline

		❶	Task Name	Duration	Start	Finish	redecessor	Jun 18, '06
	1		⊞ **Planning meetings and conference calls**	63 days?	Mon 6/19/06	Fri 9/15/06		
	18		⊞ **Budget funding and tuition**	65.7 days?	Mon 6/19/06	Wed 9/20/06		
	24		⊞ **Vendor support**	65.7 days?	Mon 6/19/06	Wed 9/20/06		
	38		⊞ **Lunches/breaks**	65.7 days?	Mon 6/19/06	Wed 9/20/06		
	43		⊞ **Coordinate hospitality**	65.7 days?	Mon 6/19/06	Wed 9/20/06		
	61		Conference begins	0 days	Wed 9/20/06	Wed 9/20/06	60	

FIGURE 3.21

9 | Click **S**how, All Subtasks.

Notice that Task 3 is the recurring task and all its subtasks (meetings) are displayed, which is not necessary.

10 | Click the minus sign on the left of the Task Name field Task 3.

The task collapses. To expand it again, click the plus sign.

11 | Double-click Task 1 (*Planning meetings and conference calls*) and then click the Advanced tab.

Notice that the WBS code of *1* is automatically applied to the task (see Figure 3.22).

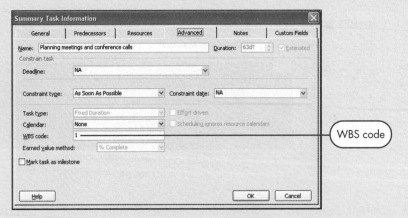

FIGURE 3.22

12 **View the WBS codes for Task 2 (*Schedule bi-weekly status meetings*) and Task 28 (*Site/hotel*).**

The WBS code for Task 2 is 1.1, and the WBS code for Task 28 is 3.3.1 (see Figure 3.23). Each code is assigned a sequential outline number indicating the hierarchical position the task holds within the overall project plan. WBS codes cannot be modified unless the entire scheme is changed.

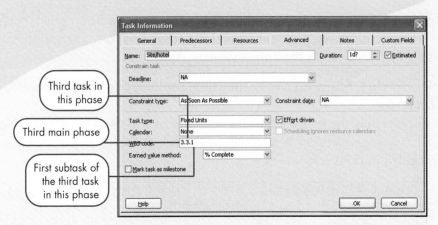

FIGURE 3.23

13 **Click OK to close the Task Information dialog box, and save the file.**

You have successfully created an outline to visually identify the various phases of the project.

Keep the *Conference_Plan* project file open and continue with the next lesson, or close the file and exit Microsoft Project.

TO EXTEND YOUR KNOWLEDGE . . .

WORKING WITH THE OUTLINE FEATURES

There are several other ways to outline a task list besides using the Formatting toolbar. You can use the Project Guide, which is a good idea if you are new to using the program. You can use the mouse to drag the task left or right. To do so, place the mouse over the first letters of the task name until it appears as a double arrow. Drag the pointer to the left or right to change the indent or outdent level of the task. Alternatively, choose <u>P</u>roject, <u>O</u>utline, <u>I</u>ndent or <u>O</u>utdent; or press `Alt`+`⬆Shift`+`→` to indent or `Alt`+`⬆Shift`+`←` to outdent.

SETTING UP CUSTOM WBS CODES

By default, WBS codes are created like outline numbers. Some companies rely heavily on WBS codes and have created custom schemes tailored to the specific needs of the organization. To modify the default scenario created by Microsoft, select <u>P</u>roject, <u>W</u>BS, <u>D</u>efine code. Enter any prefix used in front of the code in the Project Code <u>P</u>refix box, and then specify whether the sequence is a letter or number, specify the length of this level of code, and the type of separator between this level and the next. Repeat this process for each level of the hierarchical structure for the custom WBS codes until all codes are created.

LESSON 6: Applying a Calendar to a Task

In addition to creating a project base calendar, you can also specify unique calendars for individual tasks. By default, all tasks use the project base calendar you create; however, if there are tasks that are independent of the project calendar, you can apply an additional calendar to them. Task calendars provide control over the schedule for particular tasks and do not affect the overall project calendar. Assigning a task calendar to a recurring task affects all occurrences of the task. Assigning a task calendar has the potential to affect the schedule of related predecessor or successor tasks as well as a summary tasks. However, assigning a task calendar to a summary task does not affect the schedule for subtasks nor does it change the schedule for the summary task.

In this lesson, you apply a different calendar to the meeting tasks because some of your team members are in Bangkok. Your team meetings must be at 9:00 P.M. EST to accommodate the time difference.

To Apply a Calendar to a Task

1 **Open *Conference_Plan,* if necessary; then double-click Task 3 (*Weekly sub-team meeting*) and click the Cale<u>n</u>dar drop-down arrow.**

A list of calendars in the project file open in the Recurring Task Information dialog box (see Figure 3.24).

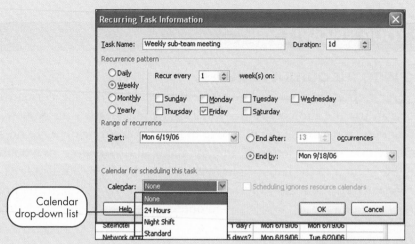

FIGURE 3.24

2 | Choose *24 Hours* and then click OK.

3 | Click the plus sign to the left of the Task 3 Task Name to expand the group, and then point your mouse in the Indicator column of Task 4.
A *constraint icon* appears in the Indicator field next to each occurrence, showing that a scheduling constraint has been applied. Notice that the summary task as well as all the subtasks utilize the 24 Hours calendar (see Figure 3.25).

3		⊟ **Weekly sub-team meeting**	253 days	Fri 6/23/06	Fri 9/15/06	
4		Weekly sub-team meeting 1	1 day	Fri 6/23/06	Fri 6/23/06	
5		This task has a 'Start No Earlier Than'	1 day	Fri 6/30/06	Fri 6/30/06	
6		constraint on Fri 6/23/06.	1 day	Fri 7/7/06	Fri 7/7/06	
7		The calendar '24 Hours' is assigned to	1 day	Fri 7/14/06	Fri 7/14/06	
8		the task. Weekly sub-team meeting 5	1 day	Fri 7/21/06	Fri 7/21/06	
9		Weekly sub-team meeting 6	1 day	Fri 7/28/06	Fri 7/28/06	
10		Weekly sub-team meeting 7	1 day	Fri 8/4/06	Fri 8/4/06	
11		Weekly sub-team meeting 8	1 day	Fri 8/11/06	Fri 8/11/06	
12		Weekly sub-team meeting 9	1 day	Fri 8/18/06	Fri 8/18/06	
13		Weekly sub-team meeting 10	1 day	Fri 8/25/06	Fri 8/25/06	
14		Weekly sub-team meeting 11	1 day	Fri 9/1/06	Fri 9/1/06	
15		Weekly sub-team meeting 12	1 day	Fri 9/8/06	Fri 9/8/06	
16		Weekly sub-team meeting 13	1 day	Fri 9/15/06	Fri 9/15/06	

Note about the constraint and task calendar

Constraint icon

Task calendar icon

FIGURE 3.25

4 | Select Tasks 59 (*Registration*) and 60 (*Presenter check-in*).

5 | Click Task <u>I</u>nformation on the Standard toolbar and then click the Advanced tab.

6 | Choose *24 Hours* in the C<u>a</u>lendar list box and then click OK.
The calendar is applied to both selected tasks.

7 | Save *Conference_Plan*.
You have added individual calendars to a recurring summary task and to multiple tasks.
Keep the *Conference_Plan* project file open and continue with the next lesson. If you prefer to complete the project later, close the file and exit Microsoft Project.

TO EXTEND YOUR KNOWLEDGE . . .

USING BASE CALENDARS VERSUS TASK CALENDARS

To distinguish the task calendars from the base calendars, it is a good idea to name each calendar with some identifier, such as a prefix. Doing so makes it easier to find the calendar you need when assigning calendars.

CREATING A CUSTOM CALENDAR FOR A TASK

You can create a custom task calendar for individual tasks. To do so, choose Tools, Change Working Time. Click Create New Calendar and name your calendar. Click *Create new base calendar,* then click OK. Make your changes, just as you did to create your project calendar.

LESSON 7: Setting Constraints

Constraints are restrictions applied to the start or finish date of a task. *Flexible constraints* are not tied to a task on a specific date. There are four flexible constraints. The *As Soon As Possible (ASAP)* constraint allows you to start a task as soon as possible in relation to the scheduled start date. By default, Project assigns an ASAP constraint to all tasks in project files that are scheduled from the start date, because it is the most flexible constraint. The opposite of ASAP is the *As Late As Possible (ALAP)* constraint, which allows you to start a task as near as possible to the scheduled project finish date. By default, Project assigns an ALAP constraint to all tasks in projects that are scheduled from the finish date, because it is the most flexible constraint for this type of project file. The *Finish No Earlier Than (FNET)* constraint requires that a task finish on or after a specific date. *Finish No Later Than (FNLT)* schedules a task to finish on or before a specified date. All flexible constraints take into account other task dependencies and constraints. Tasks with flexible constraints display a blue dot in the constraint icon in the Indicator column.

Inflexible constraints tie a task to a specific date. They are generally applied to tasks controlled by external or outside factors. External factors might include drop-dead deadlines or availability of an asset, such as a crane. There are four inflexible constraints. *Must Finish On (MFO)* has an associated date that controls when a task finishes. *Must Start On (MSO)* has an associated date that controls when a task starts. Start No Earlier Than (SNET) schedules the task to start on or after a specified date. *Start No Later Than (SNLT)* schedules the task to start on or before a specified date. Tasks with inflexible constraints display a red dot in the constraint icon in the Indicator column.

In the event that a constraint and a task link conflict, Microsoft Project honors the constraint and ignores the link.

In this lesson, you assign constraints to those tasks that have specific scheduling restrictions not addressed by the automatic scheduling utilized in Microsoft Project.

To Set Constraints

1 **Open *Conference_Plan,* if necessary; then double-click Task 17 (*Arrange core-team site visit*).**

Because this task involves a business trip and is the starting point for many of the other tasks in the project plan, you apply a flexible constraint indicating that the task must be completed by June 21, 2006.

2 **Click the Advanced tab, if necessary, then click the *Constraint type* drop-down arrow.**

A list of constraint types displays (see Figure 3.26).

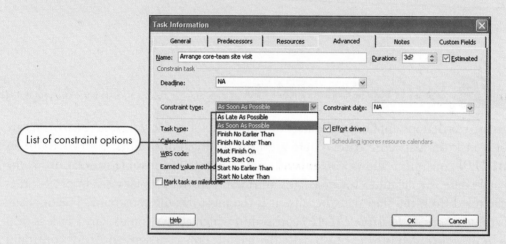

List of constraint options

FIGURE 3.26

3 **Choose *Finish No Later Than,* click OK, and then deselect the task.**

A calendar icon appears in the Indicator column, signifying the task constraint.

4 **Double-click Task 17 again.**

Notice that the entry in the *Constraint date* text box has been completed for you (see Figure 3.27). When using flexible constraints, Microsoft Project automatically applies the correct date as based on the current project plan's estimated task duration. Recall that a red dot in the constraint icon represents an inflexible constraint.

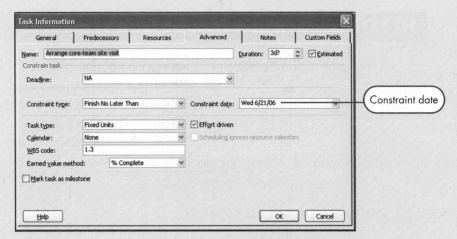

FIGURE 3.27

5 | Click Cancel to close the dialog box.

6 | Double-click Task 36 (*Approve contract with hotel*) and then apply the Must Finish On constraint.

7 | Click in the Duration column for Task 36 and change the duration to *11 days;* then press ⏎Enter.

The Planning Wizard dialog box appears because of the constraint applied to this task (see Figure 3.28).

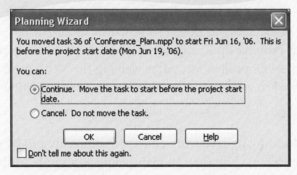

FIGURE 3.28

8 | Click the first option and then click OK.

Because of the constraint, the finish date of the task is not modified; instead, the task's start date is changed to June 16, 2006, which is earlier than the project's start date of June 19. This does not make sense.

9 | Click Undo on the Standard toolbar to return the duration of Task 36 to 10 days, and then click Save.

Leave Microsoft Project open if you plan to continue with the end-of-project exercises; otherwise, exit Microsoft Project.

TO EXTEND YOUR KNOWLEDGE . . .

CHANGING THE SCHEDULE TO A FIXED FINISH DATE

If you want to change scheduling for a project from a fixed start date to a fixed finish date, you may also desire to change the default constraint type. To do so, use the Replace feature. Choose Edit, Replace. Type **As Soon As Possible** in the *Find what* box, and then type **As Late As Possible** in the *Replace with* box. Select *Constraint Type* in the *Look in* Field drop-down list and select *equals* in the Test box.

DOCUMENTING A CONSTRAINT

Because constraints can create conflicts in the schedule, you should use the Note field in the Task Information dialog box to document the purpose of a constraint. Notes are especially helpful in alleviating confusion if you are sharing the project file or if someone else assumes the responsibility of the project.

SUMMARY

In this project, you entered tasks into the task table and specified task durations. Your actions included organizing tasks by inserting new blank rows and cutting and pasting tasks into different locations within the project file, creating a recurring task, and specifying two milestone tasks. Task links provided the next area of focus. You learned to specify predecessors to create links between related tasks, and you observed how this modified the start and finish dates of linked tasks. Microsoft Project's outline features enabled you to create summary tasks and subtasks to visually organize the project file. After viewing the WBS codes assigned by Microsoft Project, you learned how to assign unique calendars to a task and how to set scheduling constraints.

You can extend your learning by reviewing concepts and terms and by practicing variations of skills presented in the lessons. Use the following table as a guide to the numbered questions and exercises in the end-of-project learning opportunities.

LESSON	MULTIPLE CHOICE	DISCUSSION	SKILL DRILL	CHALLENGE	DISCOVERY ZONE
Entering Tasks and Specifying Durations	1, 6	1	1	1	1
Organizing Tasks	2		2		1
Creating Milestone and Recurring Tasks	3, 9		3	1	1
Linking Tasks by Specifying Task Predecessors	5, 10	3	4	3	1
Using Outline Features and Viewing Work Breakdown Structure (WBS) Codes	7	2	2	2	1
Applying a Calendar to a Task	8		5	4	1
Setting Constraints	4		5	4	2

KEY TERMS

As Late As Possible (ALAP)

As Soon As Possible (ASAP)

constraint icon

deliverables

Finish field

Finish No Earlier Than (FNET)

Finish No Later Than (FNLT)

Finish-to-Finish (FF)

Finish-to-Start (FS)

flexible constraints

ID field

inflexible constraints

lag time

lead time

Must Finish On (MFO)

Must Start On (MSO)

noncontiguous link

overflow markers

phase

predecessor task

Predecessors field

recurring task

Resource Names field

Start field

Start No Earlier Than (SNET)

Start No Later Than (SNLT)

Start-to-Finish (SF)

Start-to-Start (SS)

successor task

Task Name field

Work Breakdown Structure (WBS) codes

CHECKING CONCEPTS AND TERMS

SCREEN ID

Label each element of the Project screen shown in Figure 3.29 [L1–L7]

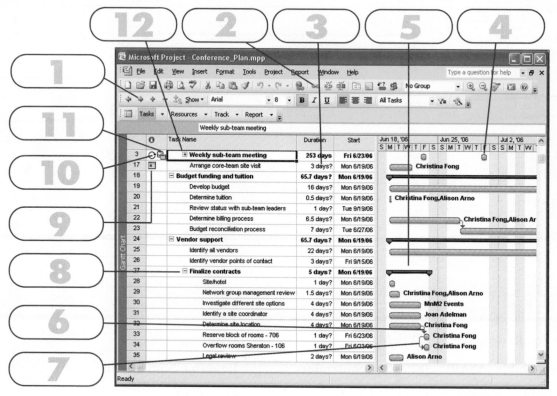

FIGURE 3.29

A. Recurring task symbol

B. Collapsed phase

C. FS link

D. Summary task Gantt bar

E. Indent button

F. Estimated duration

G. Constraint symbol

H. Task calendar symbol

I. SS link

J. Recurring task in Gantt chart

K. Expanded phase

L. Link Tasks button

MULTIPLE CHOICE

Circle the letter of the correct answer for each of the following.

1. Which of the following does not designate a task duration type? [L1]

   a. d

   b. mo

   c. w

   d. y

2. What happens when you try to paste a task into a row with existing data? [L2]

   a. The existing task is deleted automatically.

   b. A new row is inserted and the task being moved is placed in that row.

   c. A warning box appears concerning the deletion of existing data.

   d. You cannot paste a task in a row with existing data.

3. Which task type has no duration? [L3]

   a. Recurring

   b. Summary

   c. Milestone

   d. Subtasks

4. What is the default constraint type for new tasks? [L7]

   a. ALAP

   b. ASAP

   c. FNET

   d. FNLT

5. Which task is the first in a task link? [L4]

   a. Milestone

   b. Summary

   c. Successor

   d. Predecessor

6. Which of the following is not a default field in the task table? [L1]

   a. Budget

   b. Predecessor

   c. Task Name

   d. Duration

7. Which field cannot be modified in a summary task? [L5]

   a. Task Name

   b. Duration

   c. Resource

   d. Predecessor

8. Which of the following is true of a task calendar? [L6]

   a. It affects the schedule of all occurrences in a recurring task.

   b. It affects the schedule of all subtasks when applied to a summary task.

   c. It affects the schedule of all summary tasks in the project file.

   d. It never affects any task other than the selected task.

9. Which task below would be most appropriately formatted as a recurring task? [L3]

   a. Risk assessment

   b. Job interviews

   c. Holidays

   d. Company picnic

10. Suppose your project file includes the tasks for painting a house. Task 1 is painting the first coat and Task 2 is painting the second coat. Which type of link should you use? [L4]

    a. Finish-to-Start

    b. Finish-to-Finish

    c. Start-to-Finish

    d. Start-to-Start

DISCUSSION

1. The duration of a task can be measured in minutes, hours, days, weeks, or months. Give one example of how to use each different duration type. [L1]

2. Some project managers develop a project plan by creating phases and then determining the detailed subtasks. Other project managers do the reverse—meaning they group the tasks after they are created. Discuss the advantages and disadvantages of each method. [L5]

3. Suppose you are building a home, and you are contracting the work yourself. You decide to use Microsoft Project to help you keep track of the various activities. Give an example of each task link type (FS, FF, SF, SS). [L4]

SKILL DRILL

Skill Drill exercises reinforce project skills. Each skill reinforced is the same, or nearly the same, as a skill presented in the project. Detailed instructions are provided in a step-by-step format.

You should complete exercises 2–5 in sequence. Skill Drill exercise 1 is independent of the others and can be worked at any time.

While working with the Skill Drill exercises, a Planning Wizard dialog box may appear suggesting a faster method to perform the current action. You can close this dialog box by clicking OK.

1. Entering Tasks

You and your spouse are members of a social club. The social club is planning to take a cruise as a group. You have been asked to organize the club's efforts in finding a cruise, booking it, and making other necessary arrangements. You are considering becoming a cruise specialist for a travel agency and decide to use Microsoft Project to determine if it is the right tool for managing cruises for clientele.

To create a new project and enter tasks, follow these steps:

1. Start Microsoft Office Project 2007, close any open side panes, and then open a new project file.

2. Choose Project, Project Information.

3. Select *Thu 12/1/05* as the Start date and then click OK.

4. Click in the first row in the Task Name column and type **Research cruises online**.

5. Press Tab, and type **1w**.

6. Click in the Task Name box in row 2 and type **Consult travel agent**.

7. Press Tab, and type **3h**.

8. Complete typing the remaining tasks and durations as shown in the following table.

Task Name	Duration
Choose travel dates	1wk
Choose the cruise	1d?
Downpayment on cruise	1d?
Obtain birth certificate	6wks
Choose onshore excursions	4d
Book transportation/hotel to port	1d?
Pack for the cruise	2d
Bon Voyage	1d?

9. Save the file as **Cruise_Planning** and then close it.

2. Organizing Tasks

As the committee leader for the cruise planning committee, you have created a project file to track the progress of the cruise preparations you created in the previous exercise. During the last committee meeting, the members made some suggestions for other tasks that need to be added to the plan. They also pointed out where some tasks were in the wrong location.

To organize and outline tasks, follow these steps:

1. Start Microsoft Project, if necessary.

2. Open *EPr1_0302* and save it as **Club_Cruise**, and then close any open side panes.

3. Click Task 1 and choose Insert, New task.

4. Type **Research** as the task name.

5. Click within Task 7 (*Choose travel dates*); then press Insert.

6. Type **Narrow cruise choices to 2 - 3 cruises** as the task name.

7. Press Tab and type **3d?**.

8. Insert a row above Task 14 (*Obtain birth certificate*), and then type **Obtain necessary paperwork** as the task name using the default duration.

9. Click the row heading for Task 12 (*Choose the cruise*), and choose Edit, Cut Task.

10. Click the row heading for Task 9 (*Compare prices of cabins*), and then choose Edit, Paste.

11. Select Task 14 (*Obtain necessary paperwork*) through Task 16 (*Obtain passport*).

12. Click Cut Task on the Standard toolbar.

13. Click in Task 7 (*Narrow cruise choices to 2 - 3 choices*) and click Paste on the Standard toolbar.

14. Save *Club_Cruise*, and leave it open for the next exercise.

3. Outlining Tasks

Now that you have a complete list of tasks for the cruise committee, you need to outline the tasks into summary tasks and subtasks.

To outline tasks, follow these steps:

1. Open *Club_Cruise,* if necessary, and then highlight Task 2 (*Research cruises online*) through Task 5 (*Choose departure port*) and click Indent on the Formatting toolbar.

2. Select Task 8 (*Obtain birth certificate*) and Task 9 (*Obtain passport*), and then click Indent.

3. Select Task 14 (*Choose type of cabin*) and Task 15 (*Choose deck of cabin*), and then click Indent.

4. Select Task 18 (*Book onshore excursions*) and click Indent.

5. Select Task 20 (*Purchase any clothing or necessities*) and click Indent.

6. Click <u>S</u>how on the Standard Toolbar and choose *Outline Level 1.*

7. Click <u>S</u>how and then <u>A</u>ll subtasks.

8. Click the minus sign to the left of Task 1 (*Research*).

9. Double-click Task 14 (*Choose type of cabin*); then click the Advanced tab, if necessary, look at the WBS code, and close the dialog box.

10. Save *Club_Cruise,* and leave it open for the next exercise.

4. Assigning Recurring Tasks and Milestones

As you work with the cruise plan and the project file, you realize you need to add two different recurring meetings to the plan: the regular club meeting once a month and the cruise committee's bi-weekly meetings. You also realize that two of the listed tasks do not actually include work; they are milestones.

To create recurring tasks and milestones, follow these steps:

1. Open *Club_Cruise*, if necessary.

2. Click Task 1 (Research).

3. Choose <u>I</u>nsert, <u>R</u>ecurring Task; then type **Cruise Committee meeting** in the <u>T</u>ask Name text box.

4. Under Recurrence pattern, select <u>W</u>eekly, if necessary; then check T<u>u</u>esday, and select *Recur every 2 week(s) on:*

5. Choose February 28, 2006, as the *End <u>b</u>y* date and then click OK.

6. Click <u>I</u>nsert, <u>R</u>ecurring Task; then type **Club meetings** in the <u>T</u>ask Name text box.

7. Under *Recurrence pattern,* select Mont<u>h</u>ly and then select *Th<u>e</u> first Monday of every 1 months.*

8. Choose February 6, 2006, as the *End <u>b</u>y* date, and then click OK.

9. Click in the Duration column of Task 24 (*Choose the cruise*), type **0** to change this task to a milestone, and then press ⏎Enter.

10. Make Task 36 (*Bon Voyage*) a milestone task by changing the duration to zero.

11. Save *Club_Cruise,* and leave it open for the next exercise.

5. Setting Constraints and Linking Tasks

The project file for the cruise is almost finished. Now, you just need to create links to make sure the timing of the tasks is correct. The downpayment for the cruise is due 60 days before the cruise departure date. The departure date is also inflexible. Both of these tasks need constraints.

To set constraints and link selected tasks, follow these steps:

1. Open *Club_Cruise*, if necessary, and drag the split bar between the Task table and the Gantt chart to the right so that you can see the Predecessors column.

2. Click in the Predecessors column for Task 15 (*Choose cruise line*), type **14**, and then press ↵Enter.

3. Continue creating links as listed in the table below (all are Finish-to-Start links).

   Link between:

Task	Predecessor
Task 18	Task 17
Task 21	Task 20
Task 22	Task 18
Task 24	Task 23
Task 26	Task 22
Task 27	Task 22
Task 30	Task 28
Task 33	Task 28
Task 36	Task 35

4. Click anywhere on Task 16 (*Choose travel route*); choose Project, Task Information, and then click the Predecessors tab.

5. Click in the Task Name column, and then click the drop-down arrow.

6. Choose the *Choose cruise line* task.

7. Click the Type column drop-down arrow, choose *Start-to-Start (SS),* and then click OK.

8. Locate Task 17 (*Choose departure port*), click in the Predecessors column, type **16SS**, and then press ↵Enter.

9. Double-click Task 23 (*Choose travel dates*) to view the Task Information dialog box and click the Predecessors tab, if necessary.

10. In the Task Name column, click the drop-down arrow and then choose *Narrow cruise choices to 2 - 3 cruises.*

11. Choose *Start-to-Start (SS)* as the task type, and then click OK.

12. Create an SF link between Tasks 34 (*Pack for the cruise*) and 36 (*Bon Voyage*), using Task 34 as the predecessor task.

13. Double-click Task 36 (*Bon Voyage*), and click the Advanced tab.

14. Click the *Constraint type* drop-down arrow, choose *Must Finish On,* select *Mon 3/6/06* in the *Constraint date* box, and then click OK.

15. Choose the 3rd option (*Continue. A Must Finish On constraint will be set.*) in the warning box, and then click OK.

16. Double-click Task 20 (*Obtain birth certificate*), and then apply the Finish No Later Than constraint type with a date of January 11, 2006.

17. Double-click Task 28 (*Downpayment on cruise*), and then apply the Must Finish On constraint with a constraint date of January 6, 2006.

18. Save the *Club_Cruise* file and close it.

CHALLENGE

Challenge exercises expand on or are somewhat related to skills presented in the lessons. Each exercise provides a brief narrative introduction, followed by instructions in a numbered-step format that are not as detailed as those in the Skill Drill section.

Exercises 2–3 should be worked in order. Exercises 1 and 4 are independent of the others and can be worked at any time.

While working with the Challenge exercises, a Planning Wizard dialog box may appear onscreen, suggesting a faster method to perform the current action. You are encouraged to read the suggestion and then try suggested method.

1. Creating a New Project File and Entering Tasks and Milestones

You are a graphic designer assigned to create several brochures, banners, and a variety of give-away gifts, such as T-shirts and coffee mugs, for a new apartment complex opening in your community. This apartment complex is targeted toward the university in your city, and the promotional items you are creating need to be available prior to the start of the new school year.

To create a new project plan to manage the many aspects of this ongoing project, follow these steps:

1. Create a new project file and save it as **Signs_Graphics**.

2. Specify May 2, 2005, as the date to schedule from, and create a project base calendar using the Standard calendar template.

3. Define the general working times to begin at 9:00 A.M. and to end at 5:30 P.M., with a 30-minute lunch and a standard 8-hour day.

4. Add Memorial Day, July 4th, and Labor Day as nonworking days.

5. Enter the following tasks and durations into the plan, using estimated duration:

ID	Task Name	Duration
1	Develop overall look and style	15d
2	Develop logo and slogan	15d
3	Design stationery	10d
4	Provide mock-up to marketing director	1d
5	Receive feedback and make changes	2d
6	Receive green light	1d

7	Provide logo to web designer	1d
8	Design opening banner for bldg 1	10d
9	Design community event banner	10d
10	Provide all banners to printer	1d
11	Leasing office sign	2d
12	Provide leasing materials to print shop	1d
13	Select giveaways	5d
14	Marketing director approval	5d

6. Change Task 6 (*Receive green light*) to a milestone.

7. Insert a new milestone task at the bottom of the plan called **Community Lease-up**.

8. Change the start date of the new milestone task to August 1, 2005. (If a smart tag appears, accept the constraint.)

9. Insert a new recurring task after Task 1 and name it **Weekly Meeting**, to occur each Tuesday starting on May 3, 2005, and ending by July 29, 2005.

10. Click Yes in response to the dialog box that warns there are some nonworking holidays in the plan and some of the meetings will need to be rescheduled.

11. Save *Signs_Graphics* and close it.

2. Creating Summary Tasks and Using the Outline Features

Your work on the apartment complex lease-up has grown, and additional tasks and responsibilities have been entered into the plan. To further refine the project, you want to insert new summary tasks to create phases and then use the outline features in your plan.

To insert new summary tasks and use the outline features in your plan, follow these steps:

1. Open *EPr1_0303* and save it as **Apartment_Artwork**.

2. Insert the following new summary tasks:

   Insert a new Task 1 with the name **Templates and graphics**.

   Insert a new task above Task 23 (*Design opening banner for bldg 1*) with the name **Signs and banners**.

   Insert a new task above Task 27 (*Leasing office sign*) with the name **Leasing materials**.

   Insert a new task above Task 41 (*Provide leasing materials to print shop*) with the name **Giveaways**.

3. Now use Microsoft Project's outline features to demote the appropriate groups of tasks listed below the summary tasks you inserted, to create an outline showing the different phases of your project plan.

   You should end up with four groups of tasks demoted below each summary task, and then the final task, which is a milestone and should not be demoted.

4. Save *Apartment_Artwork* and leave it open for the next exercise.

3. Linking Tasks

Now that you've outlined your *Apartment_Artwork* project plan, you need to create links between those tasks that have dependencies so that the task durations will calculate correctly.

To link tasks, follow these steps:

1. Open *Apartment_Artwork,* if necessary, and widen the task table to display the Predecessors column.

2. Link Task 2 (*Develop overall look and style*) and Task 17 (*Develop logo and slogan*) with the default Finish-to-Start link.

3. Link the following tasks, all with the Finish-to-Start link type, using the first task listed as the predecessor task:

    Task 17 (*Develop logo and slogan*) to Task 19 (*Provide mock-up to marketing director*)

    Task 19 (*Provide mock-up to Marketing Director*) to Task 20 (*Receive feedback and make changes*)

    Task 20 (*Receive feedback and make changes*) to Task 21 (*Receive green light*)

    Task 21 (*Receive green light*) to Task 22 (*Provide mogo to Web Designer*)

    Task 25 (*Design Community Event banner*) to Task 26 (*Provide all banners to printer*)

    Task 33 (*Community information sheet*) to Task 34 (*Notes on our community*)

    Task 34 (*Notes on our community*) to Task 35 (*Map of community*)

    Task 35 (*Map of community*) to Task 36 (*Sheet with local listings*)

    Task 36 (*Sheet with local listings*) to Task 42 (*Provide leasing materials to print shop*)

    Task 43 (*Select giveaways*) to Task 44 (*Marketing Director approval*)

4. View the Task Information dialog box for Task 25 (*Design Community Event banner*) and create a Start-to-Start link with Task 24 (*Design opening banner for Bldg 1*).

5. Create a Finish-to-Finish link for Task 28 (*Leasing office sign*) with Task 26 (*Provide all banners to printer*).

6. Save and close *Apartment_Artwork.*

4. Setting Constraints and Assigning Task Calendars

You are on a team developing a new internal training Web portal where employees of your company can go to download product information papers and listen to streamed media or recordings of engineers discussing the technical specifications for their products that can be played via the Internet. You will work on this project file by adding constraints and assigning task calendars.

To set constraints and assign task calendars:

1. Open *EPr1_0304* and save it as **Training_Portal**.

2. View the task information for Task 15 (*Showcase booth with test prep site*) and set a Start No Earlier Than constraint for this task so that it does not begin until November 8, 2005.

3. View the task information for Task 3 (*Review logos and identify favorite two*) and set a Finish No Later Than constraint with a date of September 13, 2005.

4. Assign a 24 Hours calendar to Task 6 (*Insert mouse overs*), Task 12 (*Document where existing links go for new UI*), and Task 13 (*Hook-up system with existing items*).

5. Enter a query in the *Type a question for help* box on creating a new task calendar, and read the Help instructions.

6. For Tasks 20 (*Determine query requirements*) through 26 (*Deliver final query solution*), create a new calendar.

    You need a task calendar that encompasses the testing and production team hours of 11:00 A.M. to 9:00 P.M. with a 1-hour lunch.

7. Save and close **Training_Portal**.

DISCOVERY ZONE

Discovery Zone exercises require advanced knowledge of topics presented in *Essentials* lessons, application of skills from multiple lessons, or self-directed learning of new skills. Each exercise is independent of the others, so you may complete the exercises in any order.

1. Creating a New Software Implementation Project File from a Template

You have the ability to deal with highly technical programmers while still being able to relate to nontechnical end users. With this unique ability, you are the perfect choice to work on the development of a new accounting software package that will allow the employees of your company to process business expense reports online. You are working with the programming team to document this new software program, provide an online training tutorial, and establish ongoing end user support as the software is rolled out in your company.

Create a new project from the Software Development template located on your computer and save it as **Accounting_Software**. Modify the start date of the schedule, to begin February 7, 2005. Because the software has already been determined as needed, there will be no analysis, design, or software requirement investigations. Remove those tasks in the template that are not necessary. Remove any additional tasks that are not representative of the scope of this project.

Add a recurring task that involves a bi-weekly meeting with the Accounting Management team. Modify existing tasks and add new tasks to cover creating an online training manual. Create links between these tasks as you see fit.

Review the Predecessors column and explore the links between the tasks as created by the template. Add additional links where needed, and remove any that do not belong.

2. Working with Task Constraints

Create a new project from any existing template located either online or on your computer and save it as **Constraint**. Use the *Type a question for help* box to research information on constraints and read about the eight different types of task constraints that are available. Using the *Constraint* project that you created, apply each constraint to eight individual tasks and modify the durations of these eight tasks to see how the constraint affects the task finish date and the overall project plan.

SCHEDULING RESOURCES AND ASSIGNING COSTS

OBJECTIVES

IN THIS PROJECT, YOU LEARN HOW TO

- View and set up resources
- Enter resource information
- Enter fixed costs
- Assign resources to tasks

- View and modify resource assignments
- Print resource allocations and project costs

WHY WOULD I DO THIS?

When creating a project plan, you must consider what resources are necessary to complete the project. These resources may include personnel, materials, equipment, outside contractors, and other assets. You may already have some resources in mind, and as you create tasks and durations, identifying resources becomes more clear. Once you assign resources, you can then review the project file to ensure that the resulting schedule meets the target date. However, part of the project management process is to handle those things that come up that affect or alter the schedule. Employees take days off, equipment breaks down, or materials are unavailable. Managing resource allocation and task durations becomes critical. Even for simple projects, assigning resources to tasks allows you to record the cost of materials and equipment and the hours allocated to each person, and you can then check for overallocations. Using resources also allows you to take advantage of the many ways you can keep track of the overall budget.

Resources and costs work hand in hand in a project plan. Each resource has the potential to have a cost attached to it. If you include the cost information for each resource, Microsoft Project automatically calculates the cost of each task. These calculations aid the project manager in figuring a budget for the entire project plan.

VISUAL SUMMARY

In this project, you use Microsoft Project to set up, assign, and monitor the resources needed to create a business plan—resources needed to perform a comparative market analysis to ensure that your business idea is viable, to determine start-up expenses including management and staffing salaries as required by the loan officer at the bank, and so forth. After you make adjustments to the project file, your resource allocation should resemble the data in Figure 4.1 below.

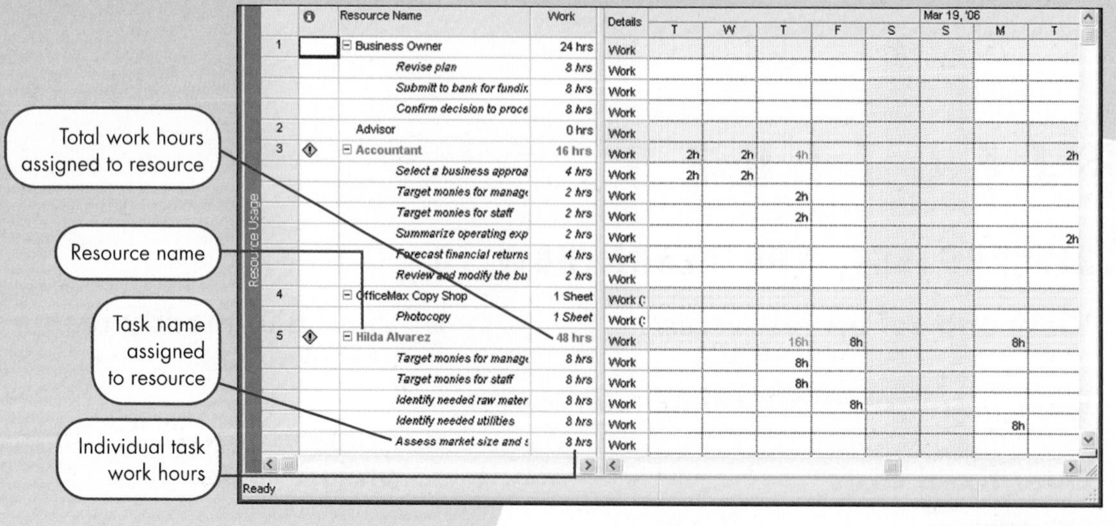

FIGURE 4.1

When you assign resources to a task, Microsoft Project considers the duration of the task as well as the working time available by the resource. At times, these two do not match. There are several views you can use to correct any conflicts that occur.

LESSON 1:   Viewing and Setting Up Resources

When creating resources for a project file, you can manually add them or import resources from another file. A list of available resources for a project plan is called the **resource pool**. A resource pool can be created either before or after tasks are defined. The resource pool contains a list of people, equipment, and materials that are available to be assigned to a task.

Resources can be any of three types: work resources, material resources, or cost resources. A **work resource** such as personnel or machinery performs work to accomplish a task. For work resources, a rate is applied per unit of time. A **material resource** is a consumable material used to complete the work required by a task. For example, if a task includes printing a newsletter, paper is a material resource. A **cost resource** does not depend on the amount of work on a task or the duration of a task, such as travel expenses. In addition, both resource types can be individuals or single items, or they can be groups of people or things. An **individual resource** is a single unit such as a person or a single asset such as a piece of raw material or equipment. A **group resource**—or **consolidated resource**—represents multiple interchangeable resources, such as a group of engineers with the same knowledge and skills concerning this project plan. When using a group resource, it is not important which specific resource within the group performs the task.

The Resource Sheet view is the easiest method to manually create resources for a project file. After you enter the resource name, Microsoft Project automatically supplies default values for many of the other fields in the table. Alternately, you can use the Resource Information dialog box to create or edit resources, or you can type in the name of a resource in the Resource Names column in Gantt Chart view or several other views. However, these options do not allow you to enter additional information such as cost data; therefore, Resource Sheet view is the preferred view for entry (see Figure 4.2).

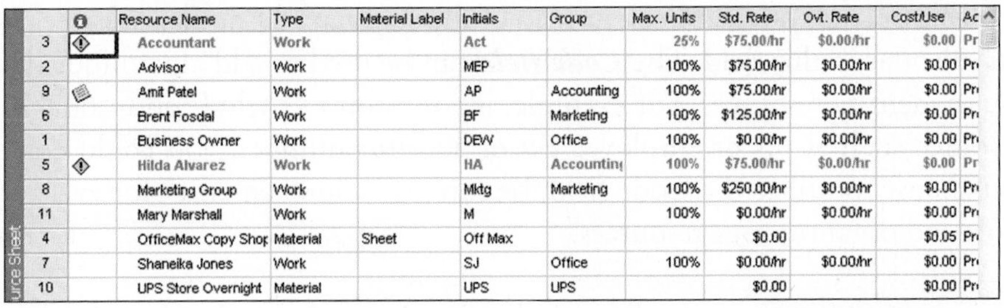

		Resource Name	Type	Material Label	Initials	Group	Max. Units	Std. Rate	Ovt. Rate	Cost/Use	Ac
3	⬥	Accountant	Work		Act		25%	$75.00/hr	$0.00/hr	$0.00	Pr
2		Advisor	Work		MEP		100%	$75.00/hr	$0.00/hr	$0.00	Pr
9	🖉	Amit Patel	Work		AP	Accounting	100%	$75.00/hr	$0.00/hr	$0.00	Pr
6		Brent Fosdal	Work		BF	Marketing	100%	$125.00/hr	$0.00/hr	$0.00	Pr
1		Business Owner	Work		DEW	Office	100%	$0.00/hr	$0.00/hr	$0.00	Pr
5	⬥	Hilda Alvarez	Work		HA	Accounting	100%	$75.00/hr	$0.00/hr	$0.00	Pr
8		Marketing Group	Work		Mktg	Marketing	100%	$250.00/hr	$0.00/hr	$0.00	Pr
11		Mary Marshall	Work		M		100%	$0.00/hr	$0.00/hr	$0.00	Pr
4		OfficeMax Copy Shop	Material	Sheet	Off Max			$0.00		$0.05	Pr
7		Shaneika Jones	Work		SJ	Office	100%	$0.00/hr	$0.00/hr	$0.00	Pr
10		UPS Store Overnight	Material		UPS	UPS		$0.00		$0.00	Pr

FIGURE 4.2

The resource sheet provides a variety of information about each resource assigned to a project plan. Recall from Project 3 that the *ID field* contains automatically supplied numbers—which cannot be edited—that are used to identify a resource. ID numbers appear down the left margin of the resource sheet much like the row numbers of a spreadsheet. The *Indicator field* displays icons that provide information about an assignment, resource, or task. For example, there is an indicator to signal that a task is completed and another to indicate that a note is attached. Look for an icon in the column headed by the single letter *i* inside a blue circle. The *Resource Name field* in the resource sheet provides a descriptive name for each resource; most users prefer this field to the nondescript ID field. Microsoft Project does not require that resource names be unique; however, it is best to make each resource name unique and easily identifiable. You use the ***Type field*** to distinguish between work, material, and cost resources. The default Type field entry is *Work.* The resource type assigned to a resource can affect the schedule for a task. For instance, a Work resource can be linked to the Resource calendar, whereas a Material resource cannot be linked.

Use the ***Material Label field*** to define the unit of measure for material resources. Units of measure are the familiar measurements such as quarts, boxes, or yards. Although the Resource Name field provides a description of a resource, the ***Initials field*** provides a brief name used in Gantt Chart view or Network Diagram view. You can use the ***Group field*** to add a keyword, such as the department name, to a resource. Group fields are extremely useful for sorting, filtering, and grouping resources. Use the ***Max. Units field*** to enter the maximum availability of a resource. It is a percentage that indicates the availability of a resource. The default entry is *100%;* however, if a person is assigned to the project and can work on the task for only half of the day, the person's max units would be 50%.

Four of the resource fields are currency fields that deal with the costs of using the resource. Use the ***Std. Rate (Standard Rate) field*** to assign the charge per unit of normal working time for a resource. The ***Ovt. Rate (Overtime Rate) field*** is used to assign charges per unit of overtime work for a resource. A ***Cost/Use field*** assigns a flat rate, such as one-time usage fees, per use of a resource. This field is generally associated with material resources. For example, one box of printer paper might be $25. The ***Accrue At field*** defines how and when resource costs are incurred and when actual costs are charged to a project. Accrue At can be either Start, End, or Prorated. By default, it is set to Prorated.

Recall that a base calendar controls a group of resources. In contrast, a ***Resource calendar*** is assigned to each resource to reflect unique scheduling considerations such as the type of work day and vacation schedules. The calendar is based on either the Standard 8-hour work day calendar, the 24 Hours calendar, or the 8-hour Night Shift calendar. In addition, you can apply any special project calendars that you created. For example, if you have a group of resources that are available only 20 hours a week instead of the standard 40-hour work week, you would specify that calendar in this field. The ***Code field*** can be used to add any unique data that you want to use to identify resources. For example, if you want to include additional information about a resource such as his or employee ID or account number, you could enter it in this field. If you choose to utilize the Code field, be sure to include an entry for every resource, to correctly sort and organize your resources.

In this lesson, you work with a partially completed resource sheet related to creating a business plan. These resources support conducting a market analysis survey and determining start-up expenses that include management and staffing salaries—data needed by the loan officer at the bank to show the planned business is viable. For now, your task is to create a resource pool for this project file.

To View the Resource Sheet and Set Up Resources

1 Open the *EPr1_0401* file and save it as `Business_Model`; then close any open side panes.

2 Drag the split bar between the task table and Gantt chart to the right until the last column, Resource Names, is visible.

Some tasks already contain resource assignments. Although you can view and create new resources from the Gantt Chart view, the Resource Sheet shows much more information.

3 Choose <u>V</u>iew, Resource <u>S</u>heet.

A grid showing resource names, resource type, resource costs, and other resource information displays (see Figure 4.3).

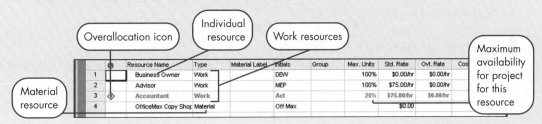

FIGURE 4.3

There are four types of information icons that can appear in the Indicator column for resources: overallocation, note, hyperlink, and response pending. An ***overallocation icon*** indicates that the resource has too much work assigned to it for the time frame involved or has been assigned to two tasks at once. A ***note icon*** provides text about the resource that the user added. A ***hyperlink icon*** associates a link to a resource or a Web page or document. A ***response pending icon*** indicates that the resource has not responded to an e-mail notification about task assignment.

4 Pause the mouse pointer over the information icon for Resource 3 (*Accountant*).

A ScreenTip appears. This resource appears in red because it is overallocated. Notice that the base calendar for the Accountant resource is the Standard calendar. The calendar has the default 8-hour work day and 40-hour work week. The Accountant works only 2 hours per day on this project, as indicated by the 25% Max. Units field.

5 Click in the first blank row after Resource 4 (*OfficeMax Copy Shop*) in the Resource Name column, type `Hilda Alvarez`, and then press `Tab⇥`.

Pressing `Tab⇥` enters the data and moves the insertion point to the next column in the resource sheet (see Figure 4.4). Default entries appear in the other resource fields.

		Resource Name	Type	Material Label	Initials	Group	Max. Units	Std. Rate	Ovt. Rate	Cost/Use	Ac
1		Business Owner	Work		DEW		100%	$0.00/hr	$0.00/hr	$0.00	Pr
2		Advisor	Work		MEP		100%	$75.00/hr	$0.00/hr	$0.00	Pr
3	◇	Accountant	Work		Act		25%	$75.00/hr	$0.00/hr	$0.00	Pr
4		OfficeMax Copy Shop	Material		Off Max				$0.00	$0.00	Pr
5		Hilda Alvarez	Work		H		100%	$0.00/hr	$0.00/hr	$0.00	Pr

Drop-down arrow for Type field

New resource

Default entries

FIGURE 4.4

6   Accept the *Work* type by pressing ⎋Tab to move to the next field.

7   Press ⎋Tab again, type **HA** in the Initials column, and then press ⏎Enter.

8   Continue entering the remaining resources listed below.

Resource Name	Type	Initials
Brent Fosdal	Work	BF
Shaneika Jones	Work	SJ
Marketing Group	Work	Mktg
Amit Patel	Work	AP
UPS Store Overnight	Material	UPS

Now that you have entered resource names, you can sort them. Sorting makes it easier to locate resources in the list.

9   Choose **P**roject, **S**ort, by **N**ame.

The list reorganizes in alphabetical order by the resource name (see Figure 4.5). Notice, however, the resource IDs do not change.

	🛈	Resource Name	Type	Material Label	Initials	Group	Max. Units	Std. Rate	Ovt. Rate	Cost/Use	Ac
3	⬧	Accountant	Work		Act		25%	$75.00/hr	$0.00/hr	$0.00	Pr
2		Advisor	Work		MEP		100%	$75.00/hr	$0.00/hr	$0.00	Pr
9		Amit Patel	Work		AP		100%	$0.00/hr	$0.00/hr	$0.00	Pr
6		Brent Fosdal	Work		BF		100%	$0.00/hr	$0.00/hr	$0.00	Pr
1		Business Owner	Work		DEW		100%	$0.00/hr	$0.00/hr	$0.00	Pr
5		Hilda Alvarez	Work		HA		100%	$0.00/hr	$0.00/hr	$0.00	Pr
8		Marketing Group	Work		Mktg		100%	$0.00/hr	$0.00/hr	$0.00	Pr
4		OfficeMax Copy Shop	Material		Off Max			$0.00		$0.00	Pr
7		Shaneika Jones	Work		SJ		100%	$0.00/hr	$0.00/hr	$0.00	Pr
10		UPS Store Overnight	Material		UPS			$0.00		$0.00	Pr

IDs remain the same

FIGURE 4.5

10   Save your changes to the *Business_Model* file.

Your project file now contains 10 resources. Keep the *Business_Model* project file open and continue with the next lesson. If you prefer to complete the project later, close the file and exit Microsoft Project.

TO EXTEND YOUR KNOWLEDGE...

MAKING A SORT PERMANENT

When sorting resources, you can make the sort permanent by reassigning the resource IDs. Choose **P**roject, **S**ort, **S**ort by. In the Sort dialog box, choose the field you want to sort the resources by, such as Name. Check the *Permanently renumber resources* check box and then click **S**ort.

ADDING RESOURCES BY USING THE PROJECT GUIDE

You can also use the Project Guide when adding resources, which is especially helpful if you are adding resources from a company address book or importing them from another external source. From Gantt Chart view, click Resources on the Project Guide and then click the *Specify people and equipment for the project* link. In the Specify Resources side pane, click the option that indicates where you are getting the resources from, and then follow the directions to complete the process.

CREATING A RESOURCE TEMPLATE

If you use a common group of resources repeatedly, it is useful to create a project template. To begin, create a blank project file; then enter the names of the resources that make up the resource pool. Choose File, Save As. Click the *Save as type* drop-down arrow and choose *Template (mpt)*.

LESSON 2:   Entering Resource Information

There are several types of costs involved in a project plan. A ***resource cost,*** the most common type of cost, is incurred due to the expense associated with using a resource. Resource costs are represented by the dollar amount entered in the Std. Rate field, the Ovt. Rate field, or the Cost/Use field (as shown in the Resource Sheet view). Microsoft Project uses resource costs in conjunction with the task duration to calculate the expense associated with a task. The cost of a material resource is based on the dollar amount entered in the Cost/Use column and the unit specified in the Material Label column. For example, if you want to track the cost of each ream of paper used in project plan, you would enter **$2.50** in the Cost/Use column and specify **Ream** in the Material Label column.

Microsoft Project calculates resource costs for a work resource by multiplying the cost per unit (i.e., hourly cost) for the resource by the amount of time the resource spends on the task (time × Std. Rate and/or Ovt. Rate). On the other hand, material resource costs are calculated solely on the number of units consumed or used up by the task. In other words, the calculation is the number of units of the resource multiplied by the per unit cost of the resource (units × Cost/Use).

In this lesson, you assign costs to each resource in the resource pool and assign groups. Additionally, you update resource information, using the Resource Information dialog box.

To Enter Resource Costs and Additional Resource Information

1 Open *Business_Model,* and choose View, Resource Sheet, if necessary.

2 Click in the Group column for Amit Patel and type `Accounting`.

3 Press `Tab` two times to move to the Std. Rate column; type 75 and then press `Enter`.

Amit Patel is now a member of the Accounting group and costs $75.00 per hour as a resource (see Figure 4.6).

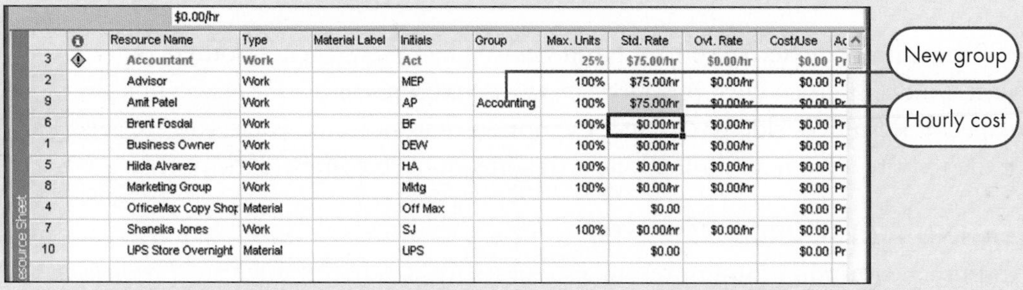

	❶	Resource Name	Type	Material Label	Initials	Group	Max. Units	Std. Rate	Ovt. Rate	Cost/Use	Ac
3	◈	Accountant	Work		Act		25%	$75.00/hr	$0.00/hr	$0.00	Pr
2		Advisor	Work		MEP		100%	$75.00/hr	$0.00/hr	$0.00	Pr
9		Amit Patel	Work		AP	Accounting	100%	$75.00/hr	$0.00/hr	$0.00	Pr
6		Brent Fosdal	Work		BF		100%	$0.00/hr	$0.00/hr	$0.00	Pr
1		Business Owner	Work		DEW		100%	$0.00/hr	$0.00/hr	$0.00	Pr
5		Hilda Alvarez	Work		HA		100%	$0.00/hr	$0.00/hr	$0.00	Pr
8		Marketing Group	Work		Mktg		100%	$0.00/hr	$0.00/hr	$0.00	Pr
4		OfficeMax Copy Shop	Material		Off Max			$0.00		$0.00	Pr
7		Shaneika Jones	Work		SJ		100%	$0.00/hr	$0.00/hr	$0.00	Pr
10		UPS Store Overnight	Material		UPS			$0.00		$0.00	Pr

New group

Hourly cost

FIGURE 4.6

4 Click in the Group column for Brent Fosdal and type `Marketing`.

5 Press `Tab` two times; type `125` and then press `⏎Enter`.
Brent Fosdal is a member of the Marketing group at a rate of $125 per hour.

6 Enter the remaining group and rate information as shown in the table below.

Resource	Group	Rate/Hr
Business Owner	Office	$0.00/h
Hilda Alvarez	Accounting	$75.00/h
Marketing Group	Marketing	$250/h
Shaneika Jones	Office	$0.00/h
UPS Store Overnight	UPS	

7 Click in the Material Label column for OfficeMax Copy Shop and type `Sheet`.

8 Click in the Cost/Use column and type `.05`.
The cost of each sheet of paper copied is 5 cents. You have added the resource costs and groups to your resource pool.

9 Double-click the Amit Patel resource.
The Resource Information dialog box opens (see Figure 4.7).

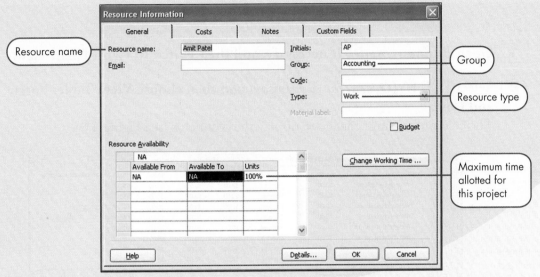

FIGURE 4.7

10 Click the Notes tab and then click in the text box.

11 Type `Promoted into Accounting department 1/06` and then click OK.
A note icon in the Indicator column signifies that a note pertaining to Amit's status on the project is in the resource information.

12 Point to the note icon.
A ScreenTip appears, showing you the note text.

13 Save your changes to the *Business_Model* file.
You have added the necessary resource information. Keep the *Business_Model* project file open and continue with the next lesson. If you prefer to complete the project later, close the file and exit Microsoft Project.

LESSON 3: Entering Fixed Costs

A *fixed cost* is a cost that is not specifically related to any one resource. It does not accrue based on work hours but is instead tied to the task to which it applies. Fixed costs are often one-time expenses, such as shipping. Fixed costs are entered into the task table as a lump sum. The sum of all resource costs and fixed costs is the *total cost* of the project plan.

In this lesson, you enter fixed costs for material resources.

To Add Fixed Costs

1 Open *Business_Model,* if necessary, and then switch to Gantt Chart view.

2 Select Task 10 (*Overnight to Advisor*) and then choose <u>V</u>iew, Ta<u>b</u>le: Entry, and <u>C</u>ost.

The column headings change to display the cost fields (see Figure 4.8).

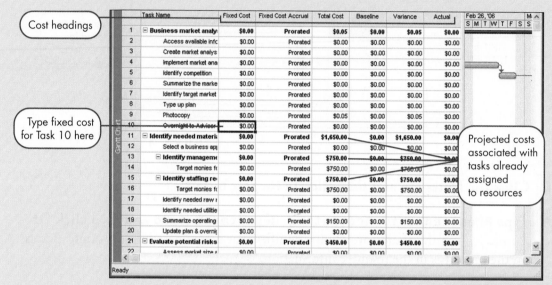

FIGURE 4.8

3 In the Fixed Cost column, type 5.50 and then press ↵Enter.

This amount is the cost to overnight a letter pack.

4 Click in the Fixed Cost column for Task 20 (*Update plan & overnight to Bus. Own*); type 6.75 and then press ↵Enter.

The fixed costs are complete (see Figure 4.9).

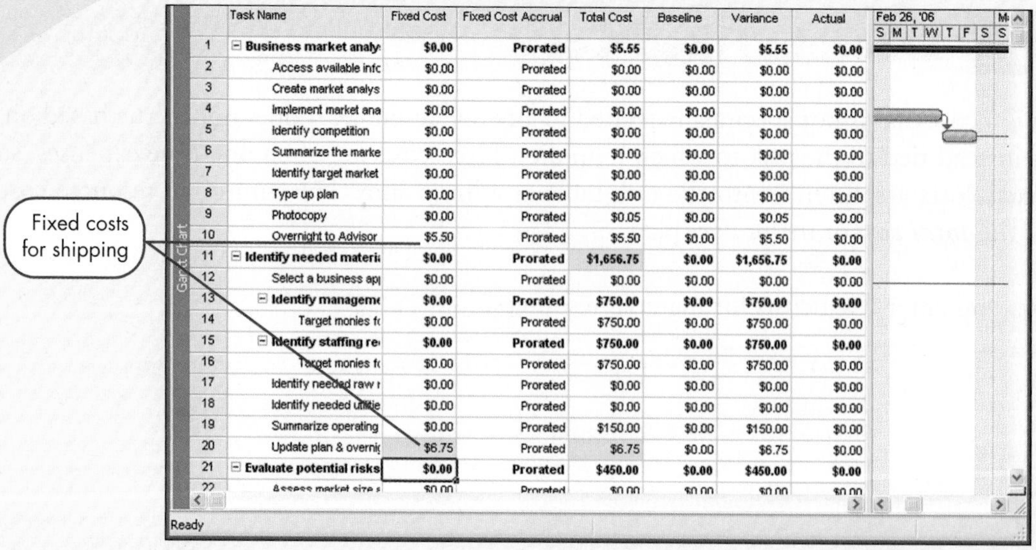

FIGURE 4.9

5 | **Choose <u>V</u>iew, Ta<u>b</u>le: Cost, and <u>E</u>ntry.**
The view changes back to the Table Entry view, which is the default.

6 | **Save your changes to the *Business_Model* file.**
You have now specified fixed costs in your project file. Keep the *Business_Model* project file open and continue with the next lesson. If you prefer to complete the project later, close the file and exit Microsoft Project.

LESSON 4: Assigning Resources to Tasks

You now know that the first step in working with Microsoft Project is to create the project base calendar by specifying the start date for the entire project plan as well as outlining the actual work hours. You also know the second step is to enter tasks and how long you think each task should take (the task duration). When you assign a resource to a task, Microsoft Project uses a ***scheduling formula*** that schedules the task according to the formula *Duration = Work / Units.* **Work** is what is assigned to a resource and also represents the total labor required to complete a task. The duration of a task can be affected by a resource assignment if the maximum units for a resource are not 100%. For example, if a resource is assigned to work 100% on a task with a 1-day duration, the work unit is 8 hours. If the work resource is working only 25%, the work unit is 2 hours.

In addition, not only do work units calculate automatically, but the overall duration for a task also automatically updates when you start assigning more than one resource. For example, if you assign two resources to a task with a duration of 1 day, each resource is assigned 4 hours of work and that task duration reduces to 1/2 day. Likewise, if you assign two resources to work on a task with a 1-day duration, each working 100%, the total work involved is 200%.

In this lesson, you assign resources to specific tasks. Then you alter the durations and resource assignments to create a schedule that allocates all resources more effectively.

To Assign Resources to Tasks

1 | **Open *Business_Model*, if necessary.**

2 | **In Gantt Chart view, click in the Resource Names column for Task 2 (*Access available information*).**

3 | **Click the drop-down arrow and choose Brent Fosdal from the list; then press ⏎Enter.**
Brent Fosdal appears in the Resource Names column and to the right of the Gantt bar in the Gantt chart (see Figure 4.10).

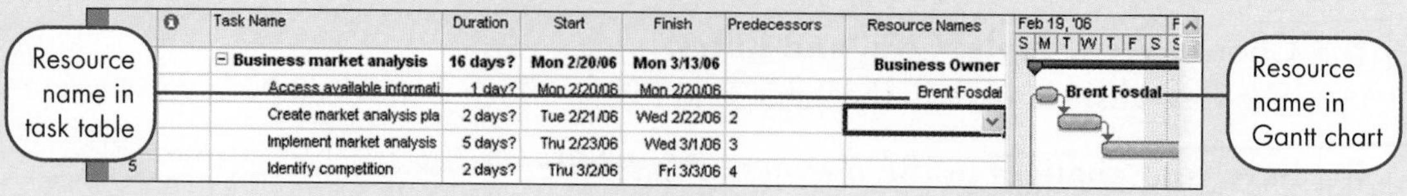

	❶	Task Name	Duration	Start	Finish	Predecessors	Resource Names	Feb 19, '06
								S M T W T F S
		⊟ **Business market analysis**	**16 days?**	**Mon 2/20/06**	**Mon 3/13/06**		**Business Owner**	
		Access available informati	1 day?	Mon 2/20/06	Mon 2/20/06		Brent Fosdal	Brent Fosdal
		Create market analysis pla	2 days?	Tue 2/21/06	Wed 2/22/06	2		
		Implement market analysis	5 days?	Thu 2/23/06	Wed 3/1 /06	3		
5		Identify competition	2 days?	Thu 3/2/06	Fri 3/3/06	4		

Resource name in task table → *Resource name in Gantt chart* → Brent Fosdal

FIGURE 4.10

4 | In the Resource Names column for Task 3 (*Create market analysis plan*), choose Brent Fosdal; then press ↵Enter.

5 | In the Resource Names column for Task 4 (*Implement market analysis plan*), choose Marketing Group, and then type , (Note: Do not press space).
You can use a comma as a separator character to add multiple resources to a task.

If you have problems . . .

If you mistakenly pressed ↵Enter at this point, click in the cell again and press F2 to edit the field.

---

6 | Click the Resource Names drop-down arrow again.

7 | Choose Brent Fosdal, and then press ↵Enter.
Two resources are assigned to the task (see Figure 4.11).

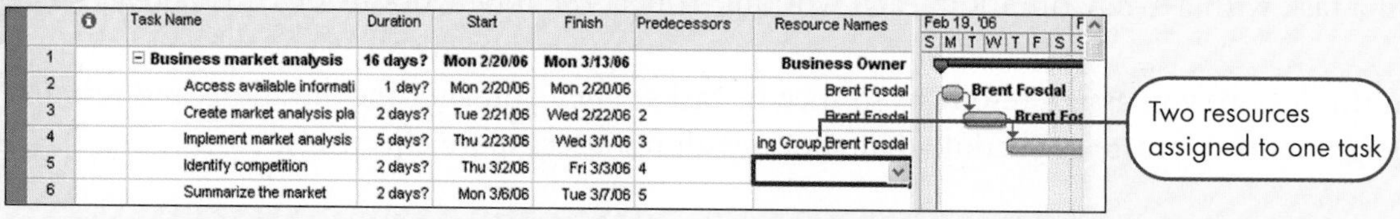

	❶	Task Name	Duration	Start	Finish	Predecessors	Resource Names	Feb 19, '06
								S M T W T F S
1		⊟ **Business market analysis**	**16 days?**	**Mon 2/20/06**	**Mon 3/13/06**		**Business Owner**	
2		Access available informati	1 day?	Mon 2/20/06	Mon 2/20/06		Brent Fosdal	Brent Fosdal
3		Create market analysis pla	2 days?	Tue 2/21/06	Wed 2/22/06	2	Brent Fosdal	Brent Fos
4		Implement market analysis	5 days?	Thu 2/23/06	Wed 3/1 /06	3	ing Group,Brent Fosdal	
5		Identify competition	2 days?	Thu 3/2/06	Fri 3/3/06	4		
6		Summarize the market	2 days?	Mon 3/6/06	Tue 3/7/06	5		

Two resources assigned to one task

FIGURE 4.11

8 | In the Resource Names column for Task 5 (*Identify competition*), type **Mary Marshall** and then press ↵Enter.
Mary Marshall is a new resource that did not exist in the resource pool. By simply typing the name of the resource in the Resource Names column, you add a new resource directly from Gantt Chart view.

If you have problems . . .

Be careful when adding a resource by typing a name in the Resource Names column in Gantt Chart view. If you duplicate an existing resource with only a change in spelling, you have two resource entries representing the same resource due to the spelling error, and the resource allocations are skewed.

You can assign resources to summary tasks, but be aware that there may be misleading information that requires explanation. For example, if you assign a manager to a summary task to show his or her ownership for that part of the project plan, that manager has the sum total for all the subtask durations, work hours, and costs rolled up and assigned to him. This may be confusing for those not closely involved with the project.

9 | Complete the remaining resource assignments as shown in the following table.

Task ID	Task Name	Resource Name
6	Summarize the market	*Marketing Group, Brent Fosdal*
7	Identify target market niche	*Marketing Group, Brent Fosdal*
8	Type up plan	*Shaneika Jones*
10	Overnight to Advisor	*UPS Store Overnight*
11	Identify needed materials and supplies	*Business Owner*
12	Select a business approach	*Accountant*
13	Identify management staff resources	*Business Owner*
15	Identify staffing requirements	*Business Owner*
20	Update plan & overnight to Bus. Own	*UPS Store Overnight*

Now that you have added resources to individual tasks, let's take a look at the Assign Resources dialog box. You can use this dialog box to add or remove a resource assignment as well as alter the work units of each resource.

To Create Work Resource Assignments

1 | **Highlight Tasks 17 (*Identify needed raw materials*) and 18 (*Identify needed utilities*).**
Notice that the duration for each of these tasks is approximately 2 days. You have two resources who share the work on these tasks.

 2 | **Click Assign Resources on the Standard Toolbar.**
The Assign Resources dialog box opens (see Figure 4.12).

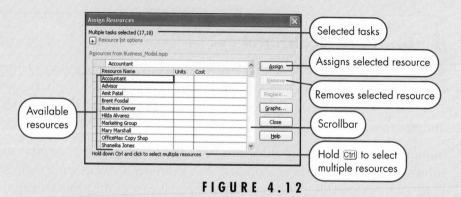

FIGURE 4.12

3 | Click *Amit Patel* and then click **Assign.**

4 | Click *Hilda Alvarez* and then click **Assign.**
Hilda Alvarez moves below Amit Patel. Check marks appear next to each assigned resource (see Figure 4.13).

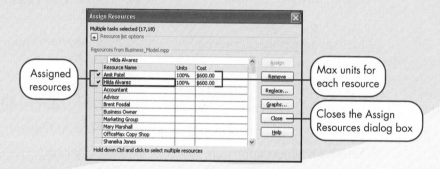

FIGURE 4.13

If you have problems . . .

If you do not want the duration to be reduced because more than one resource is assigned to a task, start by assigning just one resource. Then assign the additional resources in a separate operation.

5 | **Click Close.**
Amit Patel and Hilda Alvarez are assigned to Tasks 17 and 18. The duration for these tasks reduces to approximately 1 day each (8 hours of work). If assigned resources work at 100%, Microsoft Project divides the duration by the number of resources assigned to the task. So, when 16 hours of work is split between two resources, the duration is reduced by half and each resource is assigned 50% (see Figure 4.14).

14	Target monies for ma	5 days?	Thu 3/16/06	Wed 3/22/06			Accountant[25%]
15	⊟ **Identify staffing require**	**5 days?**	**Thu 3/16/06**	**Wed 3/22/06**	**14SS**		**Business Owner**
16	Target monies for ste	5 days?	Thu 3/16/06	Wed 3/22/06			Accountant[25%]
17	Identify needed raw mater	1 day?	Thu 3/23/06	Thu 3/23/06	16		Amit Patel,Hilda Alvarez
18	Identify needed utilities	1 day?	Fri 3/24/06	Fri 3/24/06	17		Amit Patel,Hilda Alvarez
19	Summarize operating expe	1 day?	Mon 3/27/06	Mon 3/27/06	18		Accountant[25%]
20	Update plan & overnight to	1 day?	Tue 3/28/06	Tue 3/28/06	19		UPS Store Overnight[1]
21	⊟ **Evaluate potential risks and**	**10 days?**	**Wed 3/29/06**	**Tue 4/11/06**			

Altered duration

Multiple resources assigned to task

FIGURE 4.14

6 Select Tasks 22 (*Assess market size and stability*) and 23 (*Access needed resources availability*), and then click **Assign Resources**.

7 Assign **Amit Patel** and **Hilda Alvarez** to the tasks, and then click **Close**.
Hilda Alvarez and Amit Patel are assigned to Tasks 22 and 23. The duration for these tasks reduces from approximately 2 days to 1 day each, because the total work hours to complete the task were evenly distributed between the two resources and required a shorter duration.

8 Save your changes to the *Business_Model* file.
Now you have added resources to most tasks within the project file. Keep the *Business_Model* project file open and continue with the next lesson. If you prefer to complete the project later, close the file and exit Microsoft Project.

TO EXTEND YOUR KNOWLEDGE . . .

ASSIGNING RESOURCES BY USING THE PROJECT GUIDE
You can also assign resources to tasks by using the Project Guide, which displays current resource assignment information, something that can be quite helpful if you have questions regarding how task durations are translated to work hours for a resource. To use the Project Guide, first select the task to which you want to assign a resource; then click the Resources drop-down arrow on the Project Guide toolbar and click *Assign people and equipment to tasks*. The Assign Resources side pane displays, where you select the *Assign resources* link. Follow the numbered steps in the side pane. In *Step 4 Review information*, you can view resource assignments for a selected task.

ASSIGNING RESOURCES BY USING THE ASSIGN RESOURCES DIALOG BOX
Resources can also be created from within the Assign Resources dialog box. To add a resource by using this method, click in the next blank row, type the resource name, and press ↵Enter. To assign the new resource, select the name you just created and click Assign.

VIEWING RESOURCE INITIALS ON THE GANTT CHART
You may find that the Gantt chart becomes cluttered when the full resource name is shown next to each Gantt bar. You can format the Gantt chart to display resource initials instead. In Gantt Chart view, choose Format, Bar Styles, and click the Text tab. Click in the row where you see resource names, and then click the drop-down arrow and choose *Resource Initials*. The default position of the resource name in relation to the Gantt bar is Right. Notice also that you can alter the position to Left, Top, Inside, or Bottom, if you prefer.

LESSON 5: Viewing and Modifying Resource Assignments

As defined in Lesson 4, *work* is what is assigned to a resource and also represents the total labor required to complete a task. The **work unit** is the amount of time it should take a resource to complete a task. It is automatically calculated by Microsoft Project when the task duration is translated into a unit of work for the resource. By default, Microsoft Project translates the duration of a task into hours, as indicated by the abbreviation *hrs* seen in the Resource Usage sheet and other views. Work units are the measurement of the duration (usually in hours) and are helpful in project planning, like knowing how much you weigh upon starting a diet.

For this information to calculate correctly and make sense to you, it is important that you have a good understanding of the project calendar. For example, if you created a project base calendar using the default business day from 9:00 A.M. to 5:00 P.M. with a 1-hour lunch, this translates to an 8-hour work day. So remember that when you enter estimated task durations, a duration of 1 day equals 8 hours of work in this scenario. When you assign a resource to a task with a 1-day duration, the duration translates to 8 hours of work for this resource.

In this lesson, you view resource assignments and make modifications to make a sound work schedule for the project plan.

To View Resource Assignments and Make Modifications

1   **Open *Business_Model,* if necessary; then choose View, Resource Usage.**
The view changes to Resource Usage view. This view contains a table with work hours assigned to each task by resource name and a corresponding *timephased* bar graph that displays work across time (see Figure 4.15).

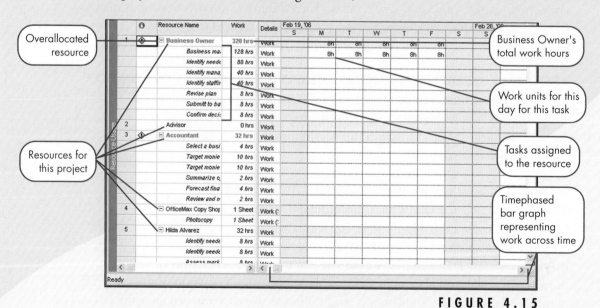

FIGURE 4.15

If you have problems . . .

If necessary, you may need to drag the split bar between the table and the timephased graph to the right to view the Work column. Also, you may need to click once on the scrollbox in the horizontal scrollbar of the timephased bar graph to view the starting date of the project in the bar graph.

Notice that the Business Owner has been assigned 320 hours of work. This is because the Business Owner is assigned to several summary tasks, which can display misleading information.

2   **Choose View, Gantt Chart.**

3   **Click in the Resource Names column for Task 1 (*Business market analysis*) and then press Del.**
The Business Owner is removed from Task 1.

4   **Select Task 11 (*Identify needed materials and supplies*) and click *Assign Resources.***
The Assign Resources dialog box opens.

5   **In the Assign Resources dialog box, select *Business Owner.***

6   **Click Remove and then click Close.**
The Business Owner is removed from Task 11.

7   **Remove the Business Owner from Task 13 (*Identify management staff resources*) and Task 15 (*Identify staffing requirements*).**

8   **Choose View, Resource Usage.**
Notice that the Business Owner is now assigned a more reasonable 24 hours of work in the project plan (see Figure 4.16).

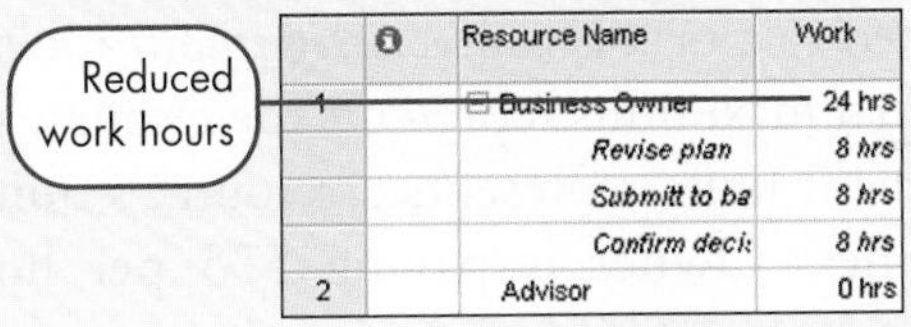

	ⓘ	Resource Name	Work
1		⊟ Business Owner	24 hrs
		Revise plan	8 hrs
		Submitt to ba	8 hrs
		Confirm deci:	8 hrs
2		Advisor	0 hrs

Reduced work hours →

FIGURE 4.16

In the next set of steps, you take a further look at analyzing the project plan and making modifications to the expenses generated by task assignments and methods to resolve overallocations. You use the Assignment Information dialog box to change the assignment units for several resources.

To Fix Resource Assignment Errors

1 **In the Indicator column, point to the overallocation icon for the Accountant resource.**

A ScreenTip appears concerning the overallocation. Too many work hours have been generated by the task assignments for the Accountant resource, and Microsoft Project recommends that you level the resource. **Leveling** refers to an automatic feature whereby Microsoft Project balances the workload for a resource by adding delays and splits in the project plan. Rather than utilizing the automatic leveling feature, however, you can adjust the resource assignments by adding additional resources to adjust task duration and overall work hours.

2 **Double-click the second task for the Accountant resource, *Target monies for management staff.***

The Assignment Information dialog box opens (see Figure 4.17).

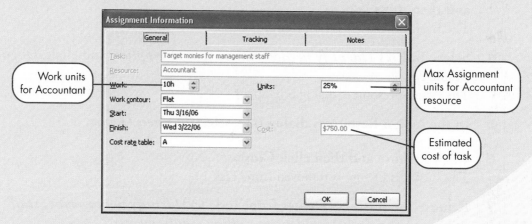

FIGURE 4.17

Recall that the original work unit was 10 hours. Since the Accountant only works 25% of an 8-hour work day on this project, he/she works just 2 hours per day, which translates to a 5 day duration (2 hours $\times$ 5 days = 10 hours work). The percentage of a resource's time allocated to a task is called **assignment units.** Assignment units differ from max. units in that max. units represents the resource's total availability on the project whereas assignment units represents a resource's units on an individual task assignment. The Business Owner is paying $75 per hour for each hour the Accountant works, currently making the cost of this task $750. You change the assignment units from 25% to 100%.

If you have problems . . .

If you are unable to view enough of the task name listed below each resource, double-click the column separator between the Resource Name and Work columns in the gray header to the right. You may also need to drag the split bar between the Resource Usage table and the bar graph to the right as well.

---

3 | Under *Units* in the Assignment Information dialog box, increase the percentage to **100%** and then click **OK**.

A green flag appears in the left corner of the task, indicating further action is required (see Figure 4.18).

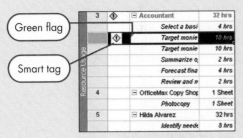

FIGURE 4.18

4 | In the Indicator column, click the smart tag.

A list of options appears (see Figure 4.19).

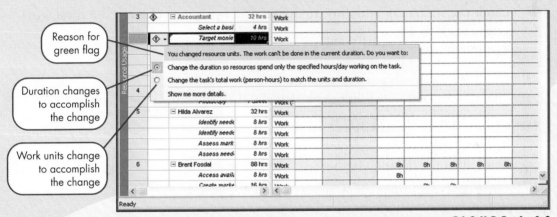

FIGURE 4.19

The first option decreases the task duration of the task to 1.25 days because the resource can now spend 100%, or the full work day of 8 hours, on this task. The second option does not change the task duration but instead increases the work hours to 40.

5 | Select the second option, *Change the task's total work (person-hours) to match the units and duration.*

The work now translates to 40 hours.

6 | Double-click *Target monies for management staff* again.

Notice that the overall cost for this task is now $3,000 if the Accountant applies 100% of his or her time to a 5-day task (see Figure 4.20).

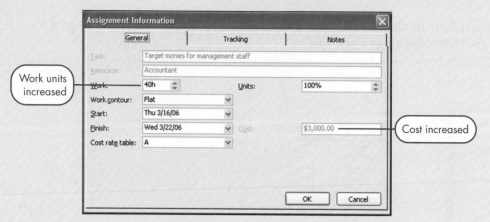

FIGURE 4.20

7 | **Change *Units* back to 25% and then click OK.**
Another green flag appears beside the task.

8 | **Click the smart tag and choose the second option to change the total work hours back to 10.**
The duration is now 5 days and the work is 2 hours per day.

9 | **Click *Hilda Alvarez* (Resource 5).**
Hilda Alvarez has only four tasks assigned to her, equaling 32 work hours.

10 | **Choose View, Gantt Chart and then select Task 14 (*Target monies for management staff*).**
Notice that the duration of this task is approximately 5 days (see Figure 4.21).

FIGURE 4.21

Currently this task is assigned to the Accountant, but the task responsibility can be shared with Hilda Alvarez.

11 | **Click *Assign Resources;* then select *Hilda Alvarez* and click Assign.**

12 | **Click Close and then click the smart tag beside the task.**
A list of options appears (see Figure 4.22).

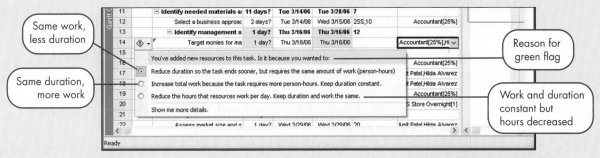

FIGURE 4.22

13 Choose the first option, *Reduce duration so the task ends sooner, but requires the same amount of work (person-hours).*

By choosing the first option, Microsoft Project divides the task duration between the two assigned resources according to their individual assignment units and recalculates the work hours. The Accountant receives a 2 hour assignment (25% of an 8-hour day), and Hilda Alvarez, who works 100% of her time on this project, receives an 8 hour assignment. The combination of the resource assignments equals 10 hours of work, thus the work can be accomplished in one day by utilizing these two resources.

14 Choose **V**iew, **Tas**k Usage, and locate Task 14 (*Target monies for management staff*).

The grid on the left shows the tasks with the specific resource assignments listed beneath them (see Figure 4.23).

FIGURE 4.23

The Task Usage view is almost identical to the Resource Usage view. This view allows you to work with resource assignment organized by task rather than by resource, and it also provides a Duration column so that you can see work hours by task as well as task duration.

Recall that with the addition of a second resource, the task duration was reduced to 1 day. The original work unit was 10 hours, which Microsoft Project translated to 2 hours of work per day for 5 days.

Normally the work hours are split equally among the two resources so each resource would be assigned 5 hours of work. However, the accountant works only 25% of the work day on this project.

15 Choose <u>V</u>iew, <u>G</u>antt Chart, and then select Task 16 (*Target monies for staff*).

16 Click *Assign Resources,* assign Hilda Alvarez to the task, and then close the dialog box.

17 Click the smart tag and choose the first option, *Reduce duration so the task ends sooner but requires the same amount of work (person-hours).*

18 Save your changes to the *Business_Model* file.

You looked at resource assignments and made modifications to level resource usage. Keep the *Business_Model* project file open and continue with the next lesson. If you prefer to complete the project later, close the file and exit Microsoft Project.

TO EXTEND YOUR KNOWLEDGE . . .

SMART TAG OPTIONS WHEN RESOURCE ASSIGNMENTS CHANGE

When you add or remove resources from a task, a smart tag appears, prompting you to reschedule the task as a result of the assignment change. You are provided three choices. The first choice, which is the default, reduces the duration of the task but keeps the amount of work units (hours) the same. The second option keeps the duration the same but increases the amount of work hours. The third option keeps the duration the same but reduces the amount of hours worked per day.

LESSON 6:   Printing Resource Allocations and Project Costs

Resource allocations and project costs represent two key areas of the project triangle, and there are many reports devoted to these areas. The **Resource Usage report** is designed to provide assignment hours for each resource by week and is very similar to the Resource Usage view. There is also a **To-do List report** that provides a particular resource with his or her assigned tasks and also provides the week the task begins and the start date of the task. There are several cost reports and each provides a different means of tracking cost issues. The **Budget report** lists all project tasks and sorts them in descending order by total cost.

In this lesson, you preview these three reports. On your own, you can also print the reports, if desired.

To Preview Resource Allocations and Project Costs

1 **Open** *Business_Model,* **if necessary; then choose Report, <u>R</u>eports.**
The Reports dialog box opens (see Figure 4.24).

FIGURE 4.24

2 **Click <u>W</u>orkload and then click <u>S</u>elect.**
A list of workload-related reports displays in the Workload Reports dialog box.

3 **Choose <u>R</u>esource Usage and then click <u>S</u>elect.**
A preview of a report appears, containing a list of tasks, by date, with Resource and work hours.

4 **Click in the report to magnify it.**
The report lists all tasks for the project file (see Figure 4.25). The tasks are organized by date and the total time involved in each task.

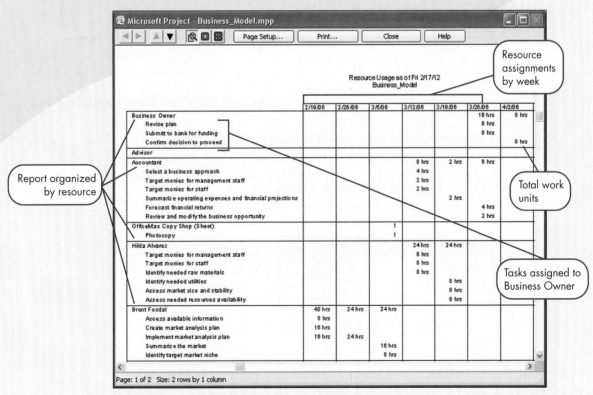

FIGURE 4.25

5 Click Close to exit without printing. (If you prefer to print, you can click the Page Setup button to first modify print settings, or you can click the Print button to immediately start the print process at default settings.)

The report closes and the Reports dialog box displays again.

6 In the Reports dialog box, click Costs and then Select.

A list of cost-related reports displays.

7 Click Budget and then click Select.

The report includes the cost of each task as well as total costs. Look at the report more closely to see the predicted costs of the project plan (see Figure 4.26).

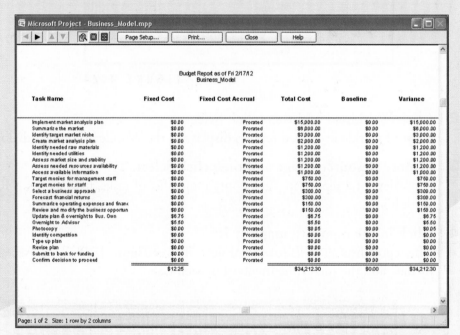

FIGURE 4.26

8 Print if desired; otherwise close the report and leave the Reports dialog box open.

9 In the Reports dialog box, select Assignments and then click Select.

A list of assignment-related reports is available.

10 Click To-do List and then click Select.

The Using Resource dialog box displays (see Figure 4.27).

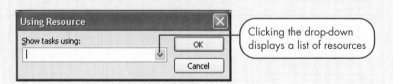

FIGURE 4.27

11 **Click the drop-down arrow and choose** *Business Owner;* **then click OK.**
A report with a list of tasks assigned to the Business Owner as well as the start dates displays (see Figure 4.28).

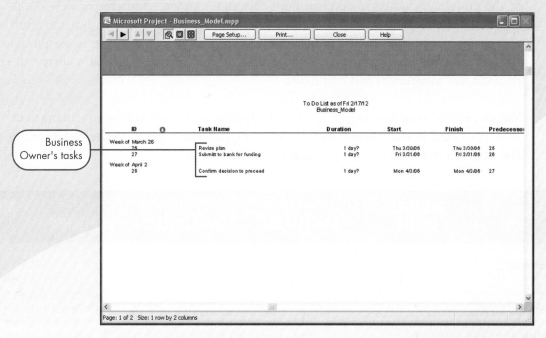

FIGURE 4.28

12 **Print if desired; otherwise close the preview window and then close the Reports dialog box.**

13 **Save your changes to the** *Business_Model* **file and close it.**

TO EXTEND YOUR KNOWLEDGE . . .

VIEWING RESOURCE ALLOCATION FROM THE PROJECT GUIDE

You can view resource allocation and task duration information in the Resources side pane. Click the Resources drop-down arrow on the Project Guide and choose *Assign people and equipment to tasks.* Click on the task whose information you want to view. The Resources side pane displays duration and work hours under *4) Review Information.*

SUMMARY

In this project you learned that adding resources enables you to work with many crucial areas of the project, including resource assignments and a budget. You created new resources and assigned them to tasks. You learned how to view resource allocations, analyze the result of your task assignments, and make modifications. By modifying resource task assignments, you affected both task duration and task cost. Finally, you looked at several reports that support resource task assignment and cost issues.

You can extend your learning by reviewing concepts and terms and by practicing variations of skills presented in the lessons. Use the following table as a guide to the numbered questions and exercises in the end-of-project learning opportunities.

LESSON	MULTIPLE CHOICE	DISCUSSION	SKILL DRILL	CHALLENGE	DISCOVERY ZONE
Viewing and Setting Up Resources	1, 2, 3, 8	1, 2, 3	1	1	1
Entering Resource Information	1	3	1	2	1, 2
Entering Fixed Costs	8	3		2	2
Assigning Resources to Tasks	4, 6, 8	2, 3	2	3	
Viewing and Modifying Resource Assignments	7, 9	2, 3	3, 4	4	
Printing Resource Allocations and Project Costs	10	2	5	4	

KEY TERMS

Accrue At field	Initials field	Resource Usage report
assignment units	leveling	response pending icon
Budget report	Material Label field	scheduling formula
Code field	material resource	Std. Rate field
consolidated resource	Max. Units field	timephased
Cost/Use field	note icon	To-do List report
cost resource	overallocation icon	total cost
fixed cost	Ovt. Rate field	Type field
Group field	resource assignment	work
group resource	Resource calendar	work resource
hyperlink icon	resource cost	work unit
individual resource	resource pool	

CHECKING CONCEPTS AND TERMS

MULTIPLE CHOICE

Circle the letter of the correct answer for each of the following.

1. Which view is used to enter resource information? [L1, L2]

   a. Resource Usage view

   b. Resource Sheet view

   c. Gantt Chart view

   d. Task Usage view

2. What is it called when a resource has too much work assigned? [L1]

   a. Overallocating

   b. Overscheduling

   c. Leveling

   d. Any of the above

3. Which of the following does *not* represent a valid work resource? [L1]

   a. Personnel

   b. Facilities

   c. Equipment

   d. Time

4. Which of the following best explains what a work unit is? [L5]

   a. The amount of time it takes to complete a task

   b. How long the resource actually spends completing a task

   c. A calculation that converts task duration to work hours when a resource is assigned to it

   d. A measurement expressed in hours

5. A cost that is not specifically related to any one resource is referred to as which of the following? [L3]

   a. Cost

   b. Resource cost

   c. Prorated cost

   d. Fixed cost

6. The amount of time a resource spends on assigned tasks is called what? [L4]

   a. Resource hours

   b. Work

   c. Assignment units

   d. Task duration

7. Which view shows a table displaying work hours assigned to each task by resource name, with a corresponding bar graph that displays work across time? [L5]

   a. Resource Usage view

   b. Gantt Chart view

   c. Resource Sheet view

   d. Task Usage view

8. Which of the following is *not* a method used to add a new resource? [L1, L4]

   a. Type the resource name in the resource sheet.

   b. Type the resource name in the Resource Names column in Gantt Chart view.

   c. Type the resource name in the Assign Resources dialog box.

   d. Type the resource name in the Gantt bar chart.

9. The amount of effort to complete a task is referred to as what? [L4, L5]

   a. Duration

   b. Work

   c. Assignment unit

   d. Force

10. Which report provides a list of costs by task and a total project cost? [L6]

    a. Task Usage report

    b. Workload report

    c. Budget report

    d. Costs report

DISCUSSION

1. There are three types of resources that work can be assigned to: people, equipment, and materials. Describe how you would determine which resource type to use for various tasks, and why. [L1]

2. With the addition of resources, tracking the progress and determining the overall accuracy of the project schedule is improved. Describe some of the things you are able to track and record when you add resources and assign them to tasks. [L1, L4-L6]

3. Take a look at the following three views in Microsoft Project: Resource Sheet, Task Usage, and Resource Usage. Describe what each of these three views shows you and the differences between them. [L1-L5]

SKILL DRILL

Skill Drill exercises reinforce project skills. Each skill reinforced is the same, or nearly the same, as a skill presented in the project. Detailed instructions are provided in a step-by-step format. The exercises relate to a single file, and you should work the exercises in order.

1. Creating Resources

The company you work at recently experienced a severe virus attack that has damaged the e-mail servers, the network, and several employee workstations. In anticipation of any recurrence, your company has created a virus recovery program that includes a project plan. Your job is to communicate the status of the clean-up operation to upper management, and to ensure that each step in your virus recovery plan is complete. You must assign tasks to the appropriate team member from the Information Systems department and track the cost of the clean-up operation.

To create a resource pool, complete the following steps:

1. Open *EPr1_0402* and save it as **Virus_Recovery**.

2. Choose <u>V</u>iew, Resource <u>S</u>heet.

3. Enter the following resource data:

Name	Type	Material Label	Initials	Group	Max Units	Std. Rate	Cost/Use
Jackie DeDios	Work		JD	IS	100%	$45	
Joe Belson	Work		JB	IS	100%	$45	
Rich Betters	Work		RB	HR	100%	$45	
Virus Software Update	Material		V	Virus			$5.00
Network downtime	Material		Net	Network			$2000.00
Recovery Manuals	Material	Dozen	Man	Virus			$120.00

4. Double-click *Network downtime* and then click the Notes tab.

5. Type **This cost per hour represents approximate cost of having the network down during virus clean-up.** Then click OK.

6. Save *Virus_Recovery* and leave it open for the next exercise.

2. Assigning Resources to Tasks

You have created the resource sheet specifying both material and nonmaterial resources in the *Virus_Recovery* project. Now, you want to assign resources to the appropriate tasks.

To assign resources, complete the following steps:

1. Open *Virus_Recovery,* if necessary, and choose <u>V</u>iew, <u>G</u>antt Chart.

2. Select Task 2 (*Virus, worm, or Trojan*) and click *Assign Resources.*

3. From the Assign Resources dialog box, select *Joe Belson* and then click the Assign button.

4. Select Task 3 (*Check Web for operating system fixes*) and click *Assign Resources.*

5. From the Assign Resources dialog box, select *Rich Betters* and then click the Assign button.

6. Complete the remaining resource assignments, as listed in the table below.

ID	Task Name	Resource Name
4	Check for virus patch	*Rich Betters*
5	Communicate with end users	*Jackie DeDios, Recovery manuals*
6	Identify affected computers	*Jackie DeDios*
8	Bring down e-mail server	*Joe Belson, Network downtime*
9	Bring down the network	*Joe Belson, Network downtime*
10	Clean server and network	*Rich Betters, Network downtime*
12	Clean-up virus	*Joe Belson*
13	Scan for virus	*Rich Betters*
14	Recover damaged mailboxes	*Joe Belson*
15	Repair damaged workstations	*Jackie DeDios*
17	Analyze affected computers	*Joe Belson*
18	Identify where the attack came from	*Joe Belson, Rich Betters*
19	Communicate with upper level	*Jackie DeDios*
20	Educate end users	*Jackie DeDios*

7. Save *Virus_Recovery* and leave it open for the next exercise.

3. Reviewing Resource Allocations

You have entered resource assignments. The next step is to take a look at the overall project and analyze the results. Then, you can make necessary changes.

To review resource allocations, complete the following steps:

1. Open *Virus_Recovery,* if necessary, and choose <u>V</u>iew, Resource <u>U</u>sage.

   Notice that the names of Joe Belson and Rich Betters are in red because they are overallocated.

2. Point to the warning icon for Joe Belson and read the message.

3. Under Jackie DeDios, double-click the *Repair damaged workstations* task.

   This task requires 32 hours of work and costs $1,440. The amount of time calculated is not reasonable for this resource.

4. Under Joe Belson, double-click the *Analyze affected computers* task.

   Notice that the cost of this task is also $1,440. You need to reduce the cost of this task.

5. Click Cancel to close the Assignment Information dialog box.

6. Choose <u>V</u>iew, <u>G</u>antt Chart and then drag the split bar between the task table and the Gantt chart to the right until you can view the Resource Names column.

7. View Task 15 (*Repair damaged workstations*) and note that this task has a 4-day estimated duration.

8. Choose <u>P</u>roject, <u>P</u>roject Information and note that the project base calendar is the Standard project calendar; click Cancel.

   Using the Standard project base calendar and the 100% maximum units of the resources, Task 15 translates to 8 hours of work each day for Jackie DeDios and requires a total of 32 hours of work. The amount of time calculated is not reasonable for this resource, given the other tasks already assigned to her.

9. Save *Virus_Recovery* and leave it open for the next exercise.

4. Leveling Resources

You have looked at your resource allocations and realize that some resources are overallocated in the virus recovery process. You need to manually level these resources to make the workloads more reasonable.

To level resource allocations, complete the following steps:

1. Open *Virus_Recovery*, if necessary, and select Task 17 (*Analyze affected computers*); then click *Assign Resources*.

2. Click in the first blank row in the Assign Resources dialog box, type **Ashish Mehta**, and then press ⏎Enter.

3. Press Up Arrow to select *Ashish Mehta*, click <u>A</u>ssign, and then click Close.

4. Click the smart tag and choose the first option, *Reduce duration so task ends sooner, but requires the same amount of work (person-hours).*

5. Select Task 18 (*Identify where the attack came from*) and then click *Assign Resources*.

6. Select *Joe Belson*, and then click <u>R</u>emove.

7. Select *Ashish Mehta*, click <u>A</u>ssign, and then click Close.

8. Click the smart tag and choose the first option in the list.

9. Select Task 15 (*Repair damaged workstations*) and click *Assign Resources*.

10. Click in the first blank row in the Assign Resources dialog box, type **Anita McKay**, and then press ⏎Enter.

11. Press Up Arrow to select *Anita McKay*, click <u>A</u>ssign, and then click Close.

12. Click the smart tag and choose the first option in the list.

13. Choose View, Resource Usage.

    Although resources are still overallocated, the work hours are more reasonable than before. Jackie DeDios is now scheduled to work 16 hours on the *Repair damaged workstations* task, rather than 32 hours; the duration is also reduced from 4 days to 2. Joe Belson is now scheduled to work 16 hours on the *Analyze affected computers* task, rather than 32 hours. Half the work on these tasks went to Ashish Mehta and Anita McKay.

14. Save *Virus_Recovery* and leave it open for the next exercise.

5. Printing Resource Allocation and Cost Reports

You have adjusted the plan the best you know how. You want to provide the creators of the virus recovery plan some reports to review. They need to see how the Information Systems department has been dispatched to handle this problem as well as review the overall costs associated with this project.

To print resource allocations and a cost report, complete the following steps:

1. Open *Virus_Recovery,* if necessary, and choose Report Reports.

2. Click Workload and then click Select.

3. Under *Workload Reports,* click *Resource Usage* and then click Select.

4. Click Print on the toolbar and then click OK.

5. In the Reports dialog box, click Costs and then click Select.

6. Under *Cost Reports,* click *Budget* and then click Select.

7. Click Print on the toolbar, click OK, and then click Close.

8. Save *Virus_Recovery* and then close it.

CHALLENGE

Challenge exercises expand on or are somewhat related to skills presented in the lessons. Each exercise provides a brief narrative introduction, followed by instructions in a numbered-step format that are not as detailed as those in the Skill Drill section.

These Challenge exercises relate to a single file and should be worked in order.

1. Adding Resources By Using the Resource Information Dialog Box

You work at a company that recently spun off a division that provides temporary employees for businesses that require extra office workers for a short period of time. Your first client requires 50 temporary employees for a huge car dealership that is being built in your area. You have received more than 500 resumes and must review these resumes for potential candidates. For legal purposes, you must verify each resume and potential candidate and conduct interviews for the group you choose. You plan to use the project plan provided by Human Resources to help you.

To add resources, complete the following steps:

1. Open the *EPr1_0403* file and save it as **Temps_Hiring_Plan**.

2. Switch to the Resource Sheet view.

3. Double-click the first empty resource row, and click the General tab, if necessary.

4. Add the resources listed in the table below. (Click OK after each resource entry and double-click the next blank row.)

Resource Name	Initials	Group	Type	E-Mail
Corporate Law	Law	Lawyers	Work	law@jkedwards.com
Dante Peeples	DP	Review Team	Work	d.peeples@tempsplus.com
Jackie Gibson	JG	HR	Work	j.gibson@tempsplus.com
Joy Ti	JT	Review Team	Work	j.ti@tempsplus.com
Letterhead paper	Letterhead	Supplies	Material	
Postage	Postage	Correspondence	Material	
Renee Thibodeaux	RT	Review Team	Work	r.thibodeaux@tempsplus.com
Saul Jeffers	SJ	Review Team	Work	s.jeffers@tempsplus.com
Testing Vendor	Vendor	Vendor	Work	kewood@questions.com
Tim Daniels	TD	HR	Work	t.daniels@tempsplus.com
UPS Overnight Store	UPS	Correspondence	Material	
Victoria Hunter	VH	HR	Work	v.hunter@tempsplus.com

5. Double-click the Corporate Law resource, and then click the Help button to learn how to use the Resource Availability table.

6. Make the Corporate Law resource available only from February 22, 2006, through March 2, 2006, and from April 3, 2006, through April 6, 2006.

7. Add a note to remind yourself that Corporate Law is involved in arbitration and other legal proceedings and will be available only on the dates specified.

8. Edit the Tim Daniels and Corporate Law resources to have a max unit of 25% each.

9. Save *Temps_Hiring_Plan* and leave it open for the next exercise.

2. Adding Costs to Material and Work Resources

Now that your resource pool is complete, you need to assign the costs to each resource. The testing vendor has quoted a set price for his services. Some resources have an hourly rate attached, while others have a per unit fee.

To add resource costs, complete the following steps:

1. Open *Temps_Hiring_Plan,* if necessary, and switch to Resource Sheet view.

2. Enter the following resource costs:

Resource Name	Std. Cost	Ovt. Cost	Cost/Use
Corporate Law	$250.00	$375.00	
Dante Peeples	$16.50	$24.75	
Jackie Gibson	$8.50	$12.75	
Joy Ti	$16.50	$24.75	
Letterhead paper			$6.50
Postage			$0.37

Renee Thibodeaux	`$16.50`	`$24.75`	
Saul Jeffers	`$16.50`	`$24.75`	
Tim Daniels	`$20.00`		
UPS Overnight Store			`$12.75`
Victoria Hunter	`$16.00`		

3. Double-click the *Letterhead paper* resource and add **Box** as the material label.

4. Switch to Gantt Chart view, and then change the Table: Entry view to the Table: Cost view.

5. Add **$2500** as the fixed cost for Task 18 (Contact testing vendor).

6. Switch back to the Table: Entry view.

7. Save *Temps_Hiring_Plan* and leave it open for the next exercise.

3. Assigning Tasks to Resources

Now that your resource pool is complete, you need to assign specific tasks to each resource. To assign resources to tasks, complete the following steps:

1. Open *Temps_Hiring_Plan*, if necessary, and click Resources from the Project Guide toolbar.

2. Click the *Assign people and equipment to task* link, and assign the following resources to the tasks. To modify the resource's assignment units, double-click aname in the Assign Resources dialog box and specify the percentage in the Units cell:

ID	Task Name	Resource/Units
2	Organize Candidate Review team	Victoria Hunter - 50%; Tim Daniels - 25%
3	Review	Victoria Hunter - 100%; Dante Peeples, Joy Ti, Renee Thibodeaux, Saul Jeffers - 80%
4	Contact candidates	Jackie Gibson - 25%; Letterhead (3); Postage (100)
6	Complete worker validity form	Victoria Hunter - 50%
7	Verify all certification and education data	Victoria Hunter - 25%
8	Receive copies of transcripts and certificates	Jackie Gibson - 10%
9	Complete education validity form	Jackie Gibson - 25%
10	Contact references	Victoria Hunter - 50%; Tim Daniels - 50%
12	Narrow down selections	Victoria Hunter - 75%; Tim Daniels - 75%
13	Provide policy and procedures	Victoria Hunter - 100%
14	Review legal issues	Corporate Law - 25%
15	Distribute candidate resumes to Review team	Victoria Hunter - 100%

16	Identify interviewing team members	Dante Peeples, Joy Ti, Renee Thibodeaux, Saul Jeffers - 100%; Victoria Hunter - 100%; Tim Daniels - 100%
17	Identify interview questions	Dante Peeples, Joy Ti, Renee Thibodeaux, Saul Jeffers - 100%; Victoria Hunter - 100%; Tim Daniels - 100%
18	Contact testing vendor	Tim Daniels -100%; UPS (1)
19	Review test questions	Dante Peeples, Joy Ti, Renee Thibodeaux, Saul Jeffers - 100%; Victoria Hunter - 100%; Tim Daniels - 100%
20	Perform 1st round interviews	Victoria Hunter - 75%; Tim Daniels - 25%
22	Meet with Review team to discuss	Dante Peeples, Joy Ti, Renee Thibodeaux, Saul Jeffers - 100%; Victoria Hunter - 100%; Tim Daniels - 100%
23	Perform 2nd round interviews	Victoria Hunter
25	Meet with Review team to discuss	Dante Peeples, Joy Ti, Renee Thibodeaux, Saul Jeffers - 100%; Victoria Hunter - 100%; Tim Daniels - 100%
27	Candidate start date	Victoria Hunter
28	Confirm with manager	Jackie Gibson
29	Confirm with candidate	Victoria Hunter

3. Select <u>V</u>iew, Tas<u>k</u> Usage.

This view shows each task and how the work involved is distributed to the assigned resources.

4. Select <u>V</u>iew, Resource <u>U</u>sage to check for overallocations.

Several resources are overallocated—namely, being assigned too much work for 1 day.

5. Save *Temps_Hiring_Plan* and leave it open for the next exercise.

4. Leveling Resource Assignments

As you know, several resources are overallocated. You need to level the resources to fit within normal working hours. Remember that the Corporate Law and Tim Daniels (the Human Resources manager) resources have a maximum unit of 25%.

To level resources, complete the following steps:

1. Open *Temps_Hiring_Plan,* if necessary, and scroll down to the Tim Daniels resource.

2. Using the timephased bar graph, look for the days on which Tim is scheduled to work for more than 2 hours.

3. Change the units for any task necessary to level Tim's time. Remember that at times it is okay to assign more hours.

4. Respond to any smart tags by changing the work to fit the change.

5. Level all other resources as you see fit.

6. Save *Temps_Hiring_Plan* and leave it open for the next exercise.

5. Changing Text in the Gantt Chart

As you look at the Gantt chart, you see how cluttered it appears. You need to shorten the text shown beside the Gantt bar. You try several options to determine which is best for you.

To change Gantt chart text, complete the following steps:

1. Open *Temps_Hiring_Plan,* if necessary, and switch to Gantt Chart view and widen the Gantt chart area.

2. Double-click the name beside the Task 10 Gantt bar.

3. Click the Text tab in the Bar Styles dialog box.

4. Click in the Right text box and then click the drop-down arrow.

5. Select *Resource initials* and close the dialog box.

6. Double-click the Gantt bar and change the bar text to *Resource Group*.

7. Save *Temps_Hire_Plan* and close it.

DISCOVERY ZONE

Discovery Zone exercises require advanced knowledge of topics presented in *Essentials* lessons, application of skills from multiple lessons, or self-directed learning of new skills. Each exercise is independent of the others, so you may complete them in any order.

1. Creating a Template with a Standard Resource Pool

Assume that you are a member of a fraternity/sorority or a civic organization. These organizations continually work on projects. To make the input easier, you can create a template that contains only a common resource pool. Decide which organization you want to use in this exercise. Create a new project and create a resource pool with at least 10 resources. Save the project file as a template. If necessary, consult Microsoft Project's Help.

2. Working with Costs

There are many different costs involved in a project, including fixed costs, variable costs, and budgets. Take some time to research costs using all available Help sources. Then add, edit, or remove costs within an existing project. Save the updated project as a separate file.

P R O J E C T 5

MODIFYING TASK INFORMATION

O B J E C T I V E S

IN THIS PROJECT, YOU LEARN HOW TO

- Edit and replace task information and check spelling

- Save a baseline

- Enter percent complete

- View percent complete

- Enter actuals

- Specify lead and lag time

- Resolve constraint conflicts and set a task deadline

WHY WOULD I DO THIS?

When tracking progress, you must decide ahead of time how you want to receive updates from your team members and how often you want to receive them. There are several levels of detail for incorporating progress, from the simple to the complex. Tracking progress at the task level is the most simple. An example of task-level progress is noting that a task is 50% complete. Assignment-level progress provides more tracking details, but it can be used only if you have assigned resources to tasks. An example of assignment-level tracking is noting how many resources are assigned to a task and the cost and work values associated with each resource. If you track progress by time period, you are interested in the progress of an assignment relative to work hours. An example of tracking progress by time period is noting the time a resource worked on a task each day or in a given week.

Once you decide on your tracking method, there are many different options for viewing progress. *Progress bars* appear in each task's Gantt bar, giving you an at-a-glance view of each task's overall status. You can view the Percent Complete column or use any of the several table views that can be applied to the Gantt Chart view so you can see additional columns of data.

VISUAL SUMMARY

As you design a project plan, modifications are necessary. After fine-tuning the project file, you save the *baseline,* a "snapshot in time" that includes all the project's original start, finish, duration, and cost estimates. Then as you begin tracking progress, you can compare baseline data against actual data. For example, you can note when you estimate a task to begin and when it actually began, or you can track the estimated work hours a resource should spend completing a task compared to the actual amount of time the resource spent completing the task. Figure 5.1 provides an example of a baseline within a project file, which you create in this project.

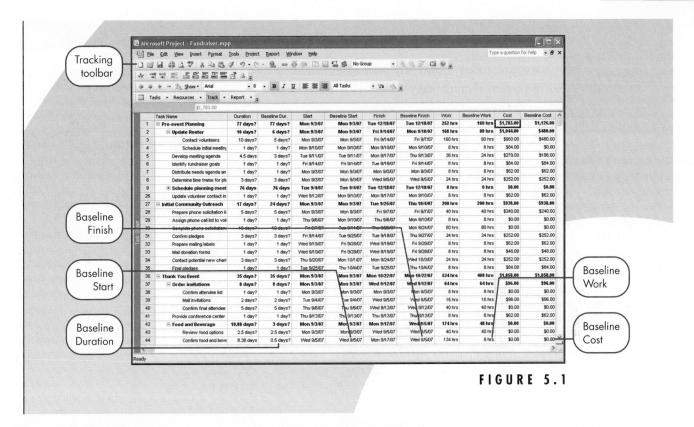

FIGURE 5.1

LESSON 1: **Editing and Replacing Task Information and Checking Spelling**

Microsoft Project utilizes ***effort-driven scheduling*** to lengthen or shorten the duration of a task based on the resources assigned to the task. The total amount of work for the task is not changed. Effort-driven scheduling is a default feature that can be turned off on a task-by-task basis for those instances in which you cannot predict the amount of work a task will generate.

Fine-tuning a project plan involves analyzing estimated task duration and how it affects the overall project completion date. You can adjust resource assignments, resource assignment units, and estimated task durations to modify task duration and thus the overall project completion date. You can check spelling and use Find and Replace features to edit language and grammar.

In this lesson, you are part of a team managing an annual fundraiser for your community's downtown events program. You are managing the tasks assigned to a group of volunteers and full-time city employees. In the first set of steps, you adjust the resources for one of the tasks to see the effect of effort-driven scheduling. In the second set of steps, you use Replace to make a global change to a word used in task descriptions, and you use the Spelling feature to find and correct spelling errors.

To Edit and Replace Task Information

1 Open the *EPr1_0501* file and save it as Fundraiser; then close any open side panes, if necessary.

2 Choose **View**, Task Usage; then drag the split bar between the Task Usage table and the bar chart to the right until the Finish column appears.

3 Select Task 3 (*Contact volunteers*).

Task 3 has a 10-day estimated duration that results in 80 hours of work for the Student Work Study Aides resource (see Figure 5.2). However, the Student Work Study Aids resource is actually two students, not one, so the assignment units need modifying.

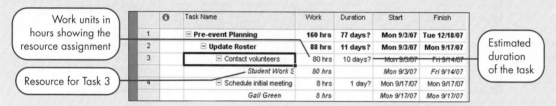

Work units in hours showing the resource assignment

Resource for Task 3

Estimated duration of the task

	❶	Task Name	Work	Duration	Start	Finish
1		⊟ Pre-event Planning	160 hrs	77 days?	Mon 9/3/07	Tue 12/18/07
2		⊟ Update Roster	88 hrs	11 days?	Mon 9/3/07	Mon 9/17/07
3		⊟ Contact volunteers	80 hrs	10 days?	Mon 9/3/07	Fri 9/14/07
		Student Work S	80 hrs		Mon 9/3/07	Fri 9/14/07
4		⊟ Schedule initial meeting	8 hrs	1 day?	Mon 9/17/07	Mon 9/17/07
		Gail Green	8 hrs		Mon 9/17/07	Mon 9/17/07

FIGURE 5.2

4 Double-click Task 3 (*Contact volunteers*).

The Task Information dialog box opens.

5 Click the Resources tab, and then click in the first Units cell.

You set the assignment units for a resource on the Resources tab in the Task Information dialog box (see Figure 5.3). To show more than one resource at 100% usage, you multiply the number of resources by 100%: 200% represents the work of the two students.

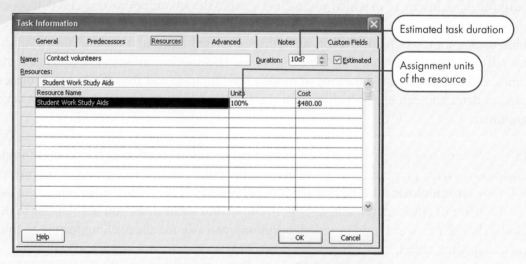

Estimated task duration

Assignment units of the resource

FIGURE 5.3

6 **Click the up-spinner until *200%* displays; then click OK.**
A smart tag appears in the Indicator column for Task 3 (see Figure 5.4).

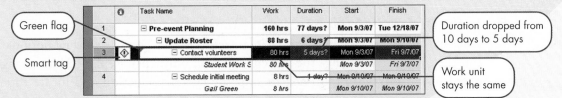

FIGURE 5.4

7 **Click the smart tag down arrow and select the first option.**
Recall that the first option is the default and reduces the duration of the task by half because each resource is assigned 40 hours of work. By ignoring the smart tag, you automatically apply the first option. The second option would increase the work hours to 160 and assign 80 hours of work to each resource, thus keeping the task duration constant at 10 days.

8 **Save your changes to the *Fundraiser* file.**

In addition to modifying task information, basic text editing tools such as Find and Replace and spell-check are available. In the next set of steps, you modify the project file by replacing "employee" with "volunteer" and then check the spelling in the file.

Using Find and Replace and Checking Spelling

1 **Choose View, Gantt Chart.**

2 **Drag the column separator between the Task Name and Duration columns to the right until you can see all of the Task Name information.**
Widening the Task Name column enables the display of full names. You can also double-click the separator line in the headings to automatically size a column to display the longest entry.

3 **Choose Edit, Replace.**
The Replace dialog box opens (see Figure 5.5).

FIGURE 5.5

4 In the *Find what* text box, type `employee`.

You plan to replace the word "employee" in the Task Name column with the word "volunteer" because the human resources in this project plan are actually volunteers.

5 In the *Replace with* text box, type `volunteer`.

After specifying the *Find what* and *Replace with* criteria, you have several options. You can click Replace to change the current selection only, click Replace All to change all occurrences, or click Find Next to skip the current selection and locate the next occurrence.

6 Click Replace All.

An information box appears letting you know that Microsoft Project replaced three occurrences (see Figure 5.6).

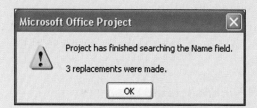

FIGURE 5.6

7 Click OK and then click Close.

8 Click Spelling on the Standard toolbar.

The Spelling dialog box opens. The Spelling tool checks content and lists as a spelling error any word not found in its dictionary. The first spelling error is "solicitaton" (see Figure 5.7). The suggestion in the *Suggestions* list is the correct spelling.

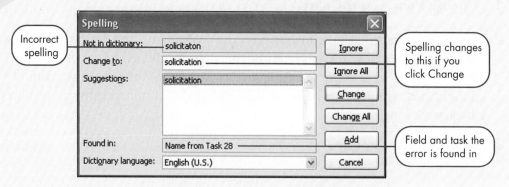

FIGURE 5.7

9 Click Change.

The second spelling error is the word *pic* in Task 50. This spelling error is not actually an error because it is an abbreviation for *picture*.

10 **Click Ignore.**

The third spelling error is a plural term that is not generally plural. In this case, the word *actuals* is a term used by managers to describe actual work and is correct. (Actuals will be discussed in more detail in Lesson 5.)

11 **Click Ignore.**

The last spelling error is *Merriweather*, the last name of a work resource.

12 **Click Ignore.**

An information box appears, telling you that the Spelling program finds no more errors (see Figure 5.8).

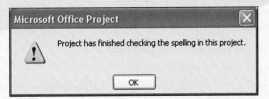

Microsoft Office Project

Project has finished checking the spelling in this project.

OK

FIGURE 5.8

13 **Click OK.**

14 **Save your changes to the *Fundraiser* file.**

You modified task information and checked for spelling errors in this project file. Keep the *Fundraiser* project file open and continue with the next lesson. If you prefer to complete the project later, close the file and exit Microsoft Project.

TO EXTEND YOUR KNOWLEDGE . . .

FINDING AND REPLACING A RESOURCE

Occasionally you may find that a resource is replaced by another resource or that you inadvertently added the same resource twice because you spelled the name differently. To resolve this problem, select the task in Gantt Chart view, and then click the Assign Resources button on the Standard toolbar. In the Resource Name column, select the resource you want to replace and then click Replace. In the Replace Resource dialog box, click the resource that is the replacement, and then click OK.

LESSON 2:   Saving a Baseline

Think of a baseline as your ideal project scenario. As explained in the Visual Summary, a baseline is your original project plan and shows the project teams' best estimations as to how long their tasks should take, the approximate cost, and the overall finish date of the entire project. You should save a baseline after you have created your project plan, assigned resources, and made all the necessary adjustments. This fine-tuned project plan becomes a "snapshot in time" and the basis with which you can view variances.

A baseline allows you to analyze key data, such as estimated task duration with actual task duration or estimated costs with actual costs. Imagine that your project plan is the rollout of a new product for a customer. Knowing the overall cost of the rollout and the product's delivery date can give other teams, such as marketing and accounting, a clear directive for putting together the budget, processing payables, and developing the advertising campaign. This information can then be used to put together much more accurate project plans in the future.

When you save a baseline, Microsoft Project copies approximately 20 pieces of information in the background about task, resource, assignment schedules, and cost data into new columns of fields that you can view. In addition, you can save up to 11 baselines within one project file. Typically, multiple baselines are used only in very long projects or in projects that have strayed so far from the original baseline that it is no longer relevant and a new baseline is warranted. A baseline is an optional component of project planning and is used only if you plan to compare estimated project data with actual project data.

In this lesson, you save a baseline for the fundraiser project file that you fine-tuned in the last project. You also view a baseline table to see what data have been recorded.

To Save a Baseline

1   **Open *Fundraiser*, if necessary, and then press** Ctrl + Home.
The cursor moves to the upper-left area of the task table.

2   **Click Track on the Project Guide toolbar.**   Track ▾
The Track side pane appears (see Figure 5.9).

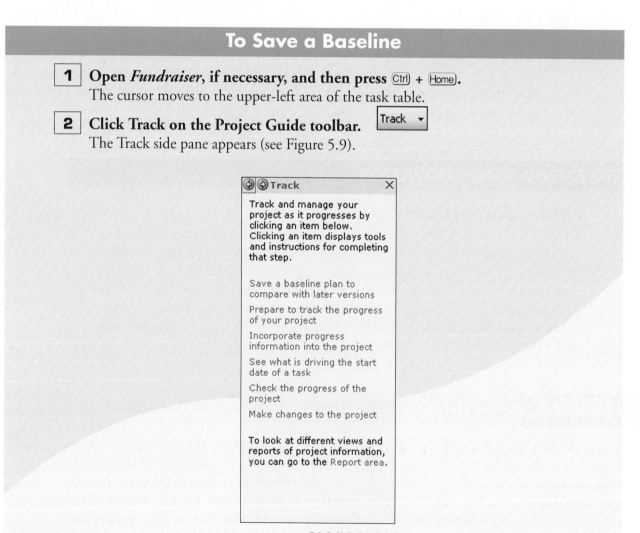

FIGURE 5.9

3   Click the first link, *Save a baseline plan to compare with later versions.*

4   Click Save Baseline.   Save Baseline

The side pane shows the date and time you saved the baseline (see Figure 5.10).

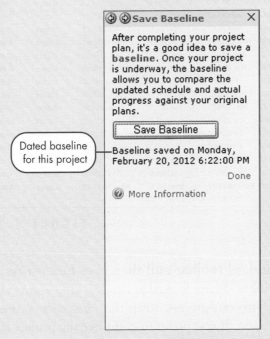

Dated baseline
for this project

FIGURE 5.10

5   Click Done.

In the background, Microsoft Project has copied the data into a set of identical baseline fields that are used for comparison purposes.

6   Close the Track side pane.

7   Choose View, Tracking Gantt.

The Tracking Gantt view displays.

8   Choose View, Table: Entry, Variance.

The Variance view appears, enabling you to view the differences between the baseline data and the actual data.

9   Drag the split bar between the task table and the Gantt chart to the right until the last column, Finish Var. (Finish Variance), displays .

The Gantt chart is not visible (see Figure 5.11). By hiding the Gantt chart portion from view, you can print only the variance table and have a copy of the baseline data upon its initial creation.

	Task Name	Start	Finish	Baseline Start	Baseline Finish	Start Var.	Finish Var.
1	⊟ Pre-event Planning	Mon 9/3/07	Tue 12/18/07	Mon 9/3/07	Tue 12/18/07	0 days	0 days
2	⊟ Update Roster	Mon 9/3/07	Mon 9/10/07	Mon 9/3/07	Mon 9/10/07	0 days	0 days
3	Contact vol	Mon 9/3/07	Fri 9/7/07	Mon 9/3/07	Fri 9/7/07	0 days	0 days
	Schedule ir	Mon 9/10/07	Mon 9/10/07	Mon 9/10/07	Mon 9/10/07	0 days	0 days
	Develop meeting	Tue 9/11/07	Thu 9/13/07	Tue 9/11/07	Thu 9/13/07	0 days	0 days
	Identify fundrais	Fri 9/14/07	Fri 9/14/07	Fri 9/14/07	Fri 9/14/07	0 days	0 days
7	Distribute needs	Mon 9/3/07	Mon 9/3/07	Mon 9/3/07	Mon 9/3/07	0 days	0 days
8	Determine time fi	Mon 9/3/07	Wed 9/5/07	Mon 9/3/07	Wed 9/5/07	0 days	0 days
9	⊞ Schedule plan	Tue 9/4/07	Tue 12/18/07	Tue 9/4/07	Tue 12/18/07	0 days	0 days
26	Update voluntee	Mon 9/10/07	Mon 9/10/07	Mon 9/10/07	Mon 9/10/07	0 days	0 days
27	⊟ Initial Community C	Mon 9/3/07	Thu 10/4/07	Mon 9/3/07	Thu 10/4/07	0 days	0 days
28	Prepare phone s	Mon 9/3/07	Fri 9/7/07	Mon 9/3/07	Fri 9/7/07	0 days	0 days
29	Assign phone ce	Mon 9/10/07	Mon 9/10/07	Mon 9/10/07	Mon 9/10/07	0 days	0 days
30	Complete phone	Tue 9/11/07	Mon 9/24/07	Tue 9/11/07	Mon 9/24/07	0 days	0 days
31	Confirm pledges	Tue 9/25/07	Thu 9/27/07	Tue 9/25/07	Thu 9/27/07	0 days	0 days
32	Prepare mailing I	Fri 9/28/07	Fri 9/28/07	Fri 9/28/07	Fri 9/28/07	0 days	0 days
33	Mail donation for	Fri 9/28/07	Fri 9/28/07	Fri 9/28/07	Fri 9/28/07	0 days	0 days
34	Contact potentia	Mon 10/1/07	Wed 10/3/07	Mon 10/1/07	Wed 10/3/07	0 days	0 days
35	Final pledges	Thu 10/4/07	Thu 10/4/07	Thu 10/4/07	Thu 10/4/07	0 days	0 days
36	⊟ Thank You Event	Mon 9/3/07	Mon 10/22/07	Mon 9/3/07	Mon 10/22/07	0 days	0 days

Tracking Gantt

Actual finish date of tasks

Variance between actual and baseline finish dates

Baseline finish date of tasks

FIGURE 5.11

10 **Click Print on the Standard toolbar and then save *Fundraiser*.**

You have created a baseline and have looked at the Tracking Gantt view. You are now ready to begin tracking project progress. Keep the *Fundraiser* project file open and continue with the next lesson. If you prefer to complete the project later, close the file and exit Microsoft Project.

TO EXTEND YOUR KNOWLEDGE . . .

ALTERNATIVE WAY TO SAVE A BASELINE

In this lesson you used a link on the Track side pane to save a baseline. You can also save a baseline by choosing Tools, Tracking, Set Baseline.

SAVING AN ADDITIONAL BASELINE

You can save up to 11 baselines in a project file. To save an additional Baseline, click Track on the Project Guide toolbar, and then click the first link, *Save a baseline plan to compare with later versions*. From the Save Baseline side pane, click the first option, *Save a new baseline*, click the selection to *Save a new baseline for: The entire project*, and then click the Save Baseline button.

LESSON 3: Entering Percent Complete

In Microsoft Project, the **percent complete** value shows how much of a task has been completed and is a percentage of the whole duration. For instance, if you complete half of a task, the percent complete is 50%. Microsoft Project calculates the percentage of work for a summary task based on the progress of its subtasks. Entering percent complete is the simplest way to monitor overall task progress.

In this lesson, you complete two sets of hands-on steps. In the first set, you enter the percent complete for several tasks by using the Task Information dialog box. In the second set, you use the *Tracking toolbar* to enter the percent complete for another task and view the % Complete column.

To Enter Percent Complete by Using the Task Information Dialog Box

1 Open *Fundraiser*, if necessary; then choose <u>V</u>iew, <u>G</u>antt Chart.

2 Double-click Task 3 (*Contact volunteers*), and then click the General tab.
You can enter the percent complete in the Task Information dialog box (see Figure 5.12).

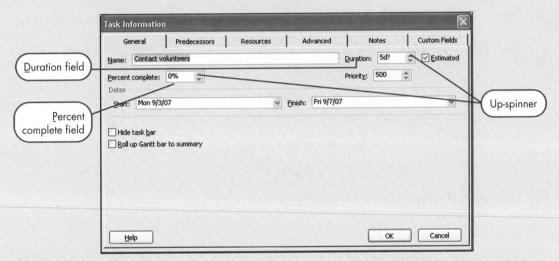

FIGURE 5.12

3 Click the *Percent complete* up-spinner until *100%* displays.

4 Click OK.
A check mark appears in the Task 3 Indicator column, and a black line runs through the corresponding Gantt bar (see Figure 5.13).

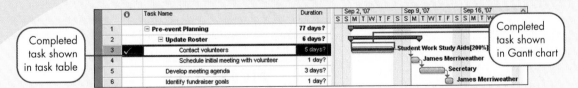

FIGURE 5.13

Task 2 is the summary task for Tasks 3 and 4. Task 3 has a 5-day duration, which is 40 hours of work. Task 4 has a 1-day duration, which is 8 hours of work.

5 Double-click Task 2 (*Update Roster*).
Note that the percent complete is now 83% to reflect the total of the subtasks below it. Because Task 3 is complete, 40 hours of work out of 48 total hours are complete.

6 | **Click OK.**

7 | **Double-click Task 4 (*Schedule initial meeting with volunteer*); change the percent complete to *100%* and click OK.**

Notice that Microsoft Project marks the summary task for Tasks 3 and 4 (Task 2) complete as well (see Figure 5.14).

FIGURE 5.14

8 | **Enter the remaining percent complete values as shown in the following table:**

Task ID	Task Name	% Complete
5	Develop meeting agenda	50%
7	Distribute needs agenda and review	100%
8	Determine time frame for planning meetings	100%
26	Update volunteer contact info	25%
28	Prepare phone solicitation list	10%

9 | **Save your changes to the *Fundraiser* file.**

You can use the Tracking toolbar to update and view project information. For example, you can click one of the predefined percentage buttons (0%, 25%, 50%, 75%, and 100%) to change the percent complete value for a task (see Figure 5.15).

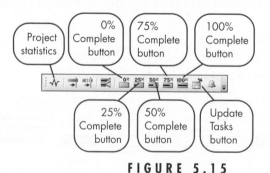

FIGURE 5.15

You can also use the Update Tasks button to manage additional functions, such as rescheduling work. Clicking the Project Statistics button opens the Project Statistics dialog box in which you can view the current project start data, project baseline data, the project finish date, and the duration, work, and cost of the overall project.

In the following steps, you use the Tracking toolbar to change the percent complete for multiple tasks.

To Enter Percent Complete by Using the Tracking Toolbar

1 **Choose View, Toolbars, Tracking.**
The Tracking toolbar appears (refer to Figure 5.15).

2 **Scroll down to show Task 42 at the top of the screen.**

3 **Select Tasks 43 (*Review food options*) and 44 (*Confirm food and beverage choices*), and then click 75% Complete on the Tracking toolbar.**

4 **Click Task 46 (*Confirm MC*), and then hold Ctrl while clicking Tasks 49 (*Review AV with conference center*) and 51 (*Hire photographer*).**

5 **Click 100% Complete.**

6 **Select Task 47 (*Confirm speakers*) and then click 25% Complete.**

7 **Double-click Task 45 (*Speakers and MC*).**
Task 45 is the summary task for Tasks 46 through 49. The estimated duration is 21 days and 14% of Task 45 is complete. This computation is automatic and reflects the 100% completion of tasks 46 (1 day) and 49 (1 day), and the marking of Task 47 as 25% complete (1 day). Thus, 3 days out of 21 days are complete, equalling 14%. The percent complete of a summary task is derived from the task duration and the percent complete of its subtasks.

8 **Click OK.**

9 **Choose View, Toolbars, Tracking.**
You turned off the Tracking toolbar.

10 **Save your changes to the *Fundraiser* file.**
Keep the *Fundraiser* project file open and continue with the next lesson. If you prefer to complete the project later, close the file and exit Microsoft Project.

TO EXTEND YOUR KNOWLEDGE . . .

MARKING RECURRING TASK OCCURRENCES COMPLETE

In the *Fundraiser* project file, Task 9 (*Schedule planning meetings*) is a recurring meeting. With tasks like this, it is important to mark each meeting as 100% complete once it has passed. Although these types of tasks have no work units associated with them, they do affect the overall percent complete for the entire project.

LESSON 4:   Viewing Percent Complete

The two easiest methods for viewing percent complete are by using the Gantt chart and by adding the percent complete column to the task table. When using the Gantt chart, pointing to a progress bar on a Gantt bar with the mouse displays a Progress information dialog box containing additional task information, including the full task name, the actual start date, and the task duration.

In addition, once you enter values in the % Complete field, Microsoft Project performs several calculations in the background to help you better track the overall progress of your project. First, ***actual duration*** is automatically calculated when you enter a value in the percent complete column by using the formula *Actual Duration = Duration * Percent Complete*. Another calculation is ***remaining duration,*** which uses the formula *Remaining Duration = Duration – (Duration * Percent Complete)*.

In this lesson, you examine the task to contact volunteers and take a closer look at viewing percent complete information in the Gantt chart. You also expand the task table by adding the percent complete column.

To View Percent Complete

1   **Open *Fundraiser*, if necessary; then select the task name of Task 3 (*Contact volunteers*).**

2   **Scroll to view the Task 3 Gantt bar, if necessary.**
A horizontal black bar appears within the Gantt bar (see Figure 5.16). This is a progress bar and shows the percent complete for a task. This task is 100% complete because the bar runs completely from left to right.

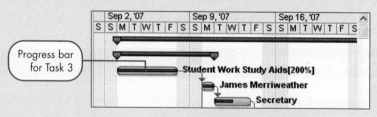

FIGURE 5.16

3   **Point to the progress bar in the Task 3 Gantt bar.**
A ScreenTip appears with Progress information (see Figure 5.17).

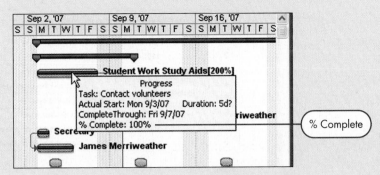

FIGURE 5.17

If you have problems . . .

To see Progress information, you must point to the black progress bar within the Gantt bar. If you point to a Gantt bar rather than the progress bar, the ScreenTip displays Task information instead.

4 | **Choose Insert, Column.**
The Column Definition dialog box opens (see Figure 5.18).

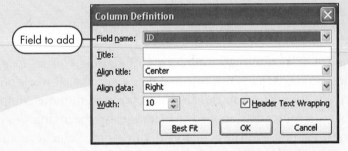

FIGURE 5.18

5 | **Click the *Field name* drop-down arrow.**

6 | **Scroll to the top of the list and select *% Complete.***
The % Complete column appears at the top of the field list because it starts with a symbol.

7 | **Click OK.**
You inserted the % Complete column to the left of the Task Name column (see Figure 5.19).

Added column

	ⓘ	% Complete	Task Name
1		38%	⊟ Pre-event Planning
2	✓	100%	⊟ Update Roster
3	✓	100%	Contact volunteers
4	✓	100%	Schedule initial meeting with volunteer
5		50%	Develop meeting agenda
6		0%	Identify fundraiser goals
7	✓	100%	Distribute needs agenda and review
8	✓	100%	Determine time frame for planning meetings

FIGURE 5.19

8 Click in the % Complete column for Task 6 (*Identify fundraiser goals*); click the up-spinner to *15%* and then press ⏎Enter.

9 Click in the % Complete column for Task 38 (*Confirm attendee list*); click the up-spinner to *5%* and then press ⏎Enter.

10 Save your changes to the *Fundraiser* file.
Keep the *Fundraiser* project file open and continue with the next lesson. If you prefer to complete the project later, close the file and exit Microsoft Project.

LESSON 5: Entering Actuals

As defined in Project 4, "Scheduling Resources and Assigning Costs," *work* is the total labor required to complete a task. Microsoft Project allows you to track work progress very simply by entering the percent complete. You can also track progress in more complex ways by tracking actual work that a resource has applied to a task or by specifying the date on which the resource should finish the task and the actual work durations. Whichever method you choose, the related fields automatically update as you enter data. By simply entering the percent complete, you are able to track remaining work, remaining task duration, and the start and finish dates of a task. ***Actual work,*** sometimes referred to as ***actuals,*** is the amount of work already completed by the resources assigned to the task. Once actual work is reported for a task, Microsoft Project calculates remaining work by using the formula *Remaining Work = Work − Actual Work*. The ***actual start*** is the date that work on a task begins, and the ***actual finish*** is the date when work on a task ends. ***Remaining work*** is the amount of hours still required to complete the task. Although percent complete is the most common means of charting progress, there are several other fields from which to choose.

There are management considerations related to the flow of project information that need to be addressed. First, you need to determine how to gather actual progress information from team members. This can be challenging. It is best to determine what kind of actual progress you need to monitor and create a form or specify a format that you can then distribute to your project team. Another important consideration that needs to be communicated to the project team is how you receive that information and its frequency. Do you want to meet face-to-face, or would you prefer receiving an e-mail update? Do you want to receive updates daily, weekly, or as they occur? Finally, it is important that you inform the team members of remaining work on the tasks that have been assigned to them once you have incorporated their progress.

In this lesson, you enter actual data into the project file, including actual duration, work, and date data. You also view the Tracking Gantt again to compare project progress against the baseline.

To Enter Actuals

1 **Open *Fundraiser*, if necessary; then choose <u>V</u>iew, <u>M</u>ore Views.**
The More Views dialog box opens (see Figure 5.20).

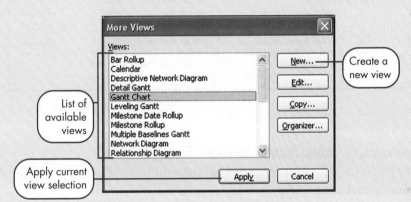

FIGURE 5.20

2 **Scroll down and select *Task Sheet* and then click Apply.**
The task sheet displays (see Figure 5.21). Only the tasks are shown, without a Gantt chart.

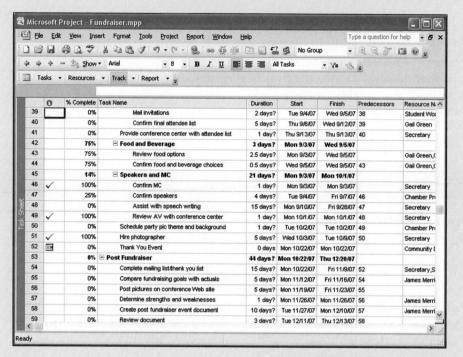

FIGURE 5.21

3 | **Choose View, Table: Entry, and Tracking.**
This view is used for entering tracking data for tasks. There are additional fields concerning actuals, including start date, finish date, duration, percent complete, cost, and work.

4 | **Right-click the Act. Dur. (Actual Duration) heading; then choose Insert Column.**

5 | **Click the *Field name* drop-down arrow; scroll up and select *Duration* and then click OK.**
The Duration column displays to the left of the Actual Duration (Act. Dur.) column (see Figure 5.22).

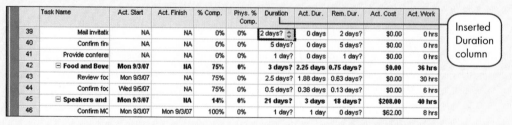

FIGURE 5.22

If you have problems . . .

There may be Duration fields with a number following them (e.g., Duration1, Duration2, and so on), which can be confusing. The Duration field that you want to use is the field without any number following it, and it is the first one in that part of the list.

6 **Select Task 5 (*Develop meeting agenda*) and view the Duration, Actual Duration, and Remaining Duration fields.**
A resource has informed you that they will need more than the 1.5 days shown in the remaining duration field to complete this task.

7 **Click in the Rem. Dur. (Remaining Duration) column, and then click the up-spinner to *3 days* and press ⏎Enter.**
Notice that the % Complete decreases from 50% to 33% for Task 5 and the Duration increases from 1.5 days to 4.5 days as a result of rescheduling the meeting from Friday to Monday (see Figure 5.23).

	Task Name	Act. Start	Act. Finish	% Comp.	Phys. % Comp.	Duration	Act. Dur.	Rem. Dur.	Act. Cost	Act. Work
1	⊟ Pre-event Planning	Mon 9/3/07	NA	37%	0%	77 days?	8.19 days	8.81 days?	$999.10	135.2 hrs
2	⊟ Update Roster	Mon 9/3/07	Mon 9/10/07	100%	0%	6 days?	6 days	0 days?	$564.00	88 hrs
3	Contact vol	Mon 9/3/07	Fri 9/7/07	100%	0%	5 days?	5 days	0 days?	$480.00	80 hrs
4	Schedule ir	Mon 9/10/07	Mon 9/10/07	100%	0%	1 day?	1 day	0 days?	$84.00	8 hrs
5	Develop meeting	Tue 9/11/07	NA	33%	0%	4.5 days	1.5 days	3 days	$93.00	12 hrs
6	Identify fundrais	Fri 9/14/07	NA	15%	0%	1 day?	0.15 days	0.85 day ⇕	$12.60	1.2 hrs

Decreased % Complete

Increased Duration

FIGURE 5.23

8 **Click in the Rem. Dur. column for Task 44 (*Confirm food and beverage choices*).**
Assume that this task will not be completed in the time remaining and the resource requires 8 additional days.

9 **Use the up-spinner to specify *8 days* and press ⏎Enter.**
The % Complete decreases from 75% to 4% and the Duration increases from .5 days to 8.38 days.

10 **View Task 3 (*Contact volunteers*) and notice that this task is already completed.**
The resource informs you that although the task was reported as complete, they continued working on the volunteer list and therefore worked longer than they said.

11 **Click the drop-down arrow in the Act. Finish (Actual Finish) column for Task 3 and select *Fri 9/14/07* on the drop-down calendar.**
Notice that the Duration and the Actual Duration increase from 5 days to 10 days, the Actual Work increases from 80 to 160 hours, and the Actual Cost changes from $480 to $960 (see Figure 5.24).

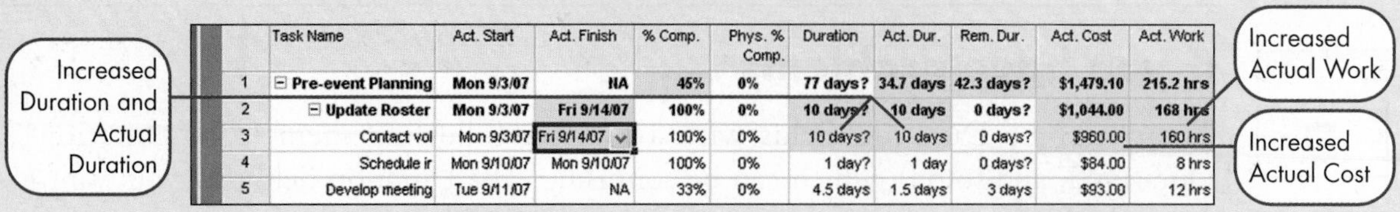

FIGURE 5.24

12 **Click in the Act. Work column for Task 6 (*Identify fundraiser goals*).**
The current Actual Work is 1.2 hours.

13 **Use the up-spinner to specify *4 hrs* and press ⏎Enter.**
Notice that the % Complete changes from 15% to 50%, the Actual Duration changes from .15 days to .5 days, the Remaining Duration from .85 days to .5 days, and Actual Cost from $12.60 to $42.

14 **Click the Act. Start (Actual Start) column drop-down arrow for Task 26 (*Update volunteer contact info*); change the date to *Wed 9/12/07* and press ⏎Enter.**

15 **Choose View, Tracking Gantt.**

16 **Select Task 3 (*Contact volunteers*) and compare the Baseline Finish and Finish dates.**
The baseline finish date is Fri 9/7/07, but the actual finish date is Fri 9/14/07. This task, if you recall, took an additional week.

17 **View the Finish Var. (Finish Variance) column for Task 3.**
Notice the variance value of *5 days* (see Figure 5.25). One week is equal to 5 days when using the default Standard calendar.

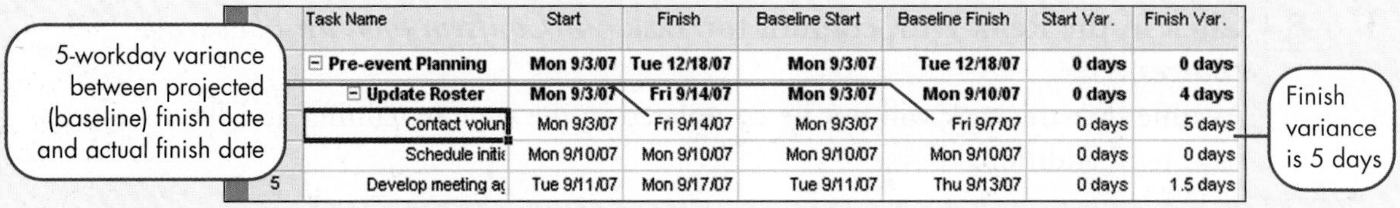

FIGURE 5.25

18 **View the Start Var. (Start Variance) column for Task 26 (*Update volunteer contact info*).**
Notice the variance of *2 days*. This task did not start on Mon 9/10/07 but rather on Wed 9/12/07 instead.

19 **Save your changes to the *Fundraiser* file.**
Keep the *Fundraiser* project file open and continue with the next lesson. If you prefer to complete the project later, close the file and exit Microsoft Project.

TO EXTEND YOUR KNOWLEDGE . . .

MODIFYING ACTUALS
When modifying Actual Work, Actual Start, Actual Finish, and Actual Duration for tasks that are not 100% complete, you create a split task, which is discussed in the next project. Split tasks appear as two Gantt bars separated by a dotted line in the Gantt chart.

LESSON 6:   Specifying Lead and Lag Time

Lead time, as you learned in Project 3, is an overlap between one task and another. For example, you can have a task that cannot begin until its predecessor is completed (finish-to-start dependency), but you later realize that the predecessor task need only be partially complete before you start the dependent task. You can specify a lead time in days in this type of scenario. To show lead time in a project, you enter a negative number because you are allowing extra time to begin a task.

Recall that *lag time* is generally time that needs to occur between two tasks but is not another task. For example, you may need a 2-day span of time between tasks due to some external delay, such as shipping or waiting for an approval or response on a deliverable. To show lag time, you enter a positive number.

In this lesson, you create lead time for two tasks and lag time for one.

To Create Lags and Lead Time

1   Open *Fundraiser*, if necessary, and then choose <u>V</u>iew, <u>G</u>antt Chart.

2   Shorten the Task Name column, and then drag the split bar between the task table and Gantt chart until the Predecessors column displays.

3   Double-click Task 29 (*Assign phone call list to volunteer*), and then click the Predecessors tab.
You enter both lag and lead time in the Lag column (see Figure 5.26). Lead time is entered as a negative number in the Lag column.

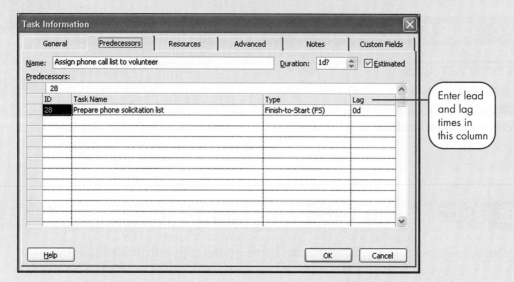

FIGURE 5.26

4   **Click in the Lag column; type -2 and then click OK.**
You can also specify lag time by clicking the down-spinner until *-2* displays. By entering a lead time of 2 days, you are specifying that the task can start earlier. Notice that the start date changes from Mon 9/10/07 to Thu 9/6/07 (see Figure 5.27). When Microsoft Project calculates the lead time, it ignores nonworking days.

8	✓	100%	Determine time frame fo	3 days?	Mon 9/3/07	Wed 9/5/07	7SS	James Merriweather
9	↻	0%	⊞ Schedule planning m	76 days	Tue 9/4/07	Tue 12/18/07		
26		25%	Update volunteer contac	1 day?	Wed 9/12/07	Mon 9/17/07	3	
27		2%	⊟ Initial Community Outreac	22 days?	Mon 9/3/07	Tue 10/2/07		
28		10%	Prepare phone solicitatic	5 days?	Mon 9/3/07	Fri 9/7/07		Student Work Study
29		0%	Assign phone call list to	1 day?	Thu 9/6/07	Thu 9/6/07	28FS-2 days	Gail Green
30		0%	Complete phone solicitat	10 days?	Fri 9/7/07	Thu 9/20/07	29	
31		0%	Confirm pledges	3 days?	Fri 9/21/07	Tue 9/25/07	30	
32		0%	Prepare mailing labels	1 day?	Wed 9/26/07	Wed 9/26/07	31	

Start date changes to Thu 9/6/07

Lead time shown in the Predecessors column

FIGURE 5.27

5   **Scroll in the Gantt chart to see the Task 29 Gantt bar, then click Undo on the Standard toolbar.**
Notice the shift in position of the Task 29 Gantt bar.

6   **Click Redo on the Standard toolbar.**
Notice the lead time line in the Gantt bar (see Figure 5.28).

8	✓	100%	Determine time frame fo	3 days?	Mon 9/3/07	Wed 9/5/07	7SS	James Merriweather
9	↻	0%	⊞ Schedule planning m	76 days	Tue 9/4/07	Tue 12/18/07		
26		25%	Update volunteer contac	1 day?	Wed 9/12/07	Mon 9/17/07	3	
27		2%	⊟ Initial Community Outreac	22 days?	Mon 9/3/07	Tue 10/2/07		
28		10%	Prepare phone solicitatic	5 days?	Mon 9/3/07	Fri 9/7/07		Student Work Study
29		0%	Assign phone call list to	1 day?	Thu 9/6/07	Thu 9/6/07	28FS-2 days	Gail Green
30		0%	Complete phone solicitat	10 days?	Fri 9/7/07	Thu 9/20/07	29	
31		0%	Confirm pledges	3 days?	Fri 9/21/07	Tue 9/25/07	30	
32		0%	Prepare mailing labels	1 day?	Wed 9/26/07	Wed 9/26/07	31	

Lead time shown in Gantt bar

FIGURE 5.28

7 | Scroll to view Task 31 (*Confirm pledges*) in the task table and the Gantt chart.
Notice that Task 31 (*Complete phone solicitations*) starts the day after Task 30 (*Confirm pledges*) ends (see Figure 5.29).

FIGURE 5.29

8 | Double-click Task 31, type -5 in the Lag column, and click OK.
This action creates a lead time of 5 days. Notice that the Gantt bar for Task 31 shifts to the left 5 days, as do its successors.

9 | Point to the join line between Tasks 30 and 31 in the Gantt chart.
A Task Link ScreenTip appears (see Figure 5.30). The lead time is noted.

FIGURE 5.30

10 | Use the horizontal scrollbar below the Gantt chart to find Task 56 (*Post pictures on conference Web site*) and select it in the task table.
Notice that Task 56 starts on Monday. You want to allow 3 extra days for the pictures to be developed, so you create lag time.

11 | Double-click Task 56, type 3 in the Lag column, and click OK.
Notice that the Predecessors column updates to reflect this change (see Figure 5.31). The Gantt bar also moves the right, moving the start of the bar 3 days later. Now the task begins on Thursday.

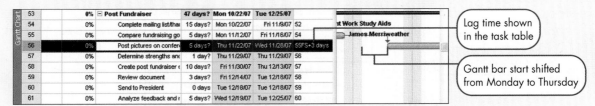

FIGURE 5.31

12 **Point to the join line between Tasks 55 and 56 in the Gantt chart.**
A ScreenTip appears, and the lag time is noted.

13 **Save your changes to *Fundraiser* and close the file.**
Continue with the final lesson. If you prefer to complete the project later, exit
Microsoft Project.

LESSON 7: Resolving Constraint Conflicts and Setting a Task Deadline

In Project 3, "Entering Tasks and Creating a Project Schedule," you learned to make changes
to constraints one task at a time. However, there are times when constraints need to be
reviewed, modified, or removed on a larger basis than task-by-task. For example, if you have a
due date for the project that you are not meeting, the first place to gain improvements is to
adjust or remove date constraints. When this involves more than one task, multiple changes
can be made at one time.

A ***deadline*** is a target date indicating when you want a task to be completed. If the deadline date
passes and the task is not completed, Microsoft Project displays an icon in the Indicator column.

In this lesson, you complete two sets of steps. In the first set, you resolve problems with date
constraints. In the second set, you set a deadline for a task.

To Correct Constraint Conflicts

1 **Open *EPr1_0502* and save the file as `Programming`.**

2 **Point to the note icon for Task 2 (*Identify presenter database fields*).**
Notice that it has a *Start No Earlier Than* constraint for Thu 6/29/00 (see
Figure 5.32).

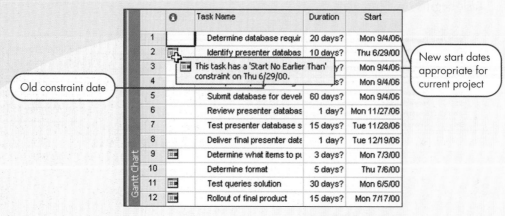

FIGURE 5.32

3   Choose <u>V</u>iew, Ta<u>b</u>le: Entry, <u>M</u>ore Tables.

4   Select Constraint Dates, and then click App<u>l</u>y.
The view shows both the constraint type and date for all tasks (see Figure 5.33), which gives you an at-a-glance tool for reviewing the constraints for all the tasks at once.

	Task Name	Duration	Constraint Type	Constraint Date
1	Determine database requir	20 days?	As Soon As Possible	NA
2	Identify presenter databas	10 days?	Start No Earlier Than	Thu 6/29/00
3	Review database project \	1 day?	As Soon As Possible	NA
4	Incorporate programming f	10 days?	As Soon As Possible	NA
5	Submit database for devel	60 days?	As Soon As Possible	NA
6	Review presenter databas	1 day?	As Soon As Possible	NA
7	Test presenter database s	15 days?	As Soon As Possible	NA
8	Deliver final presenter dat	1 day?	As Soon As Possible	NA
9	Determine what items to pt	3 days?	Start No Earlier Than	Mon 7/3/00
10	Determine format	5 days?	As Soon As Possible	NA
11	Test queries solution	30 days?	Start No Earlier Than	Mon 6/5/00
12	Rollout of final product	15 days?	Start No Earlier Than	Mon 6/5/00

Specified constraint date

F I G U R E   5 . 3 3

5   Click in the Constraint Type column for Task 2 (*Identify presenter database fields*).

6   Click the drop-down arrow; then choose *As Soon As Possible* and press ↵Enter.
Recall that with projects scheduled from the start date, the default constraint is As Soon As Possible, as in Task 1 (*Determine database requirements*). By changing the constraint type to the default, you also remove the constraint date (see Figure 5.34).

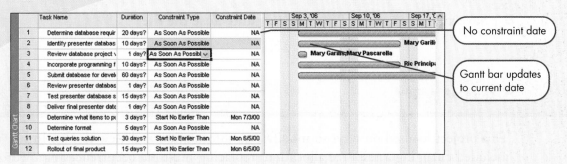

No constraint date

Gantt bar updates to current date

F I G U R E   5 . 3 4

7   Select Tasks 9 (*Determine what items to put on Web site*) through 12 (*Rollout of final product*), and then click Task Information on the Standard toolbar.

8   Click the Advanced Tab.

9   Click the *Constraint type* drop-down arrow; then choose *As Soon As Possible* and click OK.
The remaining tasks are reset to the default and the constraint dates are removed.

Now all tasks contain dates that are more current. You can now set an appropriate deadline for a specific task.

To Set a Deadline

1 Choose **V**iew, Ta**b**le: Constraint Dates, **E**ntry.

2 Double-click Task 1 (*Determine database requirements*), and then select the Advanced tab, if necessary.

3 Under *Constrain task,* type *9/29/06* in the Deadline text box.

4 Click OK.

5 Click the horizontal scroll arrow to view the entire Gantt bar for Task 1.
Notice the arrow that appears indicating the deadline you applied to this task (See Figure 5.35).

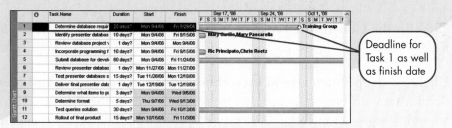

FIGURE 5.35

6 Save your changes to *Programming* and close the file.

SUMMARY

This project focused on ways to modify task information and view results. Initial activities included changing a resource allocation, replacing multiple occurrences of a word in task descriptions, checking spelling, and creating a baseline. You learned to track project progress by entering percent complete values for individual tasks and by using actual progress data. Adding a column of data to the task table facilitated the tracking of project progress. After learning about lead and lag time, you worked with global methods to resolve constraint conflicts.

You can extend your learning by reviewing concepts and terms and by practicing variations of skills presented in the lessons. Use the following table as a guide to the numbered questions and exercises in the end-of-project learning opportunities.

LESSON	MULTIPLE CHOICE	DISCUSSION	SKILL DRILL	CHALLENGE	DISCOVERY ZONE
Editing and Replacing Task Information and Checking Spelling	4, 8, 10		2, 3	1, 2	
Saving a Baseline	5	1	3	2	
Entering Percent Complete	1	3	4	3	
Viewing Percent Complete	9		4	3	2
Entering Actuals	3	3	5	4	1
Specifying Lead and Lag Time	2, 7	2	6	3	
Resolving Constraint Conflicts and Setting a Task Deadline	6		1		

KEY TERMS

actual duration	actual work	percent complete
actual finish	baseline	remaining duration
actual start	deadline	remaining work
actuals	effort-driven scheduling	Tracking toolbar

CHECKING CONCEPTS AND TERMS

MULTIPLE CHOICE

Circle the letter of the correct answer for each of the following.

1. Suppose a summary task has two subtasks each with one resource assigned at 100% max. units. The first subtask has 12 hours of work and is 50% complete. The other subtask has 6 hours of work and is 25% complete. What is the summary task's percent complete value? [L3]

   a. 40%

   b. 42%

   c. 45%

   d. 50%

2. Which of the following represents a lag time between two tasks? [L6]

   a. -2d

   b. 0d

   c. +3d

   d. <4d

3. Which term describes true data in a project plan? [L5]

   a. Actuals

   b. Baseline

   c. Work

   d. Lead time

4. Which field does Microsoft Project change to adjust for new or removed resources assigned to a task? [L1]

　　a. Work

　　b. Cost

　　c. Duration

　　d. Start date

5. What is the original, fine-tuned project plan called? [L2]

　　a. Gantt chart

　　b. Task table

　　c. Baseline

　　d. Duration

6. What happens if a task goes beyond its deadline? [L7]

　　a. The task is automatically deleted.

　　b. An e-mail notification is sent to the resource.

　　c. A notice icon appears in the Indicator column.

　　d. A popup note appears on the screen.

7. What do you add between two tasks if their duration can overlap? [L6]

　　a. Lead time

　　b. Lag

　　c. Baseline

　　d. Actuals

8. Which of the following values represents the work units for three resources working full-time on one task? [L1]

　　a. 3%

　　b. 33%

　　c. 100%

　　d. 300%

9. Which of the following formulas does Microsoft Project use to figure remaining duration? [L4]

　　a. *Duration * Percent Complete*

　　b. *Percent Complete * Duration*

　　c. *Work - Actual Duration*

　　d. *Duration - (Duration * Percent Complete)*

10. If you add a second resource to a task with a 4-day duration, which of the following should happen? [L1]

　　a. Duration increases

　　b. Duration reduces by half

　　c. Work decreases

　　d. Task splits

DISCUSSION

1. Considering a baseline, what type of analyses might you be able to perform when comparing the baseline to actual data? [L2]

2. Suppose you are working with a project to plan a wedding. Describe a few tasks that would allow lead time as well as a few that would allow lag time. [L6]

3. Discuss several methods to collect actual data from resources. [L3, L5]

SKILL DRILL

Skill Drill exercises reinforce project skills. Each skill reinforced is the same, or nearly the same, as a skill presented in the project. Detailed instructions are provided in a step-by-step format.

You should complete the six exercises in sequence.

1. Setting Constraints

As a project manager for a software company, you coordinate all software releases, including programming, distribution, manual compilation, printing, and testing of the software and the accompanying manual. Currently, you are coordinating a new software package to be distributed in September 2006. To ensure that the software and manual are both ready, you need to set some constraints. The programming, testing, and editorial staff must have 6 weeks to work on each beta of the software.

To set constraints, complete the following steps:

1. Open *EPr1_0503* and save the file as **Software_Manual**.
2. Double-click Task 9 (*Second beta software available*), and then select the Advanced tab.
3. Under *Constrain task,* set the Deadline date to *Fri 6/30/06*, and then click OK.
4. Select Task 15 (*Final software available*) and click Task Information on the Standard toolbar.
5. Set the Deadline date to *Tue 8/1/06*, and then click OK.
6. Save *Software_Manual* and leave it open for the next exercise.

2. Modifying Task Information

As you look over your project file, you realize that the resource information needs modification. Specifically, the Programmers resource represents five programmers, the Technical Writers resource represents two writers, and the Software Testers resource represents three testers. The work shown is inaccurate. You must change the assignment units to correctly reflect the work.

To modify task information, complete the following steps:

1. Open **Software_Manual**, *if necessary.*
2. Choose View, Task Usage; then drag the split bar between the Task Usage table and the bar chart to the right until the Finish column is displayed.
3. Double-click Task 3 (*Software tested*).
4. Click the Resources tab and then click in the first Units cell.
5. Click the up-spinner until *300%* displays; then click OK.
6. Click the smart tag drop-down arrow and select the second option.

7. Continue editing the assignment units as follows (leave the duration constant):

Task ID	Task Name	Resource	Unit
4	Make changes in software	Programmers	500%
7	Walk through of software	Technical writers	200%
11	Verify steps in draft manual	Technical writers	200%
16	Final run-through of steps	Technical writers;	200%
		Technical editor	50%

8. Save *Software_Manual* and leave it open for the next exercise.

3. Checking Spelling and Saving a Baseline

Now the project file is almost complete. You just need to check the spelling in the tasks and save a baseline for future reference.

To check spelling and save a baseline, complete the following steps:

1. Open *Software_Manual*, if necessary, and then choose View, Gantt Chart.

2. Press Ctrl+Home and then choose Tools, Spelling.

   The first error is the word *Software_Manual* in the project summary, which is not actually an error.

3. Click Ignore.

   The next error is *Distribute* in Task 25.

4. Click Change.

5. Click Track on the Project Guide toolbar.

6. Click the first link, *Save a baseline plan to compare with later versions*.

7. Click Save Baseline and then click Done.

8. Close the Track side pane, save *Software_Manual*, and leave it open for the next exercise.

4. Entering Percent Complete

Now, the project is under way. Some of the tasks have been partially completed. You need to enter the appropriate data to track the progress of the project.

To enter percent complete, work through the following steps:

1. Open *Software_Manual*, if necessary.

2. Double-click Task 2 (*Distribute beta to writers and testers*), and then click the General tab.

3. Click the *Percent complete* up-spinner until *100%* displays, and then click OK.

4. Double-click Task 1 (*Software beta available*) to see the percent complete, and then click OK.

5. Select the task name for Task 3 (*Software tested*), and then choose Insert, Column.

6. Click the *Field name* drop-down arrow.

7. Scroll to the top of the list and select *% Complete*.

8. Click OK.

9. Click in the % Complete column for Task 3 (*Software tested*); then click the up-spinner to *30%* and press ⏎Enter.

10. Complete the remaining percent complete values as shown in the following table:

TaskID	Task Name	% Complete
4	Make changes in software	25%
6	Read through programmers' notes	66%
7	Walk-through of software	66%

11. Save *Software_Manual* and leave it open for the next exercise.

5. Entering Actuals

With the project under way, it is time to enter actual data. Management has decided to reduce the amount of time allotted for testing the software to be sure the programmers have the time necessary to update the software. Also, during the first week of updates, there were only four programmers working on the task rather than five.

To enter actuals, complete the following steps:

1. Open *Software_Manual*, if necessary.

2. Select Task 3 (*Software tested*), and then point to the progress bar in the Task 3 Gantt bar to see the progress of the task.

3. Choose View, More Views.

4. Scroll down and select *Task Sheet* and then click Apply.

5. Choose View, Table: Entry, and Tracking.

6. Right-click the Rem. Dur. (Remaining Duration) heading, and then choose *Insert Column*.

7. Click the *Field name* drop-down arrow; then select *Duration* and click OK.

8. Click in the Duration column of Task 3; click the down-spinner to *5 weeks* and press ⏎Enter.

   The remaining duration and actual duration values adjust to reflect the new Duration.

9. Click on the smart tag and select the first option.

10. Click in the Act. Work (Actual Work) column for Task 4 (*Make changes to software*).

11. Type **260** and press ⏎Enter.

    The Actual Cost amount adjusts for the change in work.

12. Save *Software_Manual* and leave it open for the next exercise.

6. Specifying Lead and Lag Times

When programming or updating software, flexibility is essential at particular junctions. The software manual schedule must be flexible at points as well. A few tasks in your project plan are flexible in their links. You need to add lead and lag times to these tasks.

To create lead and lag times, complete the following steps:

1. Open *Software_Manual,* if necessary; then choose <u>V</u>iew, <u>G</u>antt Chart.

2. Shorten the Task Name column; then drag the split bar between the task table and Gantt chart until the Predecessors column displays.

3. Double-click Task 21 (*Choose three prototypes for manual cover*), and then click the Predecessors tab.

4. Click in the Lag column; type **6** and then click OK.

5. Double-click Task 27 (*Hyperlink on web page to manual*); type **7** in the Lag column and then click OK.

6. Double-click Task 28 (*Create Readme file for any update*); type **-3** in the Lag column and then click OK.

7. Save *Software_Manual* and close the file.

CHALLENGE

Challenge exercises expand on or are somewhat related to skills presented in the lessons. Each exercise provides a brief narrative introduction, followed by instructions in a numbered-step format that are not as detailed as those in the Skill Drill section.

You should complete the four exercises in sequence.

1. Using Spell Check and Replacing a Resource

You are managing a direct mail marketing campaign and are utilizing a template from the online Microsoft Template Gallery for the project. You have modified the tasks to fit the overall project at your own company and have set up the basic project information. Your job is to take this existing plan and finalize everything in it so that you can begin tracking overall project progress, some of which has already begun.

To check spelling and replace a resource, complete the following steps:

1. Open *EPr1_0504* and save it as **Direct_Market**; then close any open side panes.

2. Spell-check and correct any spelling errors in the project file. Note: Do not change the words *marcom* and *Ardis.*

   A few of the tasks list a person's name for the Resource Name rather than the position title, which you need to correct.

3. Use Find and look in the Resource Names field to locate all instances of the name *Patty Ardis,* writing down the Task ID # for each instance.

4. Open the Assign Resources dialog box and for each task assigned to Patty Ardis, replace *Patty Ardis* with **Media Planner**.

5. Use Replace and look in the Name field to locate all instances of the word *vertical* and replace it with nothing (to delete the word).

6. Save *Direct_Market* and leave it open for the next exercise.

2. Changing Resource Assignment Units and Saving and Viewing the Baseline

Now that you have cleaned up the tasks in your project, you need to work on the resources. Next, you need to save and print the project file baseline.

To change resources assignment units and save a baseline, complete the following steps:

1. Open *Direct_Market* if necessary, and then close any open side panes.

2. Switch to Task Usage view and select Task 32 (*Determine sales monies and calculate ROI*).

3. Change the Resource units to reflect two people working full-time on this task.

4. Choose the smart tag option to reduce the duration to 2.5 days.

5. Change the Resource Units value for Task 33 (*Compile final counts and summaries*) to reflect two people working full-time on this task, and choose the smart tag option to reduce the duration to 5 days.

6. Switch to Gantt Chart view and save a baseline for the file.

7. Use Help to learn how to view the baseline; then display the baseline and print it for future reference.

8. Save *Direct_Market* and leave it open for the next exercise.

3. Specifying Lag and Lead Time and Entering Percent Complete

Now that you have a basically sound project file, you can update the file with the progress reports that you have been receiving from the team members assigned to the project.

To specify lag and lead time and enter percent complete, complete the following steps:

1. Open *Direct_Market,* if necessary, and specify a 3-day lag for Task 13 (*Review first article samples, artwork, and drafts*).

2. Specify a 2-day lag for Task 17 (*Review and approve direct mail piece*).

3. Specify a 1-day lead for Task 4 (*Segment by industry or market*).

4. Using the Tracking toolbar, update the following tasks with the appropriate percent complete:

Task ID	Task Name	Percent Complete
3	Establish targeted markets	75%
4	Segment by industry or market	100%
5	Quantify total available market	50%
6	Define served available market	50%
10	Solicit designs from marcom vendors	25%
11	Select vendor and design	50%
12	Make format, quantity, and cost decisions for media	50%
20	Select initial markets	50%

5. Print a Current Activities report that shows tasks in progress.

6. Save *Direct_Market* and leave it open for the next exercise.

4. Entering Actual Progress Data

Once resources have been assigned to their tasks, you will need to track their progress.

To enter task progress, complete the following steps:

1. Open *Direct_Market* if necessary, and switch to Task Sheet view.

2. Switch from the Entry table to the Tracking table.

3. For Task 4 (*Segment by industry or market*), update the actual duration to 4 days.

4. For Task 5 (*Quantify total available market*), you received an update from the resources assigned to it, informing you that it will require 2 days to complete this task, not half a day. Update Task 5 to make the Actual duration 2 days .

5. You received another update from the resources assigned to Task 10 (*Solicit designs from marcom vendors*), informing you that this task is complete. Update Task 10 to reflect its completion.

6. You received an e-mail from the resource assigned to Task 20 (*Select initial markets*) stating, "Market survey data is not progressing as planned, due to a software upgrade delay. This job will require 3 more days to accurately compute the survey results." Update Task 20 to add 3 more days to the actual duration.

7. You received an e-mail from the resource assigned to Task 25 (*Enter prospects into customer relationship management database*), stating, "Shelly is no longer working on this project and it has been assigned to someone else. Please allow transition time for our new recruit." Update Task 25 to show a total of 15 days in the remaining column.

8. Switch to Gantt Chart view, and then print a Project Summary overview report.

9. Save *Direct_Market* and then close the file.

DISCOVERY ZONE

Discovery Zone exercises require advanced knowledge of topics presented in *Essentials* lessons, application of skills from multiple lessons, or self-directed learning of new skills. The exercises are independent of each other, so you may complete them in any order.

1. Learning About Project Tracking Online

Now that you have established basic proficiency in using Microsoft Project, you should explore more topics about tracking as well as creating progress reports for the different team members working on a project.

From the Help menu, choose Microsoft Office Project Help and then click the *The Project Map: Your road map to project management* hyperlink. Expand the *Track progress* topic, and then click on the *Record progress and respond to updates hyperlink.* topic and click on the *Updating Actuals* hyperlink. Read the various topics by clicking on each of the article hyperlinks.

2. Working with Views

Create a new project from any existing template located either online or on your computer, and save it as **View_Options**. Take a closer look at the View, More View options and apply each view to the project file you created. Explore the Table views in conjunction with the different views. Create a view using both view options that will show the tasks assigned to each resource and the amount of completed work and the amount of remaining work by task. Print the table.

MODIFYING TASKS USING THE GANTT CHART

OBJECTIVES

IN THIS PROJECT, YOU LEARN HOW TO

- Add a progress line to a Gantt chart

- Remove task dependencies

- Reschedule uncompleted work

- Modify and remove a split

- Use Tracking Gantt view to analyze the critical path

- Check overall project progress

WHY WOULD I DO THIS?

When working with a project plan, you must constantly check the overall status of the project. Recall from Project 1 the project triangle, which consists of the three main elements of a project: time, budget, and scope. Once your project is under way, you need to periodically check that the project goals (especially the final finish date for the entire project) are attainable, that the budget is within limits, what tasks are in progress, what tasks are not yet started, and what tasks are complete. Microsoft Project provides several tools that enable critical analysis as well as several views that provide project summary data. Once you have looked at this information, you can then decide on whatever actions are needed to adjust the project plan. You can also determine which specific tasks impact the project finish date so you can reschedule uncompleted work if necessary. In addition, there are summary reports that provide general statistics regarding the project triangle so you can distribute this information to the project team.

VISUAL SUMMARY

In this project, you are initiating an advertising campaign for the apartment complex you manage. It involves print advertising in several trade journals as well as several popular apartment advertising Web sites. You have created a project plan for this campaign to help you keep track of deliverables required for each periodical. Several of the lessons in this project involve using the Gantt chart to examine the project plan. In addition, you use several methods to adjust the Gantt bars to reschedule work.

To track the progress of your project, you view Project Statistics, print a Project Summary Report and view the critical tasks as shown in Figure 6.1. A ***critical task*** is one that, in combination with its predecessors, drives the overall finish date for the entire project.

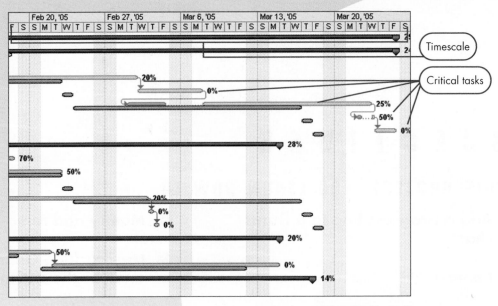

FIGURE 6.1

LESSON 1:   Adding a Progress Line to a Gantt Chart

A *progress line* is a vertical line added to the Gantt chart on a particular date of interest. It is a visual representation of the status of your project plan at that time. The intention is to draw your eyes quickly to those tasks that are either behind or ahead of schedule.

A progress line is set for a specific date (the *progress date*), which can be the current date (computer clock) or the status date and is user-specified in the Progress Information dialog box. The progress line appears in red and runs vertically from the timescale at the top of the Gantt chart. It contains spikes for tasks behind or ahead of schedule (see Figure 6.2). You can read the direction of the spikes to gauge the approximate status of work. Spikes that run to the left indicate work that is behind schedule, and spikes that run to the right indicate work that is ahead of schedule. Recall that work is the number of hours required by a resource to complete a task, not the task duration. Note that all tasks that are behind or ahead of schedule in relation to the status date are marked with a red diamond inside a circle.

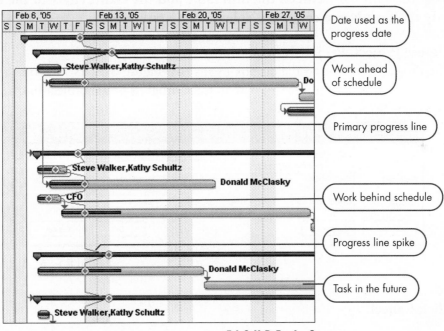

FIGURE 6.2

The distance from the primary progress line to the spike indicates the degree to which the task is ahead or behind schedule as of the specified date. For example, if a task is incomplete and behind schedule, the progress line connects to the end of the progress bar in that task's Gantt bar. Remember, the progress bar is the black bar located within each task Gantt bar that represents the percent complete. If a task with a start date in the past has no work completed, the progress line connects to the task start date. If a task is ahead of schedule, the progress line spikes on the summary task Gantt bar for that subtask, not on the actual task Gantt bar itself. The progress line ignores any past tasks that are complete or any future tasks that have not begun. Therefore, the progress line solely points out the tasks that are behind or ahead of schedule. Also, you can add multiple progress lines to a Gantt chart. The primary progress line appears in red and additional progress lines appear in black.

Summary tasks are also included in the progress line spikes. When considering progress lines in relation to summary tasks, keep in mind that progress lines are drawn down the Gantt chart based on a task's cumulative percent complete up to the date you specify. Summary tasks show the overall percent complete of the group of subtasks demoted beneath it; thus a spike may be drawn to a summary Gantt bar if any of its subtasks are ahead or behind schedule.

In this lesson, you are working to initiate an apartment advertising campaign that utilizes several trade journals and a couple of popular advertising Web sites. You add a progress line to the Gantt chart to determine which tasks are falling behind and which are ahead of schedule.

To Add Progress Lines to a Gantt Chart

1 Open the *EPr1_0601* file and save it as Ad_Campaign; then close any open side panes.

2 Drag the split bar between the task table and the Gantt chart to the left until only the Task Name column displays in the task table.

3 Choose **P**roject, **P**roject Information.
The Project Information dialog box opens (see Figure 6.3). Notice that the Status Date is *Fri 2/11/05*. You use this date to track progress of the project to date.

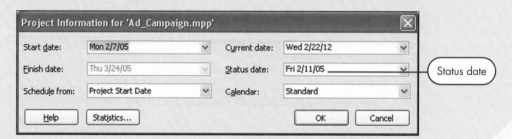

FIGURE 6.3

4 Click Cancel.

5 Choose **T**ools, **O**ptions, and click the Calculation tab.

6 Under Calculation options for, check the Edits to total task % **c**omplete will be spread to the status date check box, and then click OK.
Setting this option causes the progress line to denote specific tasks that are ahead of schedule, not just summary tasks, when the percent complete is updated.

7 Choose **T**ools, Trac**k**ing, Progress **L**ines.
The Progress Lines dialog box opens (see Figure 6.4).

8 On the Dates and Intervals tab, check the *Always display current progress line* check box.
The two date options become active. You can create a progress line to compare the current status of the project to either the current date or a status date. In this case, you want to compare progress to the status date.

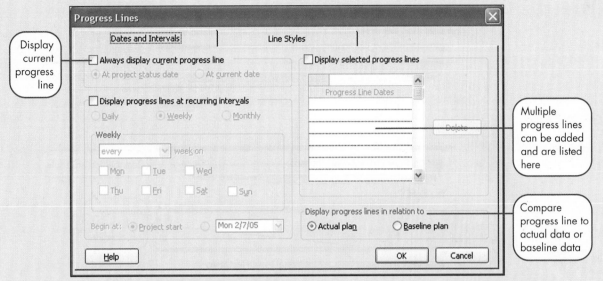

FIGURE 6.4

9 Verify that the *At project status date* option is active; then look at the two options near the lower-right corner of the dialog box (refer to Figure 6.4). You can compare the progress of the project to the actual data or to the baseline.

10 Under the *Display progress lines in relation to* section, select *Actual plan*, if necessary, and then click OK.

A vertical red progress line displays on the Gantt chart located on the date Feb 11,'05, the project status date (see Figure 6.5). If necessary to help visualize the progress, draw an imaginary line down the chart between Friday and Saturday where the primary progress line pivots or shows the spikes running to the left or to the right.

The left-pointing spikes denote specific tasks that are behind schedule; however, subtasks that are ahead of schedule are denoted by the right-pointing spike on the corresponding summary task Gantt bar. Spikes do not appear on subtasks that are ahead of schedule until you update the percent complete field for that specific task. Notice a diamond within a circle shape on the summary task that automatically marks the progress of the subtasks below.

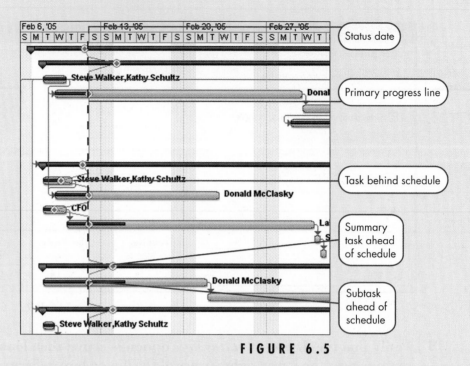

FIGURE 6.5

If you have problems . . .

You may need to use the horizontal scrollbar to display Feb 11, '05.

11 **View the progress line at Task 12 (*Sign contract*).**
Notice that the progress line is angled to the left from the original progress line, indicating work that is behind schedule (refer to Figure 6.5).

12 **View the progress line at Task 16 (*Fall 2006 covers submitted*).**
Notice that the progress line is angled to the right, indicating work that is ahead of schedule. Recall that this is a summary task, and the fact that it is ahead of schedule indicates at least some subtasks below it are ahead of schedule as well (refer to Figure 6.5).

13 **In the Gantt chart, click the Task 11 (*Determine contract*) Gantt bar, and then click Task Information.**
The Task Information dialog box opens (see Figure 6.6). The task is currently 30% complete.

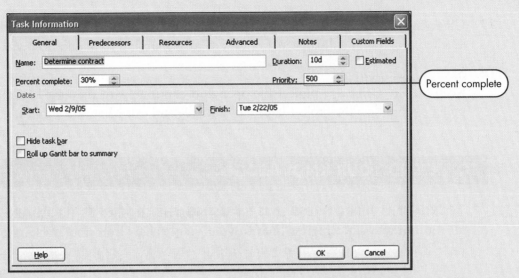

FIGURE 6.6

14 **In the _Percent complete_ box, change the number to _50%_ and click OK.**
Notice that the relatively straight line is now angled to the right, indicating the task is ahead of schedule (see Figure 6.7).

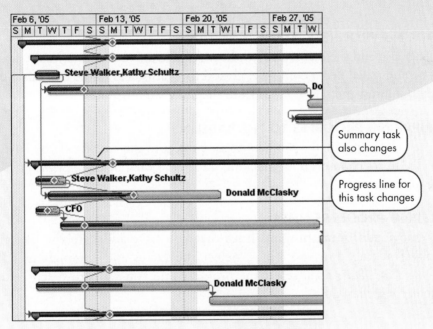

FIGURE 6.7

15 **Click Undo to view the change in the progress line; then click Redo to change the task completion back to 50%.**

16 **Choose Tools, Tracking, Progress Lines.**
The Progress Lines dialog box opens.

17 Clear the *Always display current progress line* check box, and then click **OK**.
The red progress line disappears from the Gantt chart and is hidden from view.

18 Save *Ad_Campaign*.
Keep the *Ad_Campaign* project file open and continue with the next lesson. If you prefer to complete the project later, close the file and exit Microsoft Project.

TO EXTEND YOUR KNOWLEDGE . . .

CREATING A PROGRESS LINE BY USING THE TRACKING TOOLBAR

You can also add progress lines to your Gantt chart from the Tracking toolbar. Click Add Progress Line on the Tracking toolbar. A popup displays and your mouse pointer displays as a progress line icon. Then click on the date for comparison. You can add multiple progress lines as well.

DISPLAYING PROGRESS LINES AT REGULAR INTERVALS

You may desire to track the progress of a project plan at regular intervals. To do so, select Tools, Tracking, Progress Lines. Check *Display progress lines at recurring intervals*. Then select the type of occurrence or specific date.

TRACKING PROGRESS IN THE TASK TABLE

You can also add the Status field to the task table to see which tasks are on schedule, behind schedule, or complete. To add the status field to the task table, choose Insert, Column and select Status from the *Field name* list box.

COMPARING PROGRESS TO THE BASELINE

You can also compare the progress of the project to the baseline if you have saved one. To do so, choose Tools, Tracking, Progress Lines. Select *Baseline plan* as the data to compare to.

DELETING PROGRESS LINES

To remove additional progress lines that you have added to the file, choose Tools, Tracking, Progress Lines. Select the Dates and Intervals tab. In the *Progress Line Dates* area, select the progress line you want to delete and click Delete; then click OK.

LESSON 2:   Removing Task Dependencies

At times, you may determine that a link between two or more tasks is no longer necessary. For example, in the *Ad_Campaign* project file you may find that the *Front cover submission* task is not necessarily dependent upon the completion of the *Standard Insertion Ad Full Color* task. If you decide that a task dependency is unnecessary, you can **unlink** (or remove) the dependency. When you unlink a task, the start date of the task is no longer dependent upon another task's start or finish date; therefore, the task's start date becomes the same as the project start date.

Making this type of an adjustment to your project plan can have positive results on the overall finish date for the project.

In this lesson, you remove task dependencies for several tasks that do not depend on one another for task completion. The *Determine contract* task is not necessarily dependent upon the *Standard Insertion Ad Full Color* task for both trade magazines, so you remove the task link. Likewise, there should be no link between the *Contract* task and the *Platinum property package* task. All of these links are removed by using the Unlink Tasks button or the Predecessors column in the task table.

To Remove Task Dependencies

1 **Open *Ad_Campaign*, if necessary, and scroll to the right until you can view the Task 8 (*Front cover submission*) Gantt bar and click on it.**
Clicking on a task bar is not necessary to remove a dependency but is helpful to visually locate the task with which you are working.

2 **With your mouse pointer, pause on the Gantt bar for Task 8 and view the Task ScreenTip.**
Note the start date of Wed 3/23/05. Also note that there are two join lines coming to Task 8 (see Figure 6.8).

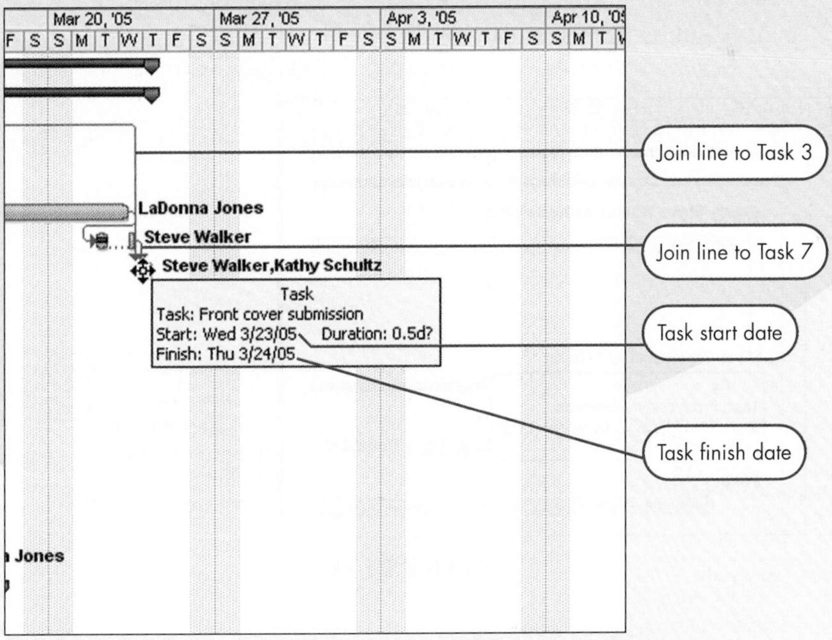

FIGURE 6.8

3 **Pause the mouse pointer on each join line to view the Link ScreenTip.**
There are Finish-to-Start links with Tasks 3 (*Standard Insertion Ad Full Color*) and 7 (*Photo page submission*) (see Figure 6.9), implying that Task 8 cannot start until these

tasks are completed. It is not necessary, however, to wait for both tasks to be completed before beginning work on this task, so you change the dependency.

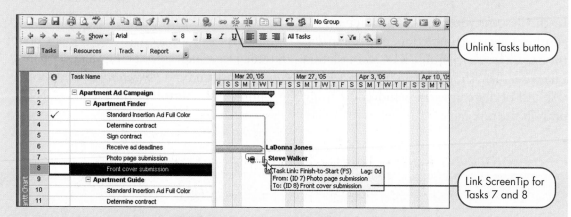

FIGURE 6.9

 4 | **Click Unlink Tasks on the Standard Toolbar.**
Notice that the join lines are removed from the Gantt chart and Task 8 is no longer visible in the area of the Gantt chart you are viewing.

5 | **Scroll left until you locate Task 8 and read the Task ScreenTip.**
Task 8 is no longer linked to Task 3 or Task 7 (see Figure 6.10). The start date changes from Wed 3/23/05 to Mon 2/7/05, which is the project start date. Using the Unlink Tasks button removes all links to a task. However, this is not what you want to happen. A link is necessary to Task 7, but not to Task 3.

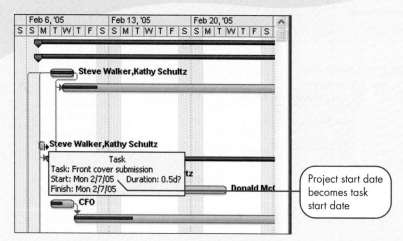

FIGURE 6.10

6 | **Click Undo.**
Task 8 is once again linked to both Tasks 3 and 7.

7 | **Click Task Information on the Standard Toolbar, and then click the Predecessors tab.**
The two links to Task 8 are listed (see Figure 6.11). To unlink only one task rather than all tasks, you must use the Task Information dialog box instead.

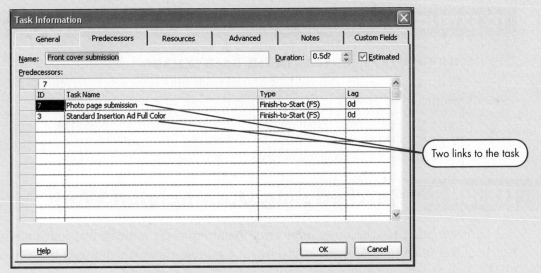

FIGURE 6.11

8 **Click on Task 3 in the _Predecessors_ list; press** Del **and then click OK.**
Task 8 remains linked to Task 7, but the link to Task 3 is removed.

9 **Point to the Task 11 (_Determine contract_) Gantt bar and read the Task
ScreenTip.**

If you have problems . . .

Be sure to point to the portion of the Gantt bar that does not contain the progress bar,
which appears as a black bar within the blue Gantt bar, to successfully view the Task
ScreenTip. When working with a Gantt bar, two ScreenTips can be viewed; the
Progress ScreenTip appears when you point at the progress bar, and the Task ScreenTip
appears when you point at any part of the Gantt bar except the progress bar.

10 **Point to the join line and read the ScreenTip.**
The join to Task 3 (_Standard Insertion Ad Full Color_) and Task 10 (_Standard Insertion
Ad Full Color_) must be removed.

11 **Click the Task 11 Gantt bar and then click Unlink Tasks.**
The links to Tasks 3 and 10 are gone.

12 **Save _Ad_Campaign._**
Keep the _Ad_Campaign_ project file open and continue with the next lesson. If you
prefer to complete the project later, close the file and exit Microsoft Project.

ALTER TASK DEPENDENCIES IN THE GANTT CHART
Task dependencies are also easily removed from the Gantt chart. To remove a task dependency or modify it, double-click the join line between two tasks on the Gantt chart. The Task Dependency dialog box opens. You can choose a different type of dependency or select None to remove the task dependency.

LESSON 3:   Rescheduling Uncompleted Work

Sometimes another task becomes more critical and resources must be reassigned temporarily. Rescheduling uncompleted work is also useful for those times when a resource cannot complete a task as scheduled or when other interruptions occur and you want to have as little impact on the overall finish date of the project as possible. For example, suppose a resource is working on a task when a business trip becomes necessary. That resource cannot work on the task during the business trip and thus there is a delay in task completion. The task can be split to allow completion around the business trip.

One alternative to rescheduling work is to literally create two tasks from the existing task, tracking each task individually. However, keep in mind that by creating two tasks, you have an additional item to track and monitor in the plan. A **split** task is one that has a time delay within it, therefore creating two or more segments. Splitting a task is the same as rescheduling work. To reschedule work in the Gantt chart, you right-click at the beginning of the incomplete portion of the task displayed in the Gantt bar, and follow onscreen instructions to split the task.

When rescheduling work, the task is split at the point where the completed portion of the task stops and the incomplete portion begins. You specify the date on which you want to resume work on the unfinished portion of the task. Splitting a task does not extend the duration but does change the finish date. A task can be split as many times as needed. Once a task is split, you can modify its duration, start date, and finish date. Even though a task is split into two or more bars, it still appears as one line item in the task table. The new start date for the rescheduled portion of a task is the **resume date.** The length of the split depends on the timescale used in the project file. If the timescale is days, a split is equal to one day. If the timescale is in hours, the split is equal to one hour. The length of the split is one unit by default, whether days or hours, but it can be lengthened, if necessary. The assigned resume date depends on whether you use the manual or automatic method for rescheduling work. Using the automatic rescheduling feature, the resume date is one unit (day, in most cases) after the status date. However, when manually rescheduling work, the resume date is specified by the user.

In this lesson, you first reschedule uncompleted work for Task 4 (*Determine contract*) because the resource requires additional days to negotiate the contract. You use the Split Task button on the Standard toolbar to complete this action. Next, you reschedule uncompleted work using the Reschedule Work button on the Tracking Toolbar.

To Manually Reschedule Uncompleted Work

1   Open *Ad_Campaign,* if necessary.

2   On the Gantt chart, point to the Task 4 (*Determine contract*) Gantt bar.
The Task ScreenTip appears. Note the start date of Wed 2/9/05 and the finish date of Tue 3/1/05. The duration is 15 days.

3   Click the Task 4 Gantt bar.
Clicking on the Task 4 bar is not necessary to reschedule work but is helpful to visually locate the task with which you are working.

4   Click Split Task on the Standard toolbar.
The Split Task information box displays, and the mouse appears as a split task pointer shape.

5   Point to the end of the progress bar in the Gantt bar.
The date in the ScreenTip is Fri 2/11/05 (see Figure 6.12).

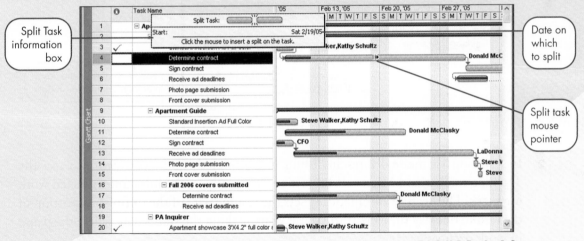

FIGURE 6.12

6   Move the mouse to the right 1/8″ on the Gantt bar.
Notice that the date in the Split Task information box changes. As you move your mouse horizontally on the Gantt bar, the date in the Split Task information box changes according to the location on the Gantt bar. The date shown in the Split Task information box is one unit (in this case, one day) prior than the proposed resume date.

7   Move the mouse on the Gantt bar until Wed *2/16/05* displays, and then click the Gantt bar.
The task is now split on Wed 2/16/05, with a dotted line linking the two Gantt bars (see Figure 6.13). Wednesday becomes a pause in work for this task, and a portion of the task is rescheduled to begin on Thursday.

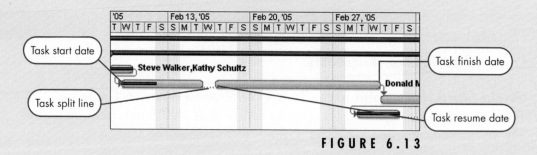

FIGURE 6.13

8 | **Pause the mouse on the right-most Gantt bar for Task 4.**

The Task ScreenTip appears (see Figure 6.15). Notice that the start date of Wed 2/9/05 remains the same as before and the finish date is Wed 3/2/05, which is one day later than the original finish date of Tue 3/1/05. There is now a one day pause in work for the completion of this task.

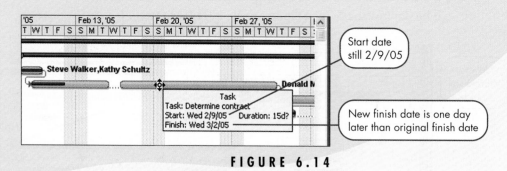

FIGURE 6.14

In addition to manually rescheduling uncompleted work, you can also use the Tracking toolbar and Microsoft Project automatically reschedules uncompleted work for a task. This feature automatically sets the resume date of the unfinished portion of the task to one day (unit) past the status date, making the status date where the pause in work occurs.

To Automatically Reschedule Uncompleted Work

1 Choose <u>V</u>iew, <u>T</u>oolbars, Tracking.

2 Point to the Task 10 (*Standard Insertion Ad Full Color*) Gantt bar and read the Task ScreenTip.
Notice the start date of Tue 2/8/05, the finish date of Thu 2/10/05, and the duration of 2.5 days (see Figure 6.16). Recall that the status date is Fri 2/11/05.

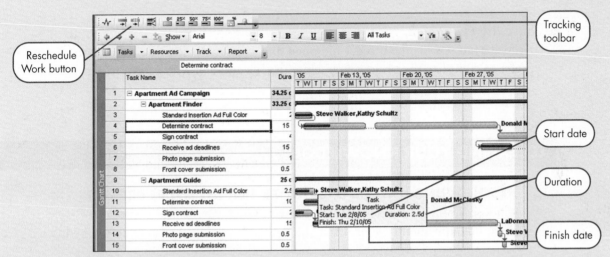

FIGURE 6.15

3 Click the Task 10 Gantt bar.

4 Click Reschedule Work on the Tracking toolbar.
The task automatically splits, adding one working day to the duration (see Figure 6.17).

FIGURE 6.16

5 Pause the mouse on the second Gantt bar for Task 10.
The Task ScreenTip appears (see Figure 6.18). Notice the new finish date of Mon 2/14/05. When using the automatic rescheduling feature, Microsoft Project selects the day after the status date as the resume date. Because the status date is a Friday, the next day is nonworking time. Monday 2/14/05 is the next working day, thus the resume date.

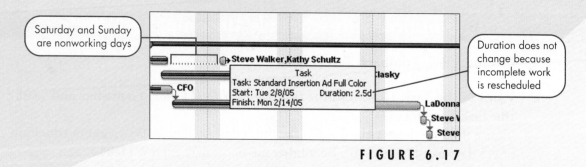

FIGURE 6.17

6 | **Save *Ad_Campaign*.**

Keep the *Ad_Campaign* project file open and continue with the next lesson. If you prefer to complete the project later, close the file and exit Microsoft Project.

TO EXTEND YOUR KNOWLEDGE . . .

RESCHEDULING UNCOMPLETED WORK FOR THE ENTIRE PROJECT

Choose Tools, Tracking, Update Project. Click *Reschedule uncompleted work to start after* and then type or select the date after which you want to reschedule all remaining work. Select the *Entire project* option button and then click OK.

LESSON 4: Modifying and Removing a Split

Sometimes, the schedule of a task alters so that it is no longer necessary to reschedule uncompleted work. For example, you may split a task because of an unexpected business trip that is removing the resource assigned to that task, but then the trip gets canceled. You may also simply find that rescheduling the uncompleted work does not have the results that you prefer. In either case, you can easily remove the split.

When you add a split to a task, Microsoft Project adds one unit to the task duration. In other words, if the project file utilizes Days in the timescale, splitting a task adds one day to the task schedule. However, there are times when you need to add more than one day between the complete and remaining work of a task that has been split. Microsoft Project provides a simple way to make changes and even remove a split from a task. You can check the resume date for the uncompleted part of the task by inserting the Resume field in the table portion of the Gantt chart, or you can drag the end of the uncompleted task Gantt bar to extend the duration.

In this lesson, you remove the split that you added to Task 4 (*Determine contract*) because it is no longer necessary. Then, you increase the delay of one day between the completed and uncompleted portions of Task 10 (*Standard Insertion Ad Full Color*) to provide additional time for the resource to resume work on Task 10.

To Modify and Remove a Split

1 | Open *Ad_Campaign,* if necessary.

2 | Click the left-most edge of the second Gantt bar of Task 4 (*Determine contract*).
The mouse becomes a four-way sizing arrow (see Figure 6.19).

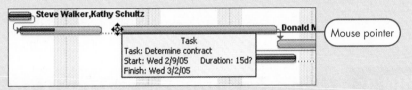

FIGURE 6.18

3 | Drag the left edge of the Gantt bar until it is flush with the right-most edge of the first Gantt bar for Task 4.
The split is removed from this task (see Figure 6.20).

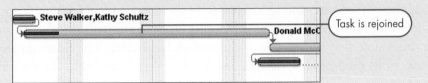

FIGURE 6.19

4 | Point to the Task 4 Gantt bar and read the Task ScreenTip.
Microsoft Project removes the split on Task 4 and the finish date is now Tue 3/1/05, which was the original date (see Figure 6.21).

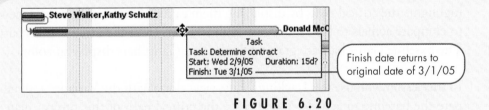

FIGURE 6.20

5 | Locate Task 10, point to the second Gantt bar, and read the Task ScreenTip.

6 | With the four-way arrow, drag the left-most edge of the second Gantt bar to the right until *Fri 2/18/05* appears in the popup.
The resume date for the second portion of Task 10 changes to Fri 2/18/05.

7 | Save *Ad_Campaign.*
Keep the *Ad_Campaign* project file open and continue with the next lesson. If you prefer to complete the project later, close the file and exit Microsoft Project.

TO EXTEND YOUR KNOWLEDGE . . .

ADDING THE RESUME FIELD TO THE TASK TABLE

You can check the resume date for the uncompleted part of a split task by inserting the Resume field in the table portion of the Gantt Chart. To insert the Resume field, choose <u>I</u>nsert, <u>C</u>olumn and select *Resume* from the *Field <u>N</u>ame* list box and then click OK.

LESSON 5: Using Tracking Gantt View to Analyze the Critical Path

The ***critical path*** represents a task and all of its predecessors as indicated by join lines on the Gantt chart (or even a single task) that dictate the overall finish date of your project plan. Each task that comprises the critical path is called a *critical task.* The terms can be a bit misleading because the critical path and its critical tasks do not necessarily represent the most important tasks in your project plan. Instead, Microsoft Project automatically chooses one task because it has a finish date that is the same as the project finish date. The finish date of this task, along with any of its predecessors, determines the critical tasks and thus the critical path. When the last task in the critical path is complete, the project is complete. It is useful to know which tasks comprise the critical path, as this lets you determine which tasks can affect your project's finish date and whether your project finishes on time.

As you know, Microsoft Project provides various views that can be customized to help keep track of the various components of a project plan. Critical tasks are best viewed in the ***Tracking Gantt view,*** which displays a baseline Gantt bar beneath the current Gantt bar and highlights the critical tasks by displaying them in red. The Tracking Gantt view allows the user to compare actuals to baseline data and thus differs from the usual Gantt chart you have seen. The baseline Gantt bars are gray, while the task Gantt bars display in color.

In this lesson, you use the Tracking Gantt view along with the Variance task table view to compare the baseline to actuals. You also see the critical path of this project plan and modify the duration of one critical task to extend the project finish date.

To Analyze the Critical Path

1 Open *Ad_Campaign,* if necessary.

2 Select <u>V</u>iew, Tracking Ga<u>n</u>tt.

If you have problems . . .

If you do not see Gantt bars in the Tracking Gantt view, use the horizontal scrollbar to scroll to the right until *Feb 6, '05* appears in the timescale.

3 | **Select <u>V</u>iew, Ta<u>b</u>le: Entry, <u>V</u>ariance.**

The Tracking Gantt chart displays (see Figure 6.22).

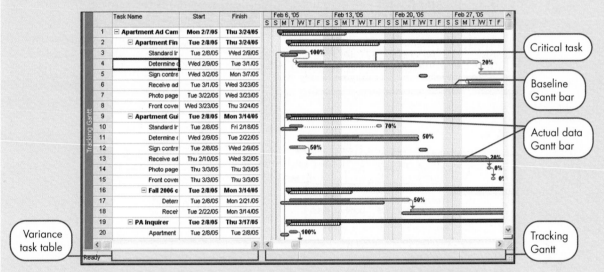

FIGURE 6.21

4 | **Point to the Task 1 (*Apartment Ad Campaign*) Gantt bar.**

A Summary ScreenTip appears. This task is the summary task for all the tasks in the plan, and it has a finish date of Thu 3/24/05 (see Figure 6.23).

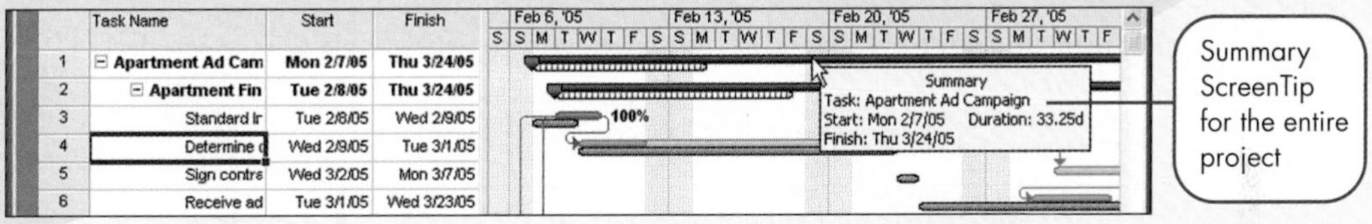

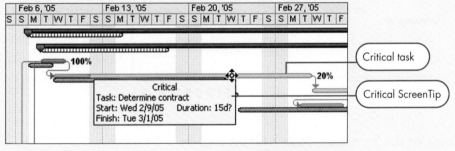

FIGURE 6.22

5 | **Point to the right side of the red Task 4 (*Determine contract*) Gantt bar.**

The Critical ScreenTip appears (see Figure 6.24). The Gantt bar is red, indicating this task is a critical task.

FIGURE 6.23

6 | **Scroll horizontally to the right until *Mar 20, '05* is visible on the timescale.**

7 **Point to the red Task 8 (*Front cover submission*) Gantt bar.**
The Critical ScreenTip appears (see Figure 6.25). Notice that this is the last task in the critical path and it has a finish date of Thu 3/24/05, which is the same as the project finish date.

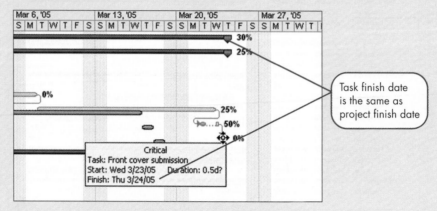

FIGURE 6.24

8 **Click the Task 8 Gantt bar and then click Task Information.**

9 **Click the General tab, and then click the *Duration* up arrow to *2d*.**

10 **Check the *Estimated* check box, and then click OK.**
The Gantt bar lengthens and the finish date for Task 8 is now Fri 3/25/05 (see Figure 6.26).

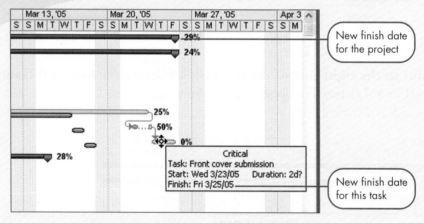

FIGURE 6.25

11 **Point to the Summary Task 1 Gantt bar.**
The Summary ScreenTip appears (see Figure 6.27). Notice the finish date for the entire project now matches the new finish date for Task 8: Fri 3/25/05.

FIGURE 6.26

12 Save *Ad_Campaign*.

Keep the *Ad_Campaign* project file open and continue with the next lesson. If you prefer to complete the project later, close the file and exit Microsoft Project.

TO EXTEND YOUR KNOWLEDGE . . .

FILTER TASKS TO VIEW THE CRITICAL TASKS

If you want to see only the critical tasks in a project, you can filter the tasks. Click the Filter button on the Formatting toolbar and select the filter you want to apply (Critical). Alternatively, select Project, Filtered For, Critical.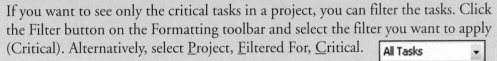

LESSON 6:   Checking Overall Project Progress

At anytime, you can review the overall status and well-being of your project and compare the baseline to the actual project plan. **Project statistics** provide up-to-the-minute statistics for the overall project plan, using actual and baseline data. These data include start and finish dates, task duration, work, cost, and percent complete. You cannot make any modifications to the data here; you can only view and print it.

The **Project Summary report** outlines actual and baseline data for the overall project plan. It is good for basic project analysis and displays the most critical project information on one page. It includes the finish dates of your project plan for both the actual plan and the baseline. The report also shows task and cost data summaries and a summary of task and resource status.

Finally, the Tracking Gantt view enables you to see task progress bars compared to baseline progress bars, with the critical path appearing in red. Some of the same statistics that are in the Project Summary report also appear in the Project Statistics dialog box; however, the report is more comprehensive and includes additional detail.

In this lesson, you view the project statistics to check the progress of the project to-date. Then, you open Project Summary report to see where the project stands concerning dates, duration, work, costs, task status, and resource status. Finally, you use ScreenTips on task Gantt bars and baseline Gantt bars to check the progress of specific tasks.

To Check Overall Project Progress

1 **Open *Ad_Campaign,* if necessary, and click Project Statistics on the Tracking toolbar.**

The Project Statistics for 'Ad_Campaign.mpp' dialog box displays (see Figure 6.28). Take a moment to look at the statistics.

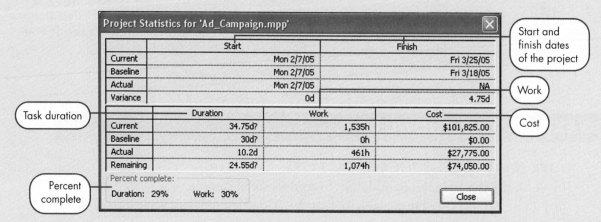

FIGURE 6.27

2 **Click Close.**

You can also view and print the Project Summary report for distribution.

3 **Choose Report Reports.**

4 **Select Overview, and then click Select.**

5 **Select Project Summary, and then click Select.**

The Project Summary report opens in Print Preview (see Figure 6.29).

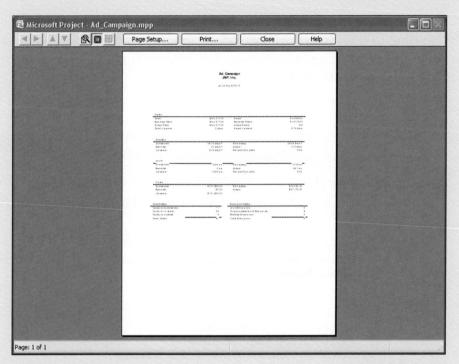

FIGURE 6.28

6 | **Click in the report to magnify it.**

The report has six sections: Dates, Duration, Work, Costs, Task Status, and Resource Status (see Figure 6.30).

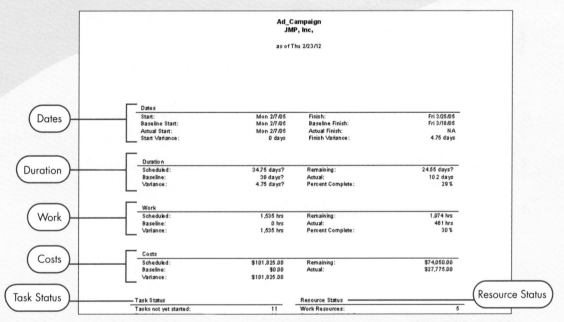

FIGURE 6.29

7 | **Click Close on the toolbar, and then click Close in the Reports dialog box.**

The report closes and you can see the project file again.

Now that you have checked the project's progress overall, you look at individual task progress. By pointing to a Gantt bar, you can read important information about a task through a ScreenTip. In the next set of steps, you view a ScreenTip for a task Gantt bar and then compare it to the baseline Gantt bar ScreenTip.

To Check Individual Task Progress

1 **View the Task 36 (*Contract: Jan 2005-March 2006*) Gantt bar.**
Notice that it is in line with the baseline bar located below it (see Figure 6.31).

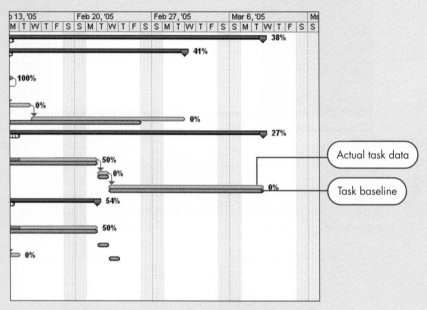

FIGURE 6.30

2 **Point to the Task 36 Gantt bar and read the Task ScreenTip.**
The start date is Wed 2/23/05, the finish date is Tue 3/8/05, and the duration is 10 days.

3 **Point to the Task 36 baseline bar and read the Baseline ScreenTip.**
The start and finish dates for both the task and the baseline are the same.

4 **View the Task 13 (*Receive ad deadlines*) Gantt bar.**
Notice that it started sooner than the baseline (see Figure 6.32).

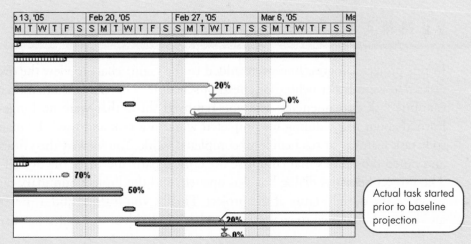

FIGURE 6.31

5 | Point to the Task 13 Gantt bar and read the Task ScreenTip.
The start date is Thu 2/10/05, the finish date is Wed 3/2/05, and the duration is 15 days.

6 | Point to the Task 13 baseline bar and read the Baseline ScreenTip.
The task actually started on Thu 2/10/05, while the baseline shows the taks scheduled to start on Thu 2/24/05.

7 | Point to the Task 17 Gantt bar (*Determine contract*) and read the Task ScreenTip.
Notice that it started later than the baseline plan (see Figure 6.33).

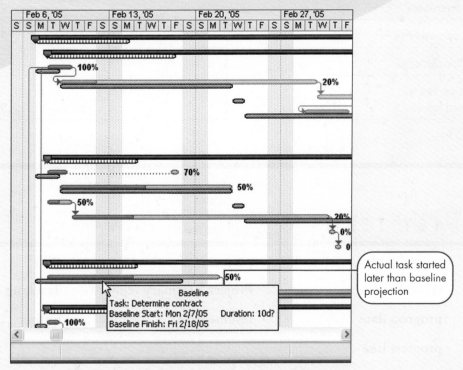

FIGURE 6.32

8 | Point to the Task 17 baseline bar and read the Baseline ScreenTip.
Task 17 was supposed to start on Mon 2/7/05 but it actually started on Tue 2/8/05.

9 | Save the *Ad_Campaign* file, and then close it.

SUMMARY

In this project, progress lines were added to the Gantt chart to view the overall status of those tasks that were either behind or ahead of schedule. The Gantt chart was critically analyzed to examine task dependencies, and you removed those that were no longer needed. You also learned about rescheduling uncompleted work in a task and used the manual and automatic split task features to reschedule uncompleted work. You viewed the critical path of a project and noted those tasks that comprise the critical path and drive the overall project finish date. The Project Statistics dialog box was opened, and the Project Summary report was previewed to check the overall status of the project. Finally, you learned about the Tracking Gantt view and how it is designed to enable you to check individual task status against the baseline.

You can extend your learning by reviewing concepts and terms and by practicing variations of skills presented in the lessons. Use the following table as a guide to the numbered questions and exercises in the end-of-project learning opportunities.

LESSON	MULTIPLE CHOICE	DISCUSSION	SKILL DRILL	CHALLENGE	DISCOVERY ZONE
Adding a Progress Line to a Gantt Chart	1, 3	1	1	1, 4	1
Removing Task Dependencies	5		2	2	
Rescheduling Uncompleted Work	2, 4	3	3	2	
Modifying and Removing a Split		3	3	2	
Using Tracking Gantt View to Analyze the Critical Path	6, 7	2	4	3	
Checking Overall Project Progress	8, 9, 10		4		2

KEY TERMS

critical path	project statistics	split
critical task	Project Summary report	Tracking Gantt view
progress date	resume date	unlink
progress line		

CHECKING CONCEPTS AND TERMS

MULTIPLE CHOICE

Circle the letter of the correct answer for each of the following.

1. Progress lines can be added to a Gantt chart and shown in relation to what types of plans? [L1]

   a. The project status date plan

   b. The actual plan or the base plan

   c. The critical path plan

   d. All of the above

2. Where are split task actions performed? [L3]

   a. On the task table

   b. From the Task Information dialog box

   c. On the Gantt chart

   d. From the Progress Lines dialog box

3. What are progress lines? [L1]

   a. Vertical lines added to the Gantt chart that show overall project progress for a particular date

   b. Horizontal black bars that display within the Gantt bars shown in the Gantt chart

   c. Red bars that display on the Gantt chart showing the most important tasks in the project plan

   d. Horizontal lines added to the Gantt chart that show overall project progress for a particular date

4. What is the difference between modifying the finish date and splitting a task? [L3]

   a. Nothing

   b. Modifying the finish date of a task extends the finish date, while splitting a task does not modify the finish date.

   c. Splitting a task breaks the task into two or more tasks that list as one item on the task sheet but are viewed as separate bars on the Gantt chart, while modifying the finish date of a task only changes the finish date of the task.

   d. None of the above

5. When you unlink a task, what happens to the task's start date? [L2]

   a. It stays the same.

   b. It returns to the project start date.

   c. A smart tag appears and you can specify whether you want to keep the start date the same or have it reset to the project start date.

   d. It changes to the total duration subtracted from the task finish date.

6. What is the critical path? [L5]

   a. The most important tasks in the overall project plan that comprise the majority of work

   b. Vertical red lines added to the Gantt chart to show progress for a particular date

   c. A task and all of its predecessors that dictate the overall finish date of a project

   d. The finish date of the project plan

7. What are critical tasks? [L5]

   a. The most important tasks in the overall project plan in terms of work and cost

   b. Each task that comprises the critical path

   c. The tasks that are falling behind schedule

   d. The tasks that appear in red because there is a scheduling problem

8. What type of data is viewed in the Project Statistics popup? [L6]

   a. The overall start and finish date of the project plan

   b. The start and finish date of the baseline

   c. Current duration work and cost

   d. All of the above

9. How are project statistics viewed? [L6]

   a. In the Project Information dialog box

   b. By clicking Project Statistics from the Tracking toolbar

   c. By selecting the Project Summary report

   d. Both b and c

10. Which option is *not* a valid section on the Project Summary report? [L6]

   a. Baseline

   b. Dates

   c. Duration

   d. Resource Status

DISCUSSION

1. What type of information can you obtain by viewing progress lines on the Gantt chart, and who on the project team would be interested in it? [L1]

2. Why is it important to periodically view the critical path and the individual tasks that comprise the critical path? What type of information can you obtain from the critical path, and how can it help you manage a project? [L5]

3. When rescheduling work (splitting a task), what often happens to the finish date of a split task? How could this impact the overall finish date of the entire project, and why is that important? [L3]

SKILL DRILL

Skill Drill exercises reinforce project skills. Each skill reinforced is the same, or nearly the same, as a skill presented in the project. Detailed instructions are provided in a step-by-step format. The exercises relate to a single file, and you should work them in order.

1. Adding Progress Lines

The company you work for utilizes a great many contractors. Part of your job is to study all bids and distribute the requests for proposals in a timely manner for project completion. You have a current construction bid process you are working on. You have customized your project file, and now you want to add a progress line.

To add a progress line, complete the following steps:

1. Open the *EPr1_0602* file and save it as **Request_For_Proposal**.

2. Drag the split bar between the task table and the Gantt chart to the left until only the Task Name column is displayed in the task table.

3. Choose <u>T</u>ools, Trac<u>k</u>ing, Progress <u>L</u>ines.

4. In the Progress Lines dialog box, click the Dates and Intervals tab.

5. Check the *Always display current progress lines* check box, and then select the *At project <u>s</u>tatus date* option button.

6. Under *Display progress lines in relation to,* select *Actual pla<u>n</u>* and then click OK.

7. View the progress line for Task 6 (*Define requirements*).

8. Turn off the progress lines for choosing <u>T</u>ools, Trac<u>k</u>ing, Progress <u>L</u>ines and then uncheck the *Always display current progress line* check box.

9. Click OK, save *Request_For_Proposal,* and leave it open for the next exercise.

2. Unlinking Task Dependencies

Now that you have viewed the overall project status in the *Request_For_Proposal* project plan, you modify the plan further by removing unnecessary task dependencies.

To unlink a task dependency, complete the following steps:

1. Open *Request_For_Proposal,* if necessary.

2. Select the Gantt bar for Task 5 (*Presolicitation Process*) and click Unlink Tasks on the Standard Toolbar.

3. Select the Gantt bar for Task 19 (*Receive oral and written proposals*) and click Task Information on the Standard Toolbar.

4. Select the Predecessors tab and click on Task 17 (Release RFP to industry) in the *Predecessors* list.

5. Press Del and then click OK.

6. Select the Gantt bar for Task 31 (*Debrief unsuccessful bidders*) and click Task Information on the Standard toolbar.

7. Select the Predecessors tab, if necessary; click on Task 28 (Debrief unsuccessful bidders) in the Predecessors list, press Del, and then click OK.

8. Save *Request_For_Proposal* and leave it open for the next exercise.

3. Split a Task and Modify a Split

Now, you work on tasks that are falling behind by rescheduling uncompleted work to allow extra time for delays that have come up.

To create and modify a split task, complete the following steps:

1. Open *Request_For_Proposal*, if necessary.

2. Click the Task 6 (*Define requirements*) Gantt bar and then click Split Task on the Standard Toolbar.

3. When you see the date of Mon 3/21/05 in the Split Task information box, click the Gantt bar to split the task.

   Note that the timescale unit is one week; thus, the new split is equal to one week (one unit).

4. From the Gantt chart, pause on the Task 14 (*Draft RFP*) Gantt bar, avoiding the black progress bar (your mouse becomes a four-way directional arrow) and read the Task ScreenTip.

   Note the start date of Mon 3/28/05 and the finish date of Mon 4/4/05.

5. Click the Task 14 Gantt bar and then click Split Task.

6. When you see the date of Wed 3/30/05 in the Split Task information box, click the Gantt bar to split the task.

7. Pause on the second Gantt bar for Task 14 and read the Task ScreenTip.

   Note the start date is Mon 3/28/05 and the finish date is Mon 4/11/05.

8. Drag the right edge of the second Gantt bar for Task 14 to the right until the finish date of Wed 4/13/05 appears.

9. Save *Request_For_Proposal* and leave it open for the next exercise.

4. View the Critical Path and Check Overall Project Progress

Now that you have made modifications to the project plan, you want to view the tasks that are driving the overall finish date of the project. You look at the critical path to determine the project finish date.

To view the critical path and check the overall progress of the project plan, complete the following steps:

1. Open *Request_For_Proposal*, if necessary, and then view Task 1 (*Request For Proposal Plan*).

   Notice that this is a summary task for all the tasks in the plan and that it has a finish date of Wed 6/1/05.

2. Choose View, Tracking Gantt.

3. Choose View, Table: Entry, Variance.

4. Scroll horizontally to the right until *Mar 20, '05* is visible on the timescale.

5. Locate the first critical task in the Gantt chart, which is Task 19 (Receive oral and written proposals).

6. Locate the last critical task in the Gantt chart, which is Task 31 (*Debrief unsuccessful bidders*), and read the Critical ScreenTip.

7. Choose View, Toolbars, Tracking, if necessary, to display the Tracking toolbar.

8. Click Project Statistics on the Tracking toolbar.

9. Click Close after viewing the project statistics.

10. Choose Report Reports, Overview, Project Summary.

    The Project Summary report loads in Print Preview.

11. Click Print, and then click OK, and then click Close.

12. If you prefer not to print, click Close on the Print Preview toolbar and then click Close again to return to Gantt chart view.

13. Save and close *Request_For_Proposal*.

CHALLENGE

Challenge exercises expand on or are somewhat related to skills presented in the lessons. Each exercise provides a brief narrative introduction, followed by instructions in a numbered-step format that are not as detailed as those in the Skill Drill section. The exercises relate to a single file, and you should work them in order.

1. Tracking Progress Against the Baseline

You are the human resources technician for a Fortune 500 bakery. Because of the vastness of the company, you have a project file that you use when orienting new employees. The orientation takes approximately two months to completely cover all issues. You have several new employees starting work in the next month, so you have updated your project file. The file has a baseline saved and you have already begun working on the orientation. Now, you need to compare what work you have done to the baseline you projected.

To track progress against baseline data, complete the following steps:

1. Open *EPr1_0603* and save it as **Orientation**; then close any open side panes.

2. Open the Project Information dialog box and note the status date.

3. Add a % Complete column in the task table and enter the percentages shown in the following table:

Task ID	Task Name	% Complete
2	New Hire Application form	100
3	Verify OPS employment form	100
4	401K savings plan	100
5	Complete 941	50
6	Emergency contact info	100
7	COBRA	50
8	Personnel Action Form	100
12	Review PPO and HMO Plans	100
13	Receive completed pkg choices	35
14	Review then submit to Benefits	50

16	Enter new hire in PeopleSoft	50
17	Update AP Dept code	90
22	Review Annual Report	20
23	Sign and return Code of Ethics	100

4. Switch to Tracking Gantt view and then choose View, Table: Entry, Variance.

5. Change the start date for Task 12 (*Review PPO and HMO plans*) to 5/23/06.

6. Choose Tools, Tracking, Progress Lines.

7. Select the option to display the progress line and to use the baseline plan for comparison.

8. Look at the progress line; then change to view the progress line using actual data.

9. View the actual progress line.

10. Turn off all progress lines.

11. Save *Orientation* and leave it open for the next exercise.

2. Modifying Task Links and Task Information

As you work with the project file, you realize that some of the tasks have dependencies that are not accurate or are not necessary. You also need to modify the schedule to allow for the Comp & Benefits Rep's one-week vacation. The vacation date is the week of June 18.

To modify a task link and task information, complete the following steps:

1. Open Orientation, if necessary, and then switch to Gantt Chart view.

2. From the Gantt chart, double-click the join line between Task 10 (*Submit the OPS PAAR form to Human Resources*)and Task 9(*Provide copies to employee*).

3. Change the join type to Start-to-Start and close the dialog box.

4. Read the join line ScreenTip to verify the change.

5. Double-click the join line between Task 24 (*Run corporate video*) and Task 23 (*Sign and return Code of Ethics*), and then select *None* as the join type.

6. Remove the join between Task 25 (*Corporate Qtr Meeting attendance*) and Task 24 (*Run corporate video*).

7. Split Task 13 at 6/20/06 (resume date of 6/21/06), and then modify the split to resume the task on 6/26/06.

   Notice the new finish date of 7/12/06.

8. Save *Orientation* and leave it open for the next exercise.

3. Filtering Critical Tasks

Sometimes it is necessary just to view the crucial tasks in a project. You can quickly do so in Microsoft Project by filtering the tasks.

To filter critical tasks, complete the following steps:

1. Open *Orientation* and then close any open side panes, if necessary.

2. Switch to Tracking Gantt view to view the critical path.

3. Switch back to Gantt Chart view.

4. Click the Filter button on the Formatting toolbar.

5. Select *Critical* on the drop-down list.

Only the critical tasks for this project are listed now.

6. Click the Filter button again and select *All Tasks*.

7. Save *Orientation* and leave it open for the next exercise.

4. Tracking Status in the Task Table

Although the Tracking Gantt view provides a quick way to see where task progress is, you may want to see it in the task table. There are two fields that you can use to see the progress of your tasks quickly: Status and Status Indicator.

To track the status of a project by using the task table, complete the following steps:

1. Open *Orientation* and then close any open side panes, if necessary.

2. Insert the Status column to the right of the Task Name column.

3. Scroll through the tasks to read the Status field for each.

4. Add another column but use Status Indicator as the new field.

5. Look at the icons in the Status Indicator column and compare them to the text in the Status column.

6. Save *Orientation* and then close the file.

DISCOVERY ZONE

Discovery Zone exercises require advanced knowledge of topics presented in *Essentials* lessons, application of skills from multiple lessons, or self-directed learning of new skills. Each exercise is independent of the other, so you may complete them in any order.

1. Using Multiple Progress Lines

At times, you may need to check the progress of a project compared to more than one date. Microsoft Project allows you to include multiple progress lines. Use Help to learn more about progress lines, particularly using the Add Progress Line button and viewing progress lines at regular intervals. Then, open one of the project files from this lesson and add at least three progress lines at a regular interval, such as every Tuesday for the first three weeks of the project.

2. Viewing Other Progress Reports

You have looked at the Project Summary report and project statistics. There are other reports that help you in tracking the progress of your project. Open one of the project files from this project and open the Reports dialog box. Look through the reports to see what reports are available. Then, open each of the following reports and view the details within each: Overview Reports – Critical Tasks and Project Summary; Current Activities – Should Have Started Tasks and Slipping Tasks.

CUSTOMIZING MICROSOFT PROJECT AND SHARING INFORMATION

OBJECTIVES

IN THIS PROJECT, YOU LEARN HOW TO

- Customize the timescale
- Create a custom field
- Create a custom view
- Create a custom report

- Use the Organizer to share custom views, reports, and calendars
- E-mail a project file
- Route a project file
- Send a schedule note message

WHY WOULD I DO THIS?

Microsoft Project enables you to create custom views and reports that fit the specifics of the project plan you are managing. Depending on the needs of your organization and project plan, you can track information and create views and reports that support specific information in which you are interested. In addition, Microsoft Project provides a tool that helps you copy these views and reports to the global template so that they are available to all project files.

Communicating information with the project team and other stakeholders in a timely and relevant manner is critical for a successful project plan. Microsoft Project supports various methods of communication to enable collaboration among members of the project team as well as individuals outside of the project team who have a vested interest, such as stakeholders. You can e-mail the entire project file, send note messages to members of the project team, or route the project file. *Routing* is a way to send the project file to one or more individuals for comments and modifications and have the file returned to you after the routing recipients have reviewed the project.

VISUAL SUMMARY

In this project, you are one of two business owners who would like to obtain approval for a plan to remodel an existing building in your historic downtown to become a restaurant. The project plan outlines the tasks you need to complete for submitting a food service operation plan prior to beginning construction.

In the first four lessons, you modify the timescale to make viewing your project plan more meaningful, and then you create a custom field, custom view, and custom report. In Lesson 5, you use the Organizer to share these customized elements. The *Organizer* is a tool that allows you to copy Microsoft Project elements such as views, reports, and project base calendars between the open file and the global template file (see Figure 7.1). Finally, you communicate the project plan by using three different methods.

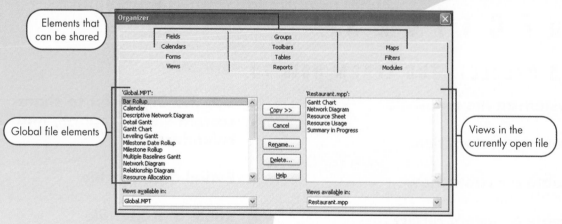

FIGURE 7.1

LESSON 1:   Customizing the Timescale

The timescale runs across the top of many views, such as the Gantt Chart, Task Usage, and Resource Graph views. You can modify the timescale to better view work within the time period that you specify. For example, you can see work within periods ranging from one minute to one year depending on the scope of the project. You may find that the timescale default setting (weeks and days) is inappropriate for a project that is entered in hours, necessitating a change to the timescale time unit format. The timescale contains three main parts: the **top tier** (top level of the timescale), the **middle tier** (middle level of the timescale), and the **bottom tier** (bottom level of the timescale). The default setting shows only the middle and bottom tiers. Besides modifying the time unit, you can also change the date label to appear with any or all tiers of the timescale and the **count,** which is the unit that appears between labels. For example, entering **3** with a time unit of *weeks* would specify that the scale is separated into 3-week segments.

In this lesson, you modify the formatting features of the timescale across the top of the Task Usage view. Then, you complete another set of steps to modify the view to include additional data and make a formatting change.

To Customize a Timescale

1 Open the *EPr1_0701* file, save it as `Restaurant`, and then close any open side panes.

2 Choose **V**iew, **V**iew Bar.
A toolbar containing the most common views appears on the left side of the screen (see Figure 7.2).

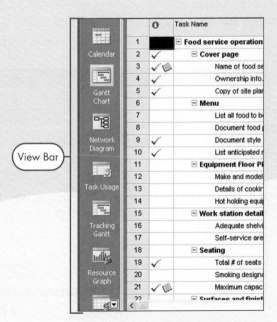

FIGURE 7.2

Resource Usage

3 **Scroll down the View Bar, and then click *Resource Usage*.**

The project displays in Resource Usage view.

4 **Click once on the scroll button on the horizontal scroll bar in the timephased bar graph window.**

The bar graph now shows *May 14, '06* in the timescale (see Figure 7.3).

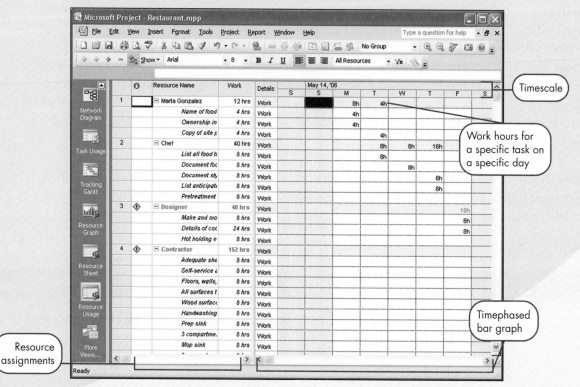

FIGURE 7.3

5 **Choose F̲ormat, T̲imescale.**

The Timescale dialog box opens (see Figure 7.4). The timescale shows two tiers: middle and bottom. By default, the Middle Tier tab is on top, with the units set to *Weeks*.

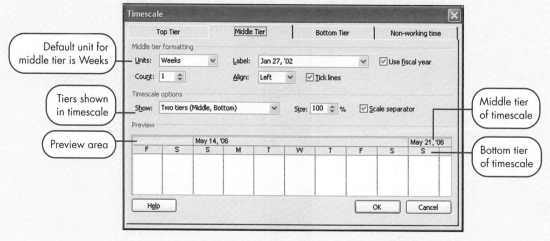

FIGURE 7.4

6 Under *Middle tier formatting*, click the *Units* drop-down arrow and select *Days*.
In the *Preview* area, you can see the changes to the timescale, showing days on the top line (the middle tier) (see Figure 7.5).

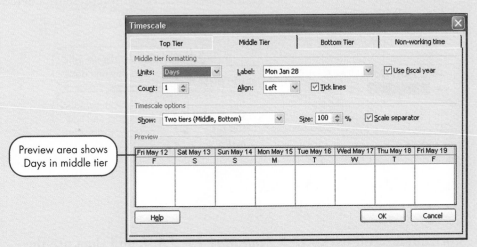

Preview area shows Days in middle tier

FIGURE 7.5

7 Click the Bottom Tier tab.
The same options are available for all three tiers. The default setting is *Days*.

8 Click the *Units* drop-down arrow and select *Hours*.
The *Preview* area displays the change (see Figure 7.6). Notice that all hours for one day do not fit under the day label in the middle tier.

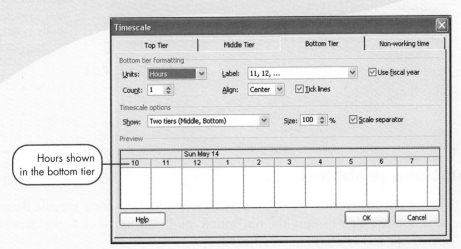

Hours shown in the bottom tier

FIGURE 7.6

9   **Click the *Label* drop-down arrow, choose the first option (*Mon Jan 28, 11 AM*), and then click OK.**

The timescale in the bar graph portion of Resource Usage view changes to show days and hours rather than weeks and days (see Figure 7.7). Each column represents a date and an hour.

Details			Mon May 15	
	Sun May 14, 10 PM	Sun May 14, 11 PM	Mon May 15, 12 AM	Mon May 15, 1 AM
Work				
Work				
Work				
Work				

New middle tier label shows day and date

New bottom tier label shows date and time

FIGURE 7.7

10   **Use the horizontal scroll bar to view *Mon May 15, 9 AM*, and then use the vertical scroll bar to view the *City* resource.**

The summary of work allocations for the City resource are shown (see Figure 7.8).

	Smoking des.	8 hrs	Work					
	Plan fee	8 hrs	Work					
	Approval lette	240 hrs	Work					
6	⊟ Fire Dept	8 hrs	Work					
	Maximum cap	8 hrs	Work					
7	⊟ City	40 hrs	Work		1h	1h	1h	
	Plan reviewec	40 hrs	Work		1h	1h	1h	
	Public health	0 hrs	Work					
			Work					
			Work					
			Work					

Summary task accounts for all work during the hour block

Work by the hour, not just by day

FIGURE 7.8

If you have problems . . .

Using the scrolling arrows may be a slow process when looking for a specific date. It may be easier and quicker to drag the horizontal scroll button to view the date you need. The date appears as a ScreenTip as you drag.

In addition to modifying the timescale, you can modify the appearance of details within a view to better match the project plan you have created. For example, the project may be defined by using hours rather than days; thus the timescale would be more appropriate if displayed as days and hours. Other projects might require quarters and months in the timescale. In the next set of steps, you add additional columns of data to the Resource Usage view and change the color of the Work row.

To Modify Resource Usage View

1 | **Choose F̲ormat, Detail S̲tyles.**

The Detail Styles dialog box opens (see Figure 7.9). The Usage Details tab displays on top.

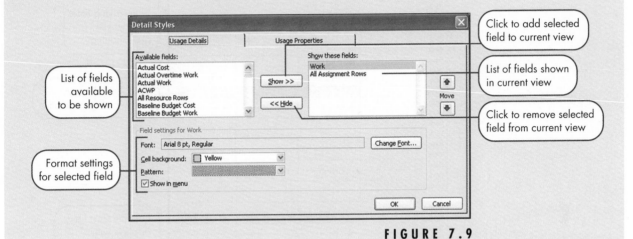

FIGURE 7.9

2 | In the *Sh̲ow these fields* list, click *Work*, if necessary.

3 | Click the *Cell background* drop-down arrow and choose the seventh color, *Blue.*

The Work field should display in the bar graph with a blue background.

Show >> **4** | In the *Available fields* list, select *Baseline Cost,* and then click the **Show button.**

The Baseline Cost field is now added to the *Sh̲ow these fields* list (see Figure 7.10). The cell background should be yellow for the Baseline Cost field.

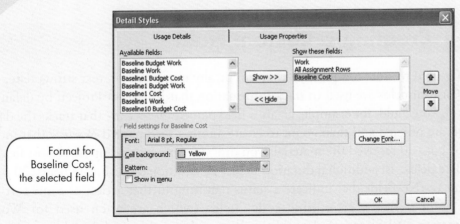

FIGURE 7.10

5 **Click OK.**

You can see the formatting changes and the additional Baseline Cost field that you added (see Figure 7.11). Notice the Baseline Cost rows are yellow, and the Work rows are blue. All nonworking time slots are gray.

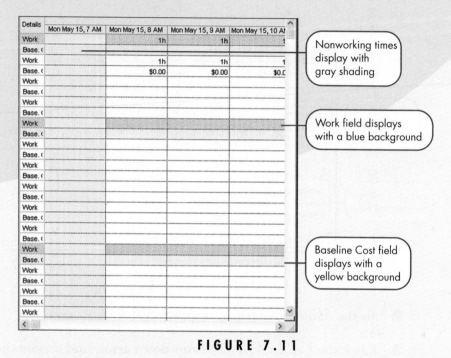

FIGURE 7.11

6 **Save your changes to the *Restaurant* file.**

You modified the timescale for Resource Usage view and changed the formatting of certain fields. Keep the *Restaurant* project file open and continue with the next lesson. If you prefer to complete the project later, close the file and exit Microsoft Project.

LESSON 2: Creating a Custom Field

A ***custom field*** is used to store unique data that can be any number, cost, text string, date, or even formula. Custom fields are used to track information that Microsoft Project, by default, does not monitor. You could, for example, create a field named *Order Date* that tracks the date certain materials are ordered and then go on to create another field named *Received* that indicates whether or not you received the materials you ordered. You can add up to 10 cost fields, 10 additional date fields, 10 additional duration fields, 10 additional finish date fields, 20 flag fields (which are Yes/No fields that indicate a status requiring further action or some sort of function), 20 number fields, 10 outline codes fields (which are often used for Work Breakdown Structure [WBS] codes), 10 additional start date fields, and 30 additional text fields. Custom fields can be added to any ***sheet view,*** which is the spreadsheet-like presentation of data such as the task table. Gantt Chart view is the most common sheet view and a likely place where you might want to add custom fields.

In this lesson, you create a custom field to display fixture prices in your remodeling project. After creating the new field, you add it to Gantt Chart view.

To Create a Custom Field

1 Open *Restaurant*, if necessary, and click *Gantt Chart* on the View Bar.

2 Choose **T**ools, **C**ustomize, Fiel**d**s.
The Customize Fields dialog box opens (see Figure 7.12). The Custom Fields tab displays on top by default.

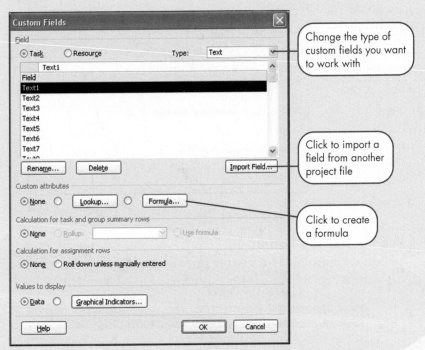

FIGURE 7.12

3 Click the *Type* drop-down arrow, select *Cost*, click *Cost1*, and then click the Rena**m**e button.
The Rename Field dialog box opens (see Figure 7.13).

FIGURE 7.13

4 Type **Fixture Price** and then click OK.
The field now has the new name you specified but also maintains the *Cost1* name in parentheses for reference (see Figure 7.14).

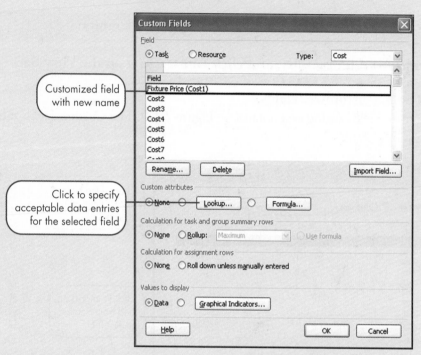

Customized field with new name

Click to specify acceptable data entries for the selected field

FIGURE 7.14

5 **Click the Lookup button.**

The Edit Lookup Table for Fixture Price dialog box opens (see Figure 7.15). Here you specify the acceptable values for this field.

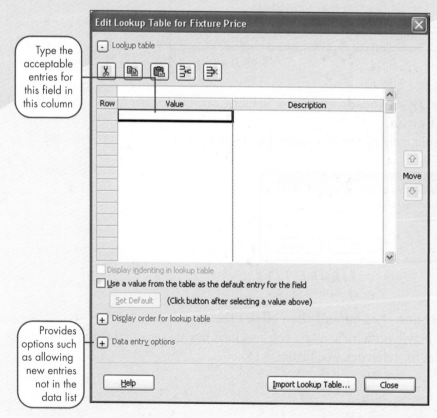

Type the acceptable entries for this field in this column

Provides options such as allowing new entries not in the data list

FIGURE 7.15

6 **Click in Row 1 in the Value column, type 100, and then press ↵Enter.**

7 Enter the following numbers, one in each cell in the column:

150

200

300

You have created the acceptable entries for this field.

8 Click the + button next to Data entry options.
Additional options are displayed.

9 Select the *Allow additional items to be entered into the fields* option.
This option lets you enter data that are not already entered in the value list.

10 Click Close, and then click OK in the Custom Fields dialog box.

11 Right-click the Indicator column heading, and choose Insert Column.
The Column Definition dialog box opens.

12 Click the *Field name* drop-down arrow, select *Cost 1 (Fixture Price)*, and then click OK.
The Fixture Price column appears on the left side of the task table (see Figure 7.16).

New custom field →

	Fixture Price	🛈	Task Name	Duration	Start
1	$0.00 ⌄		⊟ **Food service operation**	**37 days?**	**Mon 5/15/06**
2	$0.00	✓	⊟ **Cover page**	**1.5 days**	**Mon 5/15/06**
3	$0.00	✓ 🗏	Name of food se	0.5 days	Mon 5/15/06
4	$0.00	✓	Ownership info.	0.5 days	Mon 5/15/06
5	$0.00	✓	Copy of site plar	0.5 days	Tue 5/16/06
6	$0.00		⊟ **Menu**	**3 days?**	**Tue 5/16/06**
7	$0.00		List all food to b	1 day?	Tue 5/16/06

FIGURE 7.16

13 Scroll to Task 28 (*Prep sink*), and then click in the Fixture Price cell.

14 Click the Fixture Price drop-down arrow, choose *$150*, and press ⏎Enter.
The amount is accepted.

15 Click in the Fixture Price field for Task 29 (*3 compartment sink*), type **250**, and press ⏎Enter.
The entry is accepted in this field and *$250* is added to the lookup table for this field.

16 Specify a Fixture Price of *$100* for Task 30 (*Mop sink*) and *$300* for Task 31 (*3 compartment sink for bar*).

17 Save your changes to the *Restaurant* file.
You created a custom field in this lesson and inserted it into the task table of the Gantt Chart view. Keep the *Restaurant* project file open and continue with the next lesson. If you prefer to complete the project later, close the file and exit Microsoft Project.

TO EXTEND YOUR KNOWLEDGE . . .

CREATING A CALCULATED FIELD

You can use predefined functions—such as sum or average—and comparison operators—such as greater than or less than symbols—to create a custom field that involves a calculation. For example, you could create a calculated field that displays a warning message for each task that has a cost over a certain dollar amount.

To create a calculated field, select Tools, Customize, Fields. Select the field type *Text* from the *Type* drop-down list, and click the Formula button. In the Formula for Field dialog box, you can use the Field, Function and character buttons to create the calculation. After doing so, you can insert the field in the Gantt chart or any other sheet view. Challenge Exercise 1 provides an opportunity to create a calculated field.

LESSON 3:   Creating a Custom View

In addition to the number of views already available in Microsoft Project, you can also modify an existing view to create your own unique view option or use the View Definition dialog box to create an entirely new view. Project managers can better understand and manage a project plan when using a view designed to meet their specific needs. They can better see relationships between elements, analyze costs, and identify potential problems before they become serious.

There are different options in the View Definition dialog box depending on whether you are creating a single or combination view. A **single view** is a view such as the Gantt chart or Network diagram, while a **combination view** has one view in the top half of the screen and another view in the bottom half of the screen. For example, a combination view might have the Task Usage view in the top half of the window and the Task Details Form in the bottom half.

In a single view, you identify several elements or **controls** that comprise the view. The **screen control** becomes the underlying structure for the entire view. Resource Sheet view or Gantt Chart view are just two different types of screens. The **table control** is the list of fields you want in the view and is determined by the screen that you choose. For example, if you choose Gantt chart as the screen, you could select Baseline as the table and the fields from the Baseline table become the columns that comprise the view. The **group control** is a way to categorize the view. For example, you could group tasks by priority. The **filter control** either limits or highlights those tasks that fit the criteria. For example, you could filter the view to show only critical tasks.

In this lesson, you create a custom view to highlight tasks that are currently in progress. Then, you apply it in the *Restaurant* project file.

To Create a Custom View

1 Open *Restaurant*, and close any open side panes, if necessary.

2 Click *More Views* on the View Bar.

3 In the More Views dialog box, click Gantt Chart and then click <u>N</u>ew.
The Define New View dialog box opens (see Figure 7.17).

New custom field

	Fixture Price	ⓘ	Task Name	Duration	Start
1	$0.00 ▾		⊟ **Food service operation**	**37 days?**	**Mon 5/15/06**
2	$0.00	✓	⊟ **Cover page**	**1.5 days**	**Mon 5/15/06**
3	$0.00	✓ 🗐	Name of food se	0.5 days	Mon 5/15/06
4	$0.00	✓	Ownership info.	0.5 days	Mon 5/15/06
5	$0.00	✓	Copy of site plar	0.5 days	Tue 5/16/06
6	$0.00		⊟ **Menu**	**3 days?**	**Tue 5/16/06**
7	$0.00		List all food to b	1 day?	Tue 5/16/06

FIGURE 7.17

4 Click *Single view*, if necessary, and then click OK.
The View Definition in 'Restaurant.mpp' dialog box opens. Here you select options to set up the custom view.

5 Specify the options for this view as shown in the following table:

<u>N</u>ame:	`Summary in Progress`
S<u>c</u>reen:	Gantt Chart
<u>T</u>able:	Summary
<u>G</u>roup:	No Group
<u>F</u>ilter:	In Progress Tasks
Highlight filter:	Checked

6 Click OK.
The More Views dialog box reappears, and the new Summary in Progress view is selected in the list of available views.

7 Click Appl<u>y</u> in the More Views dialog box.
The Summary in Progress view displays (see Figure 7.18). Notice some tasks are blue text because a filter is applied to tasks that are in progress and you have checked the *Highlight filter* check box.

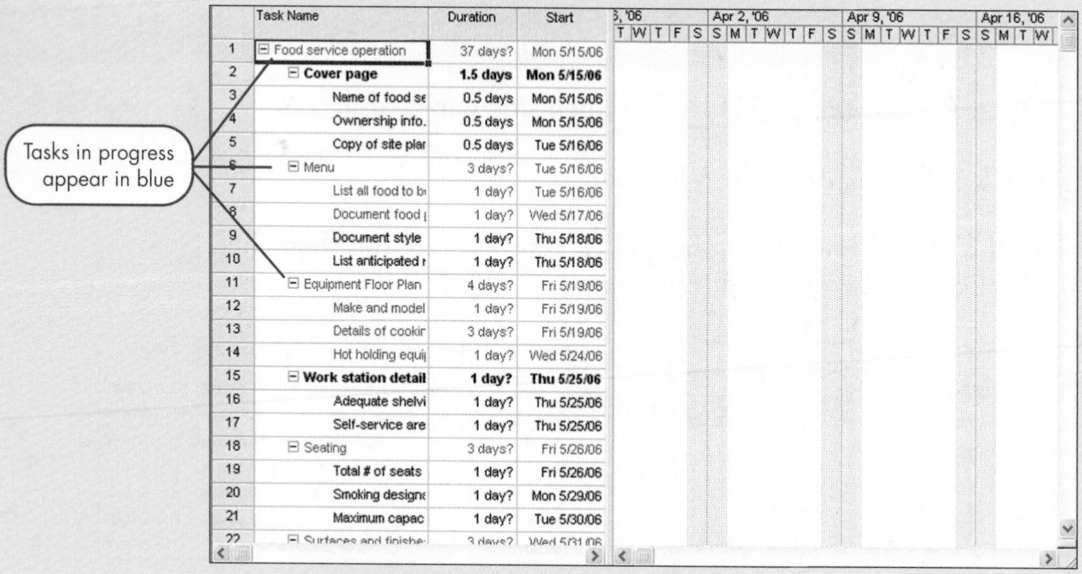

	Task Name	Duration	Start
1	⊟ Food service operation	37 days?	Mon 5/15/06
2	⊟ **Cover page**	**1.5 days**	**Mon 5/15/06**
3	Name of food se	0.5 days	Mon 5/15/06
4	Ownership info.	0.5 days	Mon 5/15/06
5	Copy of site plar	0.5 days	Tue 5/16/06
6	⊟ Menu	3 days?	Tue 5/16/06
7	List all food to b	1 day?	Tue 5/16/06
8	Document food	1 day?	Wed 5/17/06
9	Document style	1 day?	Thu 5/18/06
10	List anticipated r	1 day?	Thu 5/18/06
11	⊟ Equipment Floor Plan	4 days?	Fri 5/19/06
12	Make and model	1 day?	Fri 5/19/06
13	Details of cookir	3 days?	Fri 5/19/06
14	Hot holding equij	1 day?	Wed 5/24/06
15	⊟ **Work station detail**	**1 day?**	**Thu 5/25/06**
16	Adequate shelvi	1 day?	Thu 5/25/06
17	Self-service are	1 day?	Thu 5/25/06
18	⊟ Seating	3 days?	Fri 5/26/06
19	Total # of seats	1 day?	Fri 5/26/06
20	Smoking designa	1 day?	Mon 5/29/06
21	Maximum capac	1 day?	Tue 5/30/06
22	⊟ Surfaces and finishe	3 days?	Wed 5/31/06

Tasks in progress appear in blue

FIGURE 7.18

8 | **Scroll in the Gantt chart to see the Gantt bars.**

The Gantt bars with partial progress bars correspond to the tasks in blue text (see Figure 7.19). Notice the tasks that are 100% are not formatted in blue, nor are the tasks that have not begun.

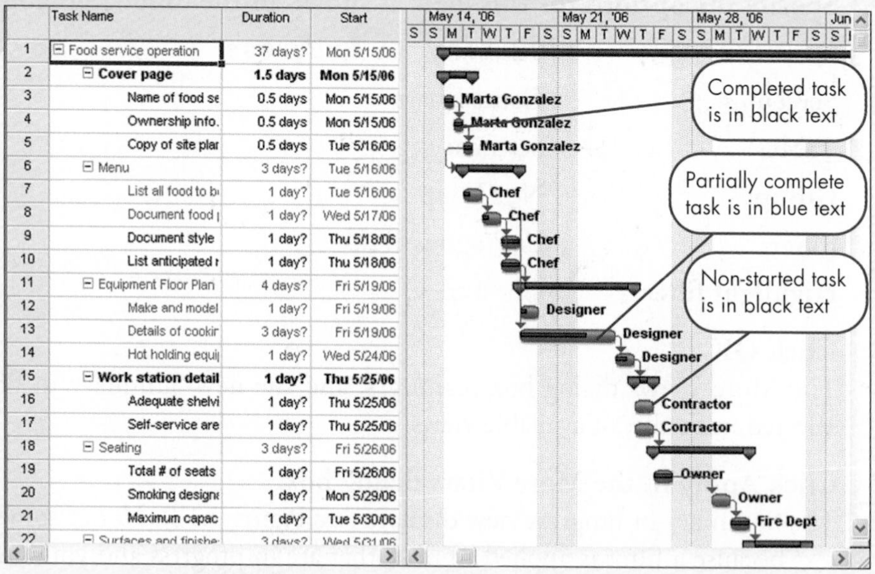

FIGURE 7.19

9 | **Save your changes to the *Restaurant* file.**

You created a custom view and applied it to the *Restaurant* project file. Keep the project file open and continue with the next lesson. If you prefer to complete the project later, close the file and exit Microsoft Project.

LESSON 4: Creating a Custom Report

Microsoft Project provides 29 predefined reports. If the information in these reports does not meet your needs, you can create your own unique report using one of the existing reports as a template. You can create custom task or resource reports, a unique monthly calendar report, or a custom crosstab report. A ***crosstab report*** is one in which the data are presented in column and row format with totals that can be applied to the column, row, or both, like a spreadsheet.

To create a custom report, you first specify the type by choosing Task, Resource, Monthly Calendar, or Crosstab and then selecting the elements it should contain. Reports are grouped into these four categories as each category requires slightly different options in the ensuing dialog boxes. When you create a custom report, you specify the table on which it is based and any filters you would like to apply. The Task and Resource reports allow you to specify a period or time frame, such as the entire project or just weeks or hours. You also have options to modify the text used for the entire report or for particular items on the report. For example, you may want to highlight critical tasks by applying bold and red text. Finally, you have the ability to sort the tasks and add elements such as borders and gridlines.

In this lesson, you create a unique, customized task usage report that allows you to filter tasks for a specific resource. You create a *Tasks and Work by Resource* report to display all tasks assigned to a specific resource, including assignment units, task durations, start and finish dates, percent complete, cost, and work (baseline, actual work, and remaining work). You then preview the report. When prompted, you select the Contractor resource and then print the report. A report displaying the tasks and work for the Contractor resource is the result of your efforts.

To Create a Custom Report

1 Open *Restaurant*, if necessary, and close any open side panes.

2 Choose Report Reports.

3 Click C**u**stom, and then click **S**elect.
The Custom Reports dialog box opens (see Figure 7.20).

FIGURE 7.20

4   **Click the New button.**

The Define New Report dialog box opens (see Figure 7.21). There are four report types available: Task, Resource, Monthly Calendar, and Crosstab.

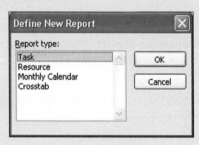

FIGURE 7.21

5   **Select Task, if necessary, and then click OK.**

The Task Report dialog box opens (see Figure 7.22). The Definition tab allows you to specify the table containing the field listing you want as well as a time period for the report and any filters you would like to apply.

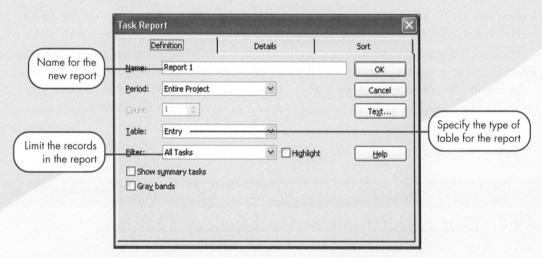

FIGURE 7.22

6   **Specify the options for this report on the Definitions tab as shown in the following table:**

Name: **Tasks and Work by Resource**

Period: Entire Project

Table: Summary

Filter: Using Resource...

7   **Click the Details tab.**

You can use the Details tab to specify additional fields you would like to include, such as *Notes* or *Predecessors*, as well as any borders or gridlines (Figure 7.23).

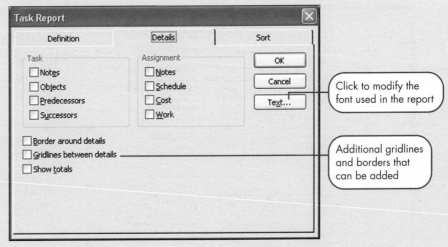

FIGURE 7.23

8 Under *Assignment*, check the *Work* check box, and then click OK.
The Custom Reports dialog box reappears and the new Task and Work by Resource report is selected in the list of available reports.

9 Click the Preview button.
The Using Resource dialog box opens (see Figure 7.24). Here you select the resource you want for the report.

FIGURE 7.24

10 Click the drop-down arrow, choose *Contractor*, and then click OK.
The new report opens (see Figure 7.25). Your report shows tasks for the contractor resource and includes work units.

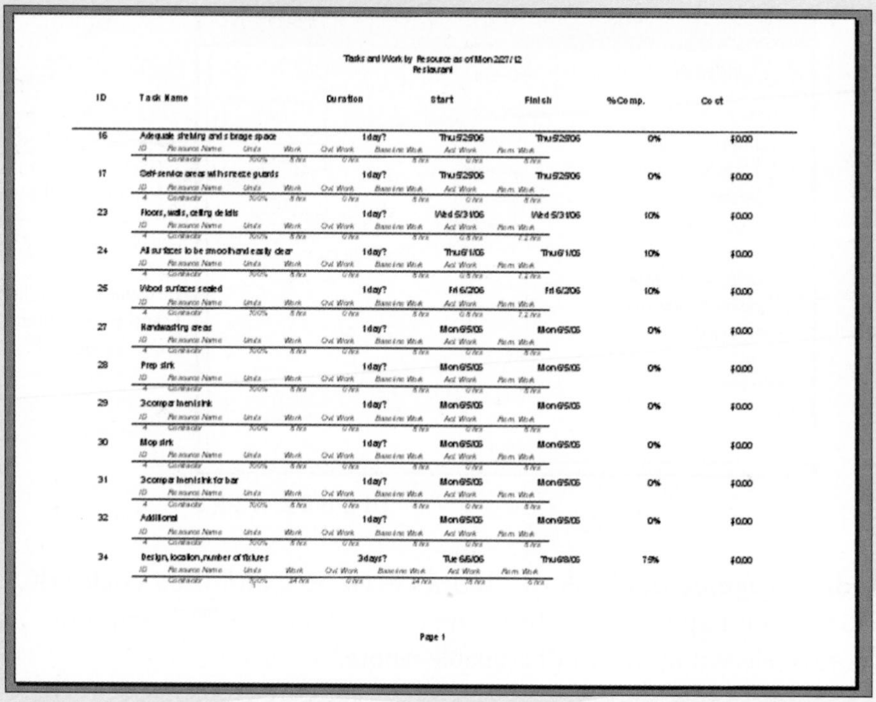

FIGURE 7.25

11 Click the Page Setup button on the Print Preview toolbar.

> Page Setup...

12 Click the Margins tab, change the left and right margins to 0.5″, and then click OK.

13 Click within the report and view the data.

14 Click Close to exit without printing. (If you prefer to print, you can click the Print button to immediately start the print process at default settings.)
After you print or close Print Preview, the Custom Reports dialog box reappears.

15 Click Close and then click Close in the Reports dialog box.

16 Save your changes to the *Restaurant* file.
You created and viewed a custom report in this lesson. Keep the *Restaurant* project file open and continue with the next lesson. If you prefer to complete the project later, close the file and exit Microsoft Project.

LESSON 5: Using the Organizer to Share Custom Views, Reports, and Calendars

The Organizer is a tool that allows you to copy certain project elements—such as fields, groups, calendars, toolbars, views, and reports—between the current project file and the global template. In addition to copying, you can rename and delete these elements as well. There are 11 tabs in the Organizer dialog box, with each tab representing an element that you can manage: Views, Reports, *Modules* (pieces of programming code that you create to perform an action),

Forms, Tables, Filters, Calendars, Toolbars, *Maps* (formats that are used when importing and exporting data between programs), Fields, and Groups.

The global file (Global.mpt) is a Microsoft Project file that contains default settings that are applied to all new project files. The global file includes settings that control the view displayed at startup, the unit in which work is displayed (hours, days, or weeks), and whether schedule calculations are manual or automatic. A *schedule calculation* is a value that Microsoft Project calculates as based on other data. For example, work units are a calculation of task duration. Once you copy custom elements to the *Global.mpt* file, they become available to all new blank project files and can also be copied to existing files. In addition to being able to copy project elements, you can use the Organizer to delete and rename elements from both the global file and the current file.

If you should alter the global file, do so with extreme caution. Changes made to the global file affect any other projects or users that utilize the Microsoft Project program. Many corporations that use Microsoft Project on a server provide policies and procedures concerning alterations to the global file. Many do not allow access to the global file except to specific users. It is best to make a copy of the global file prior to making any changes to it in case a restoration is necessary.

In this lesson, you use the Organizer to perform two sets of steps. First, you copy the Summary in Progress view, the Work by Resource report, and the Contractor calendar to the global template. Then, you verify the existence of these items in the global file by opening a new project file. Finally, you remove the custom items from the global file.

To Use the Organizer

1 **Open *Restaurant* and then choose <u>T</u>ools, Organizer.**
The Organizer dialog box opens (see Figure 7.26). Organizer allows you to copy, move, or delete views between the open project file (*Restaurant.mpp*) and the global template (*Global.mpt*).

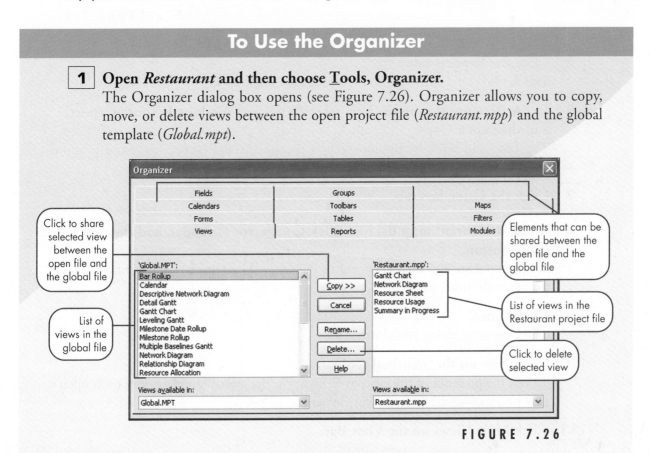

FIGURE 7.26

2 Click the Views tab, if necessary.

3 In the *'Restaurant.mpp'* list box, select the Summary in Progress view, and then click the **C**opy button.

4 Scroll through the *'Global.MPT'* list to verify that Summary in Progress view is listed.

The Summary in Progress view copies to the *Global.mpt* file (see Figure 7.27).

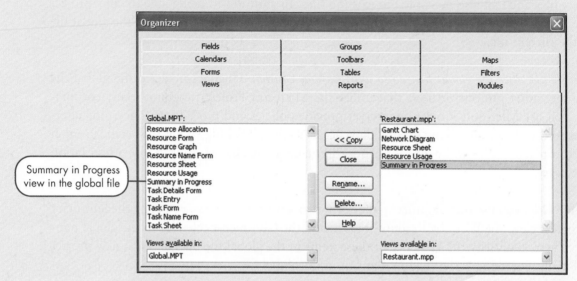

FIGURE 7.27

5 Click the Reports tab.

The Reports tab is identical to the Views tab except for the entries in the two lists.

6 In the Restaurant.mpp list box, select Tasks and Work by Resource report, and then click **C**opy.

The Tasks and Work by Resource report is copied to the *Global.mpt* template and is now available for use with future projects.

7 Click the Calendars tab.

8 In the Restaurant.mpp list box, click Contractor Calendar, and then click the **C**opy button.

The Contractor Calendar is copied to the *Global.mpt* template and is now available for use with future projects.

9 Click Close.

The Organizer dialog box closes.

10 Click New on the Standard toolbar.

To test the presence of the custom elements in the global template, you must open a new project file and look for that element.

11 Click More Views on the View Bar.

12 **Scroll through the Views list and verify that Summary in Progress is listed.**
The view is available in the new file (see Figure 7.28).

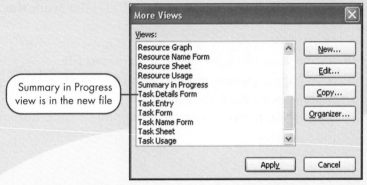

Summary in Progress view is in the new file

FIGURE 7.28

13 **Click Cancel, and then close the new project without saving changes.**
You have now made your unique custom view, report, and calendar available for each new blank project file and can be added to any existing project file.

Sometimes you may want to remove a customized element from the global file. In this case, you need to remove the custom view, report, and calendar you added in the previous set of steps so they are not available on the lab computer.

To Remove Items from the Global Template

1 **Choose Tools, Organizer and then click the Views tab, if necessary.**
The Organizer dialog box opens.

2 **In the *'Global.MPT'* list box, select *Summary in Progress* and then click Delete.**
A warning appears (see Figure 7.29).

FIGURE 7.29

3 **Click Yes.**
The Summary in Progress view is removed from the global file but remains a part of the *Restaurant* project file.

4 **Click the Reports tab.**

5 **In the *'Global.MPT'* list box, select *Tasks and Work by Resource* and then click Delete.**
A warning dialog box opens.

6 **Click Yes in the warning box.**
The Tasks and Work by Resource report is removed from the global file.

7 **Click the Calendars tab and remove the Contractor Calendar from the
'*Global.MPT*' list.**

8 **Click Close, and then save your changes to the *Restaurant* file.**
You used the Organizer to copy a custom report, calendar, and view to the global
template. Then you removed them. Keep the *Restaurant* project file open and continue with the next lesson. If you prefer to complete the project later, close the file
and exit Microsoft Project.

TO EXTEND YOUR KNOWLEDGE . . .

RENAMING ITEMS IN THE ORGANIZER
You can also use the Organizer to rename project elements. Select the element you
want to rename and click the Rename button. Type a new name and click OK;
then close the dialog box.

RESETTING THE GLOBAL FILE
The global template file (*Global.mpt*) itself cannot be opened in Microsoft Project,
as it is merely a collection of settings that are applied to all new projects. To preserve
the global file, you should copy the template to a safe location. To replace/overwrite
a changed global file, restore the backup of the original global file.

LESSON 6:   E-Mailing a Project File

Microsoft Project has several integrated MAPI-compliant e-mail features that allow you to
e-mail project plans directly from Microsoft Project by using Outlook or another MAPI e-mail
program. ***MAPI*** (Messaging Application Programming Interface) is the standard programming interface supported by Microsoft for accessing electronic messaging.

You are able to e-mail a project file to others by using Outlook or any MAPI compliant e-mail
system. E-mailing a project file is the simplest method of sharing your project with other people. E-mailing a project file can be done from within Microsoft Project and involves sending
the open file to a recipient. A ***recipient*** is simply the person to whom you are addressing the
e-mail. The open project file is sent as an ***attachment,*** which is a file that is included with an
e-mail but is not part of the e-mail message.

In this lesson, you explore using the *Send-to* feature on the File menu. You perform the setup
needed to e-mail the project file as an attachment.

To Set Up E-Mailing a Project File

1 Open *Restaurant*, if necessary, and close any open side panes.

2 Choose File, Send To, Mail Recipient (as Attachment).
Your e-mail application launches and a new e-mail message form displays, showing your project file as an attachment. A subject line displays the name of the project file (see Figure 7.30).

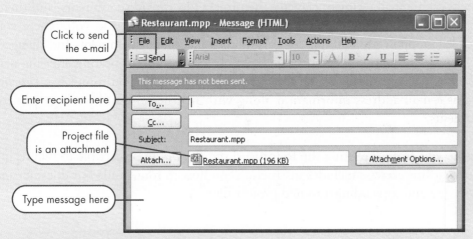

FIGURE 7.30

If you have problems . . .

Depending on the e-mail program you are using and the settings or virus protection programs in use, you may receive warning dialog boxes stating something similar to *A program is trying to access e-mail addresses you have stored in Outlook. Do you want to allow this? If this is unexpected, it may be a virus and you should choose 'No'.* Proceed by clicking Yes or as directed.

3 In the *To* text box, enter the e-mail address of a recipient.

4 In the message area, type `Attached please find the latest copy of the Restaurant project plan.`
You completed the specifications to send the current project file as an e-mail attachment. At this point, clicking Send would complete the process. Instead, you close without sending.

5 Click Close and do not save your changes to the e-mail form.
The e-mail form closes.

6 Save your changes to the *Restaurant* file.
You explored how to send the open project file as an attachment. Keep the *Restaurant* project file open and continue with the next lesson. If you prefer to complete the project later, close the file and exit.

LESSON 7: Routing a Project File

Routing a project file means sending the file to specific individuals for feedback. For example, you may require information from the designer concerning certain equipment for the kitchen, which also requires input from the contractor regarding installation feasibility. Routing sends your project plan through e-mail to a list of people—and you can specify that each individual receives the file one at a time in sequence, or you can send the file to everyone simultaneously, creating multiple copies of the project file. In general, sequential routing is ideal for review and evaluation, as each e-mail recipient can edit the project file, provide comments, and then send it along to the next recipient. Upon completion, the file is returned to you, where you can review one file (as opposed to multiple copies) and then incorporate comments and changes to it. When you receive the completed routed file, it will have a number appearing after the name to preserve the original copy of the project file. When you route a file, you complete a *routing slip* that contains e-mail address information along with instructions and message text for the e-mail recipients.

In this lesson, you create a routing slip to forward the *Restaurant* project file to two recipients. Please note that this exercise includes instructions on how to route a file but does not include steps on viewing and forwarding a routed project file.

To Route a Project File

1 Open *Restaurant*, if necessary, and close any open side panes.

2 Choose **File**, **Send To**, **Routing Recipient**.
The Routing Slip dialog box opens (see Figure 7.31).

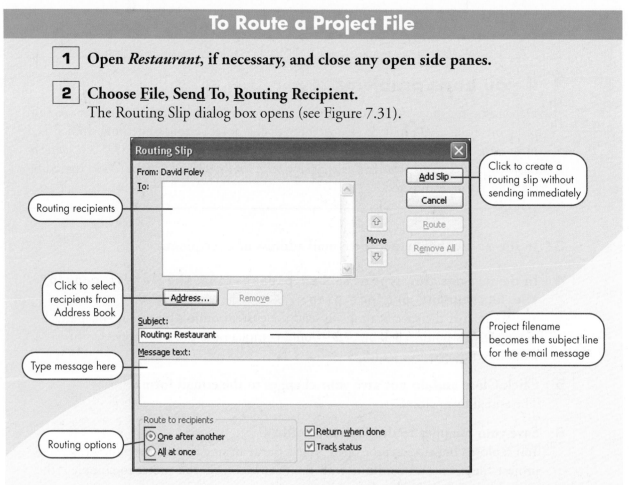

FIGURE 7.31

If you have problems . . .

Depending on the e-mail program you are using and the settings or virus protection programs in use, you may receive warning dialog boxes stating something similar to *A program is trying to access e-mail addresses you have stored in Outlook. Do you want to allow this? If this is unexpected, it may be a virus and you should choose 'No'.* Proceed by clicking Yes or as directed.

3 **Click A̲ddress.**
The Address Book dialog box opens.

4 **Select the first e-mail recipient from the list of names and click the *To* button.**

5 **Click the second e-mail recipient from the list of names, click the *To* button, and then click OK.**

6 In the *Message text* box, type `Please review Tasks 11-14 concerning equipment floor plan and update the attached file with your progress. Include a note regarding the status of this equipment installation.`

7 Under *Route to recipients*, click *O̲ne after another*, if necessary.

8 Check the *Return w̲hen done* and *Track̲ status* check boxes (see Figure 7.33).

9 **Click A̲dd Slip.**
You completed the specifications to route the current project file. At this point, clicking R̲oute rather than A̲dd Slip would add a routing slip and forward the project file simultaneously. Instead, you close without sending. The project file is ready to be routed to the first e-mail recipient in the address list. Figure 7.32 illustrates a sample routing slip.

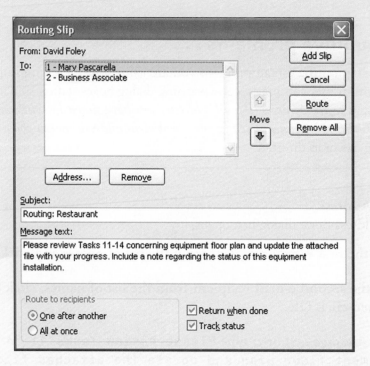

FIGURE 7.32

10 **Save *Restaurant*.**

You added a routing slip. Keep the *Restaurant* project file open and continue with the next lesson. If you prefer to complete the project later, close the file and exit.

TO EXTEND YOUR KNOWLEDGE . . .

SENDING A ROUTING SLIP

Once you have addressed and created the routing slip, you need to send it. To send a routing slip, choose File, Send To, Other Routing Recipient. From the Routing Slip dialog box, click Route and the project file is routed to the recipients as addressed.

VIEWING A ROUTING SLIP

From your e-mail program, open the routed e-mail message. The e-mail message contains the project file as an attachment. Double-click on the attachment to open the project file and launch Microsoft Project. Review and modify the project as per the message contained in the routing slip.

SENDING THE PROJECT FILE TO THE NEXT ROUTING RECIPIENT

If the creator of the routing slip has chosen the *One after another* option in the Routing Slip dialog box, the project file needs to be sent to the next recipient. These instructions can be seen in the content of the e-mail message written as: *The project below has a routing slip. When you are done reviewing this project, choose Next Routing Recipient from the Send To menu in the Microsoft Office Project File menu to continue the routing.* To send the project file to the next routing recipient, choose File, Send To, Next Routing Recipient.

LESSON 8:   Sending a Schedule Note Message

A *schedule note message* is either a picture of selected tasks or an attached project file that is automatically addressed to members of the project team. When you need to send information about critical tasks to assigned resources or ask resources to report on the status of their task assignments, you can schedule a note and send it to them as an e-mail message. This feature is useful to communicate with the project team as well as stakeholders to send or receive project information. When sending a schedule note, you can display the view, including any sheet views as well as custom fields that you require.

In this lesson, you select a range of tasks and send only those tasks as a picture to an e-mail recipient.

To Send Schedule Note Messages

1   Open *Restaurant*, if necessary, and close any open side panes.

2   Click *Task Usage* on the View Bar.

3   Highlight Tasks 41 (*Plans and approvals*) through 47 (*Construction can begin*).

4   Choose <u>F</u>ile, Sen<u>d</u> To, Mail Recipient (as S<u>c</u>hedule Note).
The Send Schedule Note dialog box appears (see Figure 7.33).

FIGURE 7.33

If you have problems . . .

Depending on the e-mail program you are using and the settings or virus protection programs in use, you may receive warning dialog boxes stating something similar to *A program is trying to access e-mail addresses you have stored in Outlook. Do you want to allow this? If this is unexpected, it may be a virus and you should choose 'No'.* Proceed by clicking Yes or as directed.

5   Under *Address message to*, uncheck the *Project manager* check box.

Now, only *Resources* should be selected (see Figure 7.34).

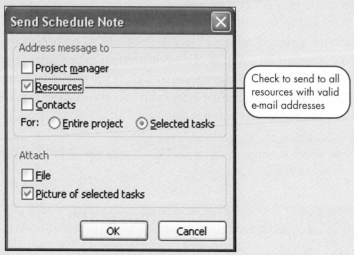

FIGURE 7.34

6   Check *Picture of selected tasks*, if necessary, and then click OK.

Your e-mail application is launched and a new e-mail message form is created with a completed *To* text box showing the e-mail addresses of each resource from the project plan. In addition, the selected tasks are attached as a BMP (bitmapped picture) file (see Figure 7.35).

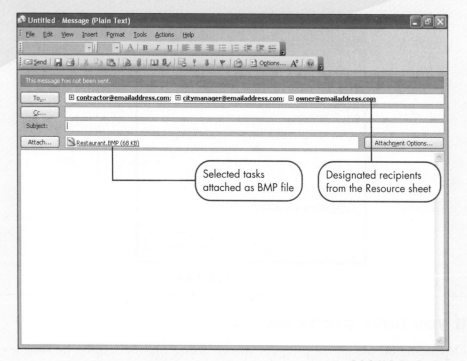

FIGURE 7.35

7 Click in the *Subject* text box, and type `ACTION: Please review the attached.`

8 In the message area, type `Attached please find several tasks. Please review to ensure this is a comprehensive list and advise me of any additions or changes you feel are necessary. Student Name (where Student Name is your name).`
You completed the specifications to send the selected tasks as a note. At this point, clicking OK would complete the process. Instead, you close without sending.

9 Click Close and do not save your changes to the e-mail form.

10 Save *Restaurant* and then close it.

TO EXTEND YOUR KNOWLEDGE . . .

ADDING E-MAIL ADDRESSES TO THE RESOURCE SHEET
You can include e-mail addresses as part of the information that you maintain with the resources data that you have entered. To add e-mail addresses, choose View, Resource Sheet and then choose Insert, Column and select *Email Address* in the *Field name* text box; click OK. The E-mail Address column is added to the resource sheet where you can then type the e-mail address for each resource.

SUMMARY

In this project, you learned many ways you can customize Microsoft Project and share information. First, you modified the timescale to display hours rather than days. Then, you also created a custom field, a custom view, and a custom report. You learned how to share a custom view, report, and calendar by copying to the *Global.mpt* file by using the Organizer so that is available to other project files. Finally, you took a look at several e-mail functions by sending a project file as an attachment, routing a file for feedback, and sending a scheduled note message to members of the project team.

You can extend your learning by reviewing concepts and terms and by practicing variations of skills presented in the lessons. Use the following table as a guide to the numbered questions and exercises in the end-of-project learning opportunities.

LESSON	MULTIPLE CHOICE	DISCUSSION	SKILL DRILL	CHALLENGE	DISCOVERY ZONE
Customizing the Timescale	5		1	2	2
Creating a Custom Field	1	2		1	
Creating a Custom View	7	1	2	3	1
Creating a Custom Report	3	1	3		
Using the Organizer to Share Custom Views, Reports, and Calendars	6, 8, 9	1		4	
E-Mailing a Project File	4			5	
Routing a Project File	10	3	4		
Sending Schedule Note Messages	2		5		2

KEY TERMS

attachment	MAPI	schedule calculations
bottom tier	maps	schedule note message
combination view	middle tier	screen control
controls	modules	sheet view
count	Organizer	single view
crosstab report	recipient	table control
custom field	routing	top tier
filter control	routing slip	
group control		

CHECKING CONCEPTS AND TERMS

MULTIPLE CHOICE

Circle the letter of the correct answer for each of the following.

1. Which of the following does *not* happen when you create a lookup table for a custom field? [L2]

   a. Data entry is restricted.

   b. Accuracy of data entry is ensured.

   c. A wizard automatically generates a list of acceptable values.

   d. Data entry is consistent.

2. Which method of communicating a project plan would you use if you only want to include a small portion of a project plan? [L8]

   a. E-mail the project file

   b. Routing slip

   c. Scheduled note message

   d. Instant messaging

3. Which report type presents data in column and row format with totals? [L4]

   a. Task report

   b. Resource report

   c. Calendar report

   d. Crosstab report

4. What happens to a project file when you e-mail it? [L6]

   a. It is inserted as part of the message text.

   b. It is sent as an attachment to the e-mail message.

   c. A routing slip is attached to the project file.

   d. The project file becomes shared and changes from multiple users are incorporated.

5. What is the default setting for the timescale? [L1]

   a. Top tier = Week, Middle tier = Day, Bottom tier = Hour

   b. Middle tier = Week, Bottom tier = Day

   c. Middle tier = Day, Bottom tier = Hour

   d. Top tier = Year, Middle tier = Month, Bottom tier = Day

6. Why would you want to copy a custom report to the global file? [L5]

   a. It automatically appears in all existing projects.

   b. It is available in all new project files.

   c. It can be accessed in any Microsoft Project program because it becomes part of the software code.

   d. Copying it to the global file makes it accessible via the Web.

7. What is a combination view? [L3]

   a. A view that displays two projects at once.

   b. A view that displays tasks and costs at once.

   c. A view that displays one view in the left and one view on the right.

   d. A view that displays one view in the top of the window and one view in the bottom of the window.

8. Which of the following elements cannot be copied by using the Organizer? [L5]

   a. Views

   b. Reports

   c. Tasks

   d. Calendars

9. To which file does the Organizer allow you to copy project elements? [L5]

   a. Project.mpt

   b. Global.mpt

   c. Template.mpt

   d. Project1.mpp

10. Which method would you use if you wanted to receive feedback about your project file from a group of people? [L7]

   a. E-mail

   b. Routing

   c. Scheduled note

   d. Instant messaging

DISCUSSION

1. What are the benefits of being able to create a unique customized view or report? How does the Organizer enhance the benefits of creating these unique elements, and why would you make them available to the global template file? [L3, L4, L5]

2. Provide at least two examples of some unique custom fields that you could create in your own project plans and the purposes that they would serve. Include the field name and the type of field it would be: text, date, cost, and so on. [L2]

3. Describe a scenario where using the routing feature could help you incorporate feedback from other individuals involved with your project plan. Discuss why it might be better to route a file to each individual one at a time, rather than to multiple individuals all at once. [L7]

SKILL DRILL

Skill Drill exercises reinforce project skills. Each skill reinforced is the same, or nearly the same, as a skill presented in the project. Detailed instructions are provided in a step-by-step format. The exercises relate to a single file, and you should work them in order.

1. Modifying the Resource Usage View

As the fund-raiser coordinator of a local civic organization, you organize an auction each year as a fund-raiser for charity. From past experience, you know that a project plan is necessary to keep things running more smoothly. To make it easier to visualize the status of the project plan, you decide to modify the Resource Usage view to help you see the cost of all tasks completed by each resource.

To modify the Resource Usage view, follow these steps:

1. Open the *EPr1_0702* file, save it as Fundraiser_Auction, and then close any open side panes.

2. Choose <u>V</u>iew, <u>V</u>iew Bar, and then click Resource Usage.

3. Choose F<u>o</u>rmat, T<u>i</u>mescale.

4. Under *Middle tier formatting*, click the <u>U</u>nits drop-down arrow and select *Days*.

5. Click the <u>L</u>abel down arrow and choose the first option (*Mon Jan 28, '02*).

6. Click the Bottom Tier tab, click the <u>U</u>nits down arrow, and then select *Hours*.

7. Click the _Label_ down arrow, choose the third option (_1/28 11 AM_), and then click OK.

8. Choose Format, Detail Styles.

9. In the _Available fields_ list, select _Cost_ and then click the _Show_ button.

10. Click the _Cell background_ drop-down arrow, choose _Lime_, and then click OK.

11. Scroll horizontally to the right to view _Jan 2, 8 AM_.

12. Save _Fundraiser_Auction_ and leave it open for the next exercise.

2. Creating a Custom View

As you continue to work with the fund-raiser project plan, you determine you need a custom view. You need to view the work of each resource for each task.

To create a custom view, follow these steps:

1. Open _Fundraiser_Auction_, if necessary, and then click _More Views_ on the View Bar.

2. In the More Views dialog box, click Resource Allocation and then click _N_ew.

3. Click _S_ingle View, if necessary, and then click OK.

4. Specify the options for this view as shown in the following table and then click OK.

Name:	**Work by Resource**
S**c**reen:	Resource Usage
Table:	Work
Group:	No Group
Filter:	Resources - Work
H**i**ghlight filter:	Checked

5. Click _Apply_ in the More Views dialog box.

6. Scroll to see the work for the Auction Coordinator for January 1, 2006.

7. Scroll down to view the Copy Shop resource.

   Notice the Copy Shop is black text. It is not a work resource.

8. Save _Fundraiser_Auction_ and leave it open for the next exercise.

3. Creating a Custom Report

On at least a weekly basis, you must provide a report to organization leadership concerning the assignments given to each volunteer. You decide to create a custom report that lists the volunteers and their assignments. You also want to show what work has been completed on each task.

To create a _Resource Assignments_ report, follow these steps:

1. Open _Fundraiser_Auction_, if necessary, and then choose Report _R_eports.

2. Click _C_ustom, and then click _S_elect.

3. In the _Reports_ list, select _Resource (Material)_.

4. Click the _N_ew button.

5. Select _Resource_, and then click OK.

6. Specify the options for this report on the Definitions tab as follows:

<u>N</u>ame: **Resource Assignments**

<u>P</u>eriod: Months

<u>T</u>able: Entry - Work Resources

<u>F</u>ilter: All Resources

7. Click the Details tab.

8. Check the *Schedule* check box, and then click OK.

9. Click the Preview button.

10. Click within the report and view the data.

11. Click Close to exit without printing. (If you prefer to print, you can click the Print button to immediately start the print process at default settings.)

12. Click Close, and then click Close in the Reports dialog box.

13. Save *Fundraiser_Auction* and leave it open for the next exercise.

4. Routing a Project Plan

Now that the *Fundraiser_Auction* project plan is designed, you need to send it to the organization leaders and the volunteers. You expect to receive some feedback concerning the tasks and the schedule. The easiest way to do so is to route the file to all stakeholders.

To route the *Fundraiser_Auction* project plan, follow these steps:

1. Open *Fundraiser_Auction*, if necessary, and then choose <u>F</u>ile, Send To, <u>R</u>outing Recipient.

2. Click A<u>d</u>dress.

3. Select the first e-mail recipient from the list of names, click the *To* button, and then click OK.

4. In the *Message* text box, type **Please review the attached project plan and notify me of any changes you see that are necessary. Thanks for your input.**

5. Under *Route to recipients*, click A<u>ll</u> at once.

6. Check the *Return <u>w</u>hen done* check box.

7. Click <u>A</u>dd Slip.

8. Save *Fundraiser_Auction* and leave it open for the next exercise.

5. Sending Schedule Note Messages

You need to regularly send reminders to volunteers and leaders concerning their specific tasks. A note message is most appropriate in this case to highlight tasks that need attention. Now you want to send a copy of the advertisement tasks to the project manager.

To send a scheduled note message, follow these steps:

1. Open *Fundraiser_Auction*, if necessary, and then click *Gantt Chart* on the View Bar.

2. Highlight Tasks 25 (*Coordinate advertisements*) through 32 (*Distribute yard signs*).

3. Choose <u>F</u>ile, Send To, Mail Recipient (as Sc<u>h</u>edule Note).

4. Under *Address message to*, uncheck all boxes except *Project manager*.

5. Check *Picture of selected tasks*, if necessary, and then click OK.

6. Click in the *Subject* text box, and type **Auction advertisement.**

7. In the message area, type **Attached are the tasks necessary to properly advertise our auction fundraiser. Please be certain that each task is handled promptly. Thank you.**

8. Click Close and do not save your changes to the e-mail form.

9. Save *Fundraiser_Auction* and then close it.

CHALLENGE

Challenge exercises expand on or are somewhat related to skills presented in the lessons. Each exercise provides a brief narrative introduction, followed by instructions in a numbered-step format that are not as detailed as those in the Skill Drill section. The exercises relate to a single file, and you should work them in order.

1. Creating a Customized Calculated Field

You are an insurance claims processing specialist and a member of the Provider Information Maintenance System (PIMS) team. Your job is to assist the project manager by maintaining the deliverables of a software implementation in Microsoft Project. The PIMS team is testing and implementing a new software program to be used by your company. This software maintains data on physician records, Medicare, and procedure codes. The data and their accuracy are vital to how claims are processed. The project file is tracking a test upload of provider information in an effort to gather data on how long it should take the mainframe system and the claims processing specialists to review and clean up a data download of provider updates.

Now, you need to add a calculated custom field to determine which task items are over the budgeted amount of $100. To create a custom field, follow these steps:

1. Open *EPr1_0703*, save it as **PIMS**, and then close any side panes, if necessary.

2. Use Help to research custom calculated fields and how to use them.

3. Create a new custom field called **Cost Warning** using the Text1 field.

4. Click Formula in the Custom Fields dialog box.

5. In the Formula for 'Cost Warning' dialog box, click the Function button, point to General, and click *IIf(expression, truepart, falsepart)*.

   The formula is added to the *Cost Warning* = text box.

6. Double-click the word *expression*, click the Field button, point to *Cost*, and then point to *Cost* in the second column and click it.

7. Click the greater than symbol (>), and type **100**.

8. Double-click the word *truepart* and type **"Overbudget"** (making sure you include the quotation marks).

9. Double-click the word *falsepart* and type **"On Target"** (making sure you include the quotation marks).

The formula appears as *IIf([Cost]>100,"Overbudget","On Target")*

10. Click OK, click OK on the warning screen that appears, then click OK again to return to the Gantt chart.

11. Add the Text 1 (Cost Warning) field to the left of the Duration field in Gantt Chart view and then add the Cost field to the left of the Duration field as well.

Notice that for each item over $100 a message appears that the task is over budget, while the other tasks that are under $100 have a message stating the task is on target.

12. Save *PIMS* and leave it open for the next exercise.

2. Creating a Custom Crosstab Report

As you are working with the project plan, you decide you need to compare the tasks in the project to their costs. You need to know which tasks' costs are higher than a specified goal. You want to look at the tasks for this month only.

To create a custom crosstab report, follow these steps:

1. Open *PIMS* and close any side panes, if necessary.

2. Use Help to research the use of a crosstab query and how to create one.

3. Open the Reports dialog box and create a new report called **Costs Greater Than Specified Amount** based on the Crosstab report type.

4. Use Tasks and Cost for the row data and 1 month for the column data.

5. Use the Cost Greater Than filter, and include totals for the Row and Column data.

6. Preview the report, specify $150 when prompted, and then close it.

7. Save *PIMS* and leave it open for the next exercise.

3. Creating a Custom View That Includes Baseline and Progress Lines

In Lesson 3, you created a custom single view. Now you create a specific view that includes baseline data and progress lines to better track and compare the amount of time it is taking the new PIMS software to complete the tasks in this test run. A single view is not complete; thus you create a custom combination view.

To create a custom view, follow these steps:

1. Open *PIMS* and close any side panes, if necessary.

2. Create a new combination view and name it **Software Upgrade**.

3. The top portion of the view should display the Resource Usage view and the bottom portion of the view should display the Task Details Form.

4. Apply the view to the PIMS project plan.

5. Click on each specialist's name, view the Task Details Form portion of the view, and note how it changes.

6. Modify the view so that the top portion displays Task Usage and the Bottom portion of the view displays the Resource Sheet; then apply the view.

7. Switch to Gantt Chart view and remove the horizontal split bar.

8. Save *PIMS* and leave it open for the next exercise.

4. Copying Custom Views Using Organizer

You need to create a new custom view that includes progress lines and a modified timescale. You also want to copy this view to the global template so that it is available for all Microsoft Project files.

To create and copy a custom view, follow these steps:

1. Open *PIMS* and close any side panes, if necessary.

2. Move the split bar so that more of the Gantt chart is visible.

3. Create a new single view named **Software Progress** with the following options:

S<u>c</u>reen:	Gantt Chart
<u>T</u>able:	Summary
<u>G</u>roup:	No Group
<u>F</u>ilter:	All Tasks

4. Apply the view and modify the timescale so that the middle and bottom tiers of the Gantt chart units are expressed in days.

5. Add progress lines that are displayed in relation to the baseline.

6. Using the Organizer, copy the Software Progress view to the *Global.mpt* file.

7. Open any existing lesson file that you have already created; apply the Software Progress view to it; and then close the file without saving your changes.

8. Open the Organizer and remove the Software Progress view from the *Global.mpt* file.

9. Save *PIMS* and leave it open for the next exercise.

5. E-Mailing Resource Information

You would like to receive some input on the resources that are currently assigned to the PIMS project and plan to e-mail this information to the project manager. Because you need the project manager to review the entire project plan, you send the project file as an attachment to your inquiry e-mail.

To set up sending resource information via e-mail, follow these steps:

1. Open *PIMS* and close any side panes, if necessary.

2. View the Resource Sheet and select all of the resources.

3. Send the selected resources as a schedule note message to e-mail recipients.

4. Under *Address message to*, uncheck the *Resources* check box.

5. E-mail the highlighted resources as a picture.

6. In the body of the e-mail message form, type **Review Resource Assignment** as the subject.

7. In the message text box, type **Please review the attached picture and let me know if you think we should add people to the project team as I suspect the workload is becoming too great for some.**

8. Close the e-mail message without sending it and do not save the e-mail message.

9. Save *PIMS* and close the project file.

DISCOVERY ZONE

Discovery Zone exercises require advanced knowledge of topics presented in *Essentials* lessons, application of skills from multiple lessons, or self-directed learning of new skills. The exercises are independent of each other, so you may complete them in any order.

1. Researching View Help Topics on Microsoft Online

In this project, you have learned about custom views and other custom elements. You used both single views and combination views. Another important view to learn about is the Network Diagram view. Select Microsoft Office Project <u>H</u>elp from the <u>H</u>elp menu and click the *View Management* link. Click the *Available views* link and research the *Network Diagram* topic under *Task Views*. Again from *View management*, click the *Available groups* link and research task groups. Research other topics on views that look interesting to you.

2. Sending a Schedule Note of a PERT Analysis View

You have learned about different e-mail options that allow you to send the entire project file or certain pieces of it to mail recipients. In this exercise, you try working with a new view and sending a picture of it to the Project Manager. Type **PERT** in the *Type a question for help* box and look through the Help topics that appear. Open *EPr1_0702* and save it as **PERT**. Turn on the PERT Analysis toolbar and then click PERT Entry Sheet from the PERT toolbar and enter some optimistic, expected as well as pessimistic durations in the appropriate fields for some of the tasks. Select all the tasks and send them as a picture to the project manager, using the *Scheduled Note Message* option. When you get to the actual *Send* option in your e-mail program, save the message instead and close it without sending.

INTEGRATING PROJECT DATA

OBJECTIVES

IN THIS PROJECT, YOU LEARN HOW TO

- Import a task list from Excel

- Export task sheet information into an Excel worksheet

- Copy and paste a Gantt chart

- Link and embed Project data into Word and Excel

- Insert objects into task notes and add hyperlinks to tasks

- Use the Outlook address book to add resources

WHY WOULD I DO THIS?

Project data can be shared between Microsoft Project and other applications such as Microsoft Word, Excel, and PowerPoint. When you are creating new project files, some of the data you would like to use might be contained in another application file. Microsoft Project provides the tools that allow you to use information from other programs quite easily. The fact that you don't have to retype the data is a big time-saver and, more importantly, eliminates the chance of introducing typing errors. In addition to being able to use information from another application file, you can also share project data with other programs. This can be helpful when you would like to share information from your project file with other individuals, who might not have Microsoft Project on their system. Perhaps you would simply like to share a snapshot of a Gantt chart as a picture or present the task list in a Word document. Microsoft Project also provides menu options to easily share data contained in Microsoft Outlook. You can utilize the address book in Outlook to create your resource pool, including contact information such as e-mail addresses.

VISUAL SUMMARY

In this project, you are a member of an external consulting team that specializes in streamlining corporations to make them more cost-effective and efficient. Your team has been hired by a company that is in the process of reorganizing its corporate management staff in an effort to improve internal processes. The project file you are using is in the final stages of creation. Tasks have been entered, but you need to add more. Resources have not yet been entered or assigned to tasks and no work progress has been entered. Your efforts in this project file include importing and exporting task sheet data, linking and embedding data with other programs so that it can be used in new ways, and adding resources from Microsoft Outlook. You use the Export Wizard and use a map to transfer data between Microsoft Project and Microsoft Excel. Also, you copy and paste the Gantt chart into an Excel worksheet, link the task sheet to a Word document so that it automatically updates, embed a pie graph into the project file, and import contacts from the Outlook address book into the resource sheet (see Figure 8.1).

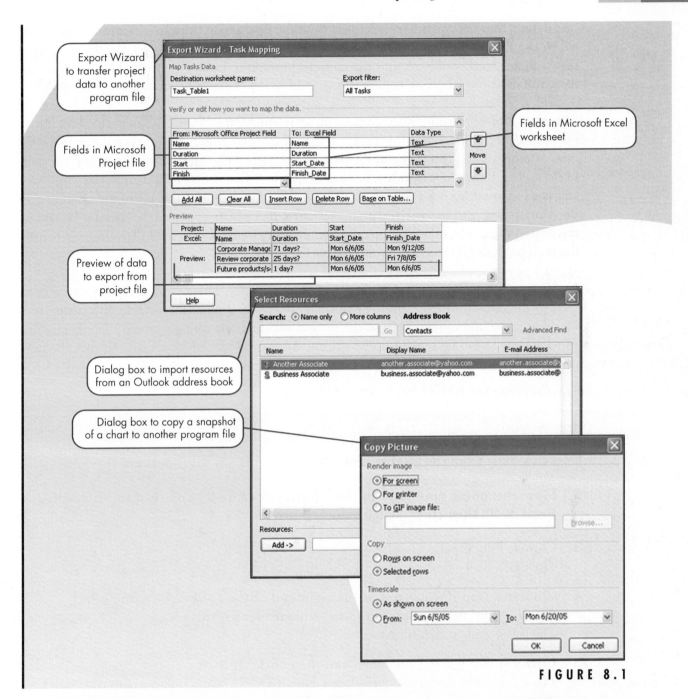

FIGURE 8.1

LESSON 1:   Importing a Task List from Excel

Generally, a project plan involves a group of resources working toward the same goal. That being the case, it is possible that some project data have been entered into another application file by one team player and could easily be imported into the project file. To ***import*** data into Microsoft Project means transferring the data from another application file into Microsoft Project. Importing data is a useful feature that can save you quite a bit of time because you can recycle information without having to type it again. Importing also eliminates the chance of making typos. To import data, you utilize a ***map,*** which is a set of instructions that defines the data you import, the order, and the destination fields in Microsoft Project into which the data will be imported. For example, you might have a list of tasks that you have stored in an Excel workbook and the column heading is Task. When you import the Excel data, you must map the Task column from Excel to the Name column in Microsoft Project.

Microsoft Project provides three choices for importing data. You can import the data into a new blank project file. Doing so makes creating the initial project file quicker and more accurate. Another option is to *append* the data to the active file—meaning that you add the data to the end of the active project file. For example, a list of tasks may exist in an Excel worksheet and need to be added to an existing project file. You could append this list to the task table. A third alternative is to *merge* the data to the active file, which also adds the data to the end of the active project file. However, merging requires a *primary key* (a field that uniquely identifies each task) and for that reason this option is not used very often.

In this lesson, you first view a worksheet in Microsoft Excel. Then, you use the Import Wizard to map the data from Excel into Microsoft Project and append the data to an existing file. Merging is not appropriate because the project file does not contain primary key fields. You conclude the lesson by making some editing changes to the imported data so that the new information flows smoothly with the existing data already in the task table.

To Import a Task List from Excel

1 Click Start from the taskbar and move the mouse to All Programs.

2 Move the mouse pointer to the Microsoft Office folder and then to Microsoft Excel 2010; then click the left mouse button.

3 Choose File, Open.
The Open dialog box opens.

4 Click the drop-down arrow at the right end of the *Look in* box, and select the drive and folder containing the student files for this text.
The list of student data files displays.

5 Click the *EPr1_0801* filename, and then click Open.
The *EPr1_0801* workbook opens (see Figure 8.2). The workbook contains only one sheet of data, with a list of tasks. When importing data, it is not necessary for the source and destination files to reside in the same folder.

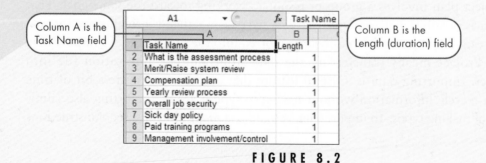

FIGURE 8.2

6 Choose File, Save As; then navigate to the location of your solution files, click in the *File name* text box, type Assessment, and then click Save.

7 View the data contained in the Excel worksheet.

There are two column headings in this worksheet: Task Name and Length. Typically, data in an Excel worksheet include column headings to provide a description for the data within that column. These headings become field names when imported into a project file.

8 Choose File, Close and then minimize the Excel program.

Microsoft Excel is minimized and resides on the taskbar. You keep it open to use it in several other lessons in this project.

9 Start Microsoft Project, open the *EPr1_0802* file, save it as Mgmt_Review, and then close any open side panes.

10 Choose Tools, Options, click on the Security tab, and select Allow loading files with legacy or non default file formats in the Legacy Formats section (see Figure 8.3).

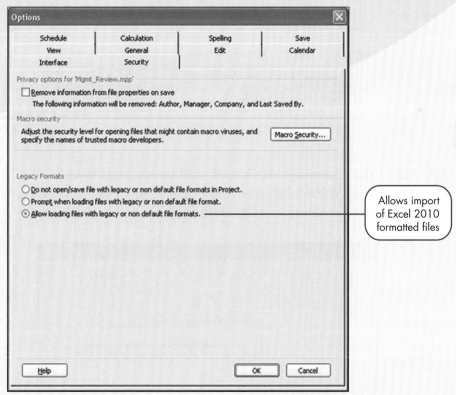

FIGURE 8.3

11 Click OK to close the Options dialog box.

12 **Choose File, Open.**

The Open dialog box opens.

13 **Click the *Files of type* drop-down arrow, select *Microsoft Excel Workbooks*, and then navigate to the folder where your solution files are located.**

The list of files changes to display only Excel (97-2003 format) workbooks (see Figure 8.4).

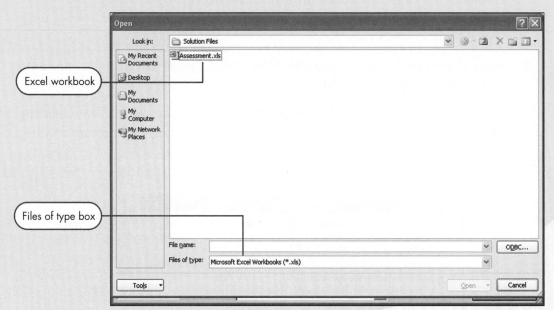

FIGURE 8.4

14 **Select the *Assessment* workbook and then click Open.**

The Import Wizard dialog box opens (see Figure 8.5). This dialog box is the first of several steps designed to walk you through importing data.

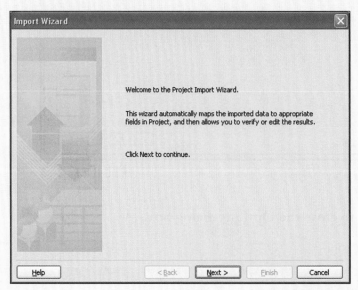

FIGURE 8.5

15 **Click Next.**
The Import Wizard – Map dialog box opens (see Figure 8.6).

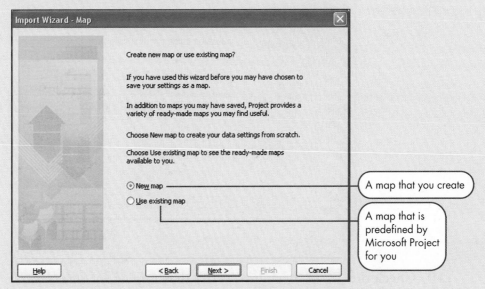

FIGURE 8.6

16 **Click the *New map* option, if necessary, and then click Next.**
The Import Wizard – Import Mode dialog box opens (see Figure 8.7).

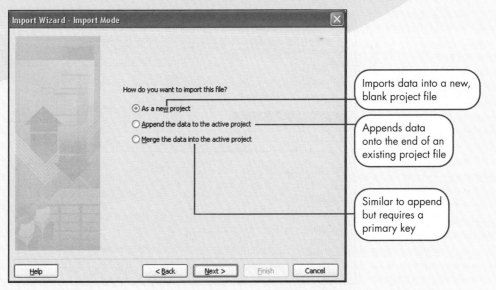

FIGURE 8.7

17 **Click the *Append the data to the active project* option, and then click Next.**
The Import Wizard – Map Options dialog box opens (see Figure 8.8).

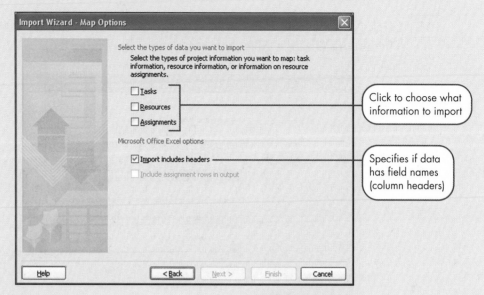

FIGURE 8.8

18 Check the *Tasks* check box, verify that *Import includes headers* is also selected, and then click **N**ext.

The Import Wizard – Task Mapping dialog box opens (see Figure 8.9).

FIGURE 8.9

19 Click the *Source worksheet name* drop-down arrow and choose **Sheet1**, which is a worksheet in the *Assignment* workbook.

The dialog box updates, showing the columns of data contained in the Excel worksheet along with the corresponding Microsoft Project field to which they will be mapped, in an area called the *mapping grid* (see Figure 8.10).

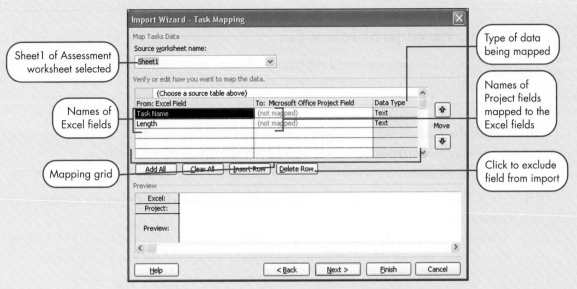

FIGURE 8.10

20 **In the mapping grid, click the Task Name field under** *To: Microsoft Office Project Field.*
A drop-down arrow appears in the Microsoft Office Project field box.

21 **Click the drop-down arrow, scroll down the list, and choose** *Name.*
Now the *Task Name* Excel field is mapped to the *Name* Microsoft Office Project field.

22 **Click in the Length field under** *To: Microsoft Office Project Field,* **click the drop-down arrow, scroll down the list, and then choose** *Duration.*
The Import Wizard–Task Mapping dialog box now should look like Figure 8.11.

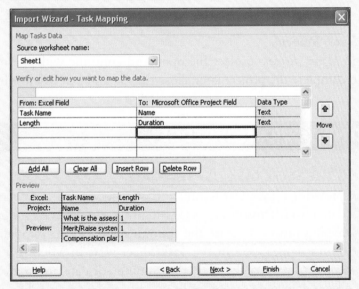

FIGURE 8.11

23 **Click** *Next* **and then click** *Finish.*
The eight tasks from the Excel worksheet are appended to the bottom of the task table in the project file.

If you have problems . . .

Sometimes blank rows precede the imported data. If so, highlight the blank rows and press Del.

---

24 **Highlight Task 27 (*Merit/Raise system review*) through Task 33 (*Management involvement/control*) and click Indent on the Formatting toolbar.**

The selected tasks become subtasks for Summary Task 26 (*What is the assessment process*).

25 **Click Task 26 (*What is the assessment process*) and click Outdent on the Formatting toolbar.**

Summary Task 26 and its subtasks are promoted to become subtasks of Task 1 (*Corporate Management Review*). The *Mgmt_Review* project file should look like Figure 8.12.

	ⓘ	Task Name	Duration	Start	Fi
20		Review function	20 days?	Mon 7/11/05	F
21		Review manage	5 days?	Mon 8/8/05	Fri
22		Determine how	20 days	Mon 8/15/05	F
23		⊟ Functional division	30 days?	Mon 6/6/05	Fri
24		Identify job cata	10 days?	Mon 6/6/05	Fri
25		Review manage	20 days?	Mon 6/20/05	Fri
26		⊟ What is the assess	1 day	Mon 6/6/05	Mo
27		Merit/Raise syst	1 day	Mon 6/6/05	Mo
28		Compensation p	1 day	Mon 6/6/05	Mo
29		Yearly review p	1 day	Mon 6/6/05	Mo
30		Overall job secu	1 day	Mon 6/6/05	Mo
31		Sick day policy	1 day	Mon 6/6/05	Mo
32		Paid training pro	1 day	Mon 6/6/05	Mo
33		Management inv	1 day	Mon 6/6/05	Mo

Imported tasks

FIGURE 8.12

26 **Save *Mgmt_Review*.**

Keep the *Mgmt_Review* project file open and continue with the next lesson. If you prefer to complete the project later, close the file and exit Microsoft Project.

TO EXTEND YOUR KNOWLEDGE . . .

USING THE EXCEL TASK LIST TEMPLATE

Excel provides a Task List template that is set up for the purpose of importing Excel data into Microsoft Project. Using this template takes the guesswork out of the mapping process because the column names in the template are the same as the column names used in the Task Sheet view in Microsoft Project. When it comes time to import the data, the columns of data automatically map because the column names are the same. To use the template, open Excel 2010 and choose File, New. Click on *Sample Templates* and then double-click the Microsoft Project Plan Import Export Template to create a new blank file with columns that correspond to the default task sheet columns in Gantt Chart view. Within this template, there are individual worksheets for each portion of a project file, including Task_Table, Resource_Table, Assignment_Table, and Info_Table.

USING AN EXISTING MAP
Microsoft Project also provides preexisting maps that you can use when importing data. These predefined maps fit specific and unique situations. The import process is the same as in the lesson, except you would choose _Use existing map_ in the Import Wizard. Some types of import maps include but are not limited to "Who Does What" Report, Default task information, Earned value information, and others.

LESSON 2: Exporting Task Sheet Information into an Excel Worksheet

To **export** data means that you transfer data from Microsoft Project to another software program. Exporting enables you to place project data into another application format, such as an Excel worksheet or Word document or even an Access database. This feature is useful for simply sharing the data in another file format or using the data for another purpose. For example, there might be information in the Microsoft Project task sheet that you want to use in an end-of-year report done in Microsoft Excel. Rather than retype the tasks, you can simply export them into the report. Maps are also used when exporting data from Microsoft Project and provide you with the opportunity to pick and choose the specific fields you want to export. Programs that support exported information from Microsoft Office Project 2007 include Microsoft Excel (as a workbook or PivotTable), another Microsoft Project file, Microsoft Access Database (MDB), and other Open Database Connectivity (ODBC) database programs. **ODBC** programs are compliant database formats that Microsoft supports. In addition, you can export data into **Extensible Markup Language (XML)** format, which allows you to publish Project 2007 data onto web pages, or the **Comma Separated Values (CSV)** format, which is a file format in which fields are separated by commas or semicolons.

In this lesson, you use the Export Wizard to map the columns in the task table that you want to export to Microsoft Excel. Then, you start Excel and view the data that you exported.

To Export Task Sheet Information into Excel

1 Open _Mgmt_Review_, if necessary, and close any open side panes.

2 Deselect any selected group of tasks, if necessary, and then choose _File_, Save _As_.
The Save As dialog box opens.

3 Navigate to the location of your solution files.

4 Click the _Save as type_ drop-down arrow and choose _Microsoft Excel Workbook (*.xls)_.
Only Excel workbooks are listed now, and a suggested filename is given for the file you are saving (see Figure 8.13), which is the same as the project filename. Note that Project 2007 does not export to Excel 2007-2010 format (*.xlsx).

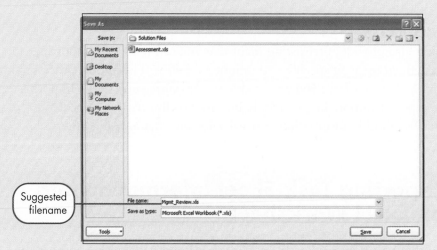

Suggested filename

FIGURE 8.13

---

5 | Click in the *File name* text box after the *w* in *Review* and type **_Export** so the filename is *Mgmt_Review_Export*; then click **S**ave.

The Excel file is saved as *Mgmt_Review_Export* and the Welcome screen for the Export Wizard dialog box opens.

6 | Click **N**ext.

The Export Wizard – Data dialog box opens.

7 | Verify that the *Selected Data* option button is selected; then click **N**ext.

The Export Wizard – Map dialog box opens (see Figure 8.14).

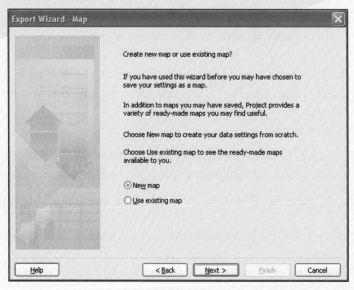

FIGURE 8.14

8 | Click the *New map* option button and then click **N**ext.

The Export Wizard – Map Options dialog box opens.

9 Check the _Tasks_ check box, verify that _Export includes headers_ is also selected, and then click _Next_.

The Export Wizard – Task Mapping dialog box opens and should appear as shown in Figure 8.15.

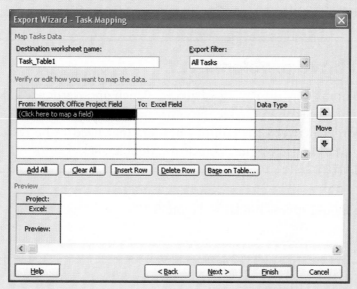

FIGURE 8.15

10 Click in the first cell under _From: Microsoft Office Project Field_.

11 Click the drop-down arrow in the cell, scroll down the list, select _Name_ from the list, and then press ⏎Enter.

The Name field is inserted into the _From: Microsoft Office Project Field_ column and is automatically added to the _To: Excel Field_ column. The data type is automatically set.

12 Continue adding fields as shown in Figure 8.16.

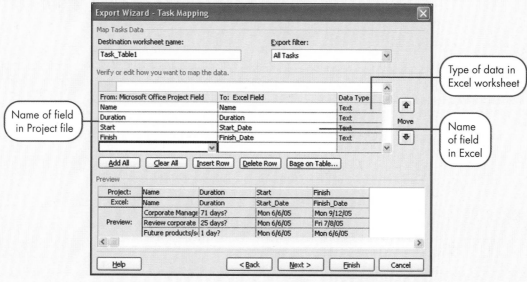

FIGURE 8.16

13 Click <u>N</u>ext and then click <u>F</u>inish.

14 Minimize Microsoft Project, and maximize Excel from the taskbar.

15 Choose File, Open; navigate to the location where your solution files are saved and select the *Mgmt_Review_Export* Excel file; then click <u>O</u>pen.

If you have problems . . .

Some columns may display crosshatches, which are overflow markers. You may also need to resize the column to see the entire name in all the columns. Move your mouse to the border between the column headers that need to be resized, and when the mouse appears as a left-right sizing arrow, double-click.

Your file should appear similar to Figure 8.17.

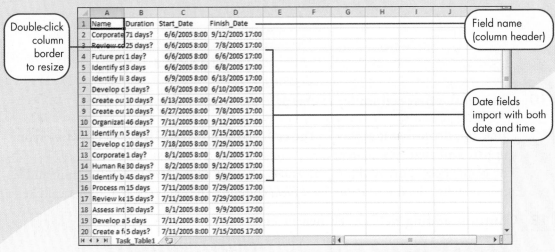

Double-click column border to resize

Field name (column header)

Date fields import with both date and time

FIGURE 8.17

16 Choose File, Close; save any changes; and minimize Excel.

If you have problems . . .

A warning box may appear concerning the Excel file version. If so, click Yes to save the file with the latest Excel file format and continue.

17 **On the taskbar, restore your project file and then save the file.**
Keep the *Mgmt_Review* project file open and continue with the next lesson. If you prefer to complete the project later, close the file and exit Microsoft Project.

LESSON 3:   Copying and Pasting a Gantt Chart

Sharing a Gantt chart with another program can be difficult because the charts tend to be oversized and often do not fit well in some file formats. It may require trial and error to get the result that you want. By default, when you choose to copy a Gantt chart, the procedure captures only what you see on the screen rather than the entire chart. You can modify this default by copying a range of tasks and specifying the begin and end dates for the timescale of the Gantt chart to capture exactly what you need. You are provided three options on how you would like to **render** the image, or capture the picture of the Gantt chart. You can choose *For screen*, which means the Clipboard captures the picture and it becomes something that you can use Edit, Paste to insert into the other program. *For printer* means it will go directly to your printer, and *To GIF image file* means that the image will be saved as a **Graphics Interchange Format (GIF)** file, a bitmapped graphics file format used by the World Wide Web.

In this lesson, you select a range of rows and specify a timescale for the Gantt chart. Then you copy it, using the *For screen* option. After you have copied the image, you paste it into a Microsoft Excel worksheet.

To Copy and Paste a Gantt Chart

1 **Open *Mmgt_Review*, if necessary, and close any open side panes.**

2 **On the Gantt chart, point to the Task 1 (*Corporate Management Review*) Gantt bar and view the Summary ScreenTip.**
Note the start date of *Mon 6/6/05* and the finish date of *Mon 9/12/05* (see Figure 8.18).

	ⓘ	Task Name	Duration	Start	Finish	Predecessors	Jun 5, '05	Jun 12, '05	Jun 1
							S M T W T F S	S M T W T F S	S M
1		⊟ Corporate Managemen	71 days?	Mon 6/6/05	Mon 9/12/05				
2		⊟ Review corporate	25 days?	Mon 6/6/05	Fri 7/8			Summary	
3		Future products	1 day?	Mon 6/6/05	Mon 6/6	Task: Corporate Management Review		
4		Identify stakehol	3 days	Mon 6/6/05	Wed 6/8	Start: Mon 6/6/05 Duration: 71d		
5		Identify lines of	3 days	Thu 6/9/05	Mon 6/13/05	4	Finish: Mon 9/12/05		
6		Develop core vs	5 days?	Mon 6/6/05	Fri 6/10/05				
7		Create outline fc	10 days?	Mon 6/13/05	Fri 6/24/05	6			
8		Create outline fc	10 days?	Mon 6/27/05	Fri 7/8/05	7			

FIGURE 8.18

3 In the task table, select Task 1 (*Corporate Management Review*) through Task 33 (*Management involvement/control*) to select all the tasks.

4 Choose Report, Copy Picture.
The Copy Picture dialog box opens (see Figure 8.19).

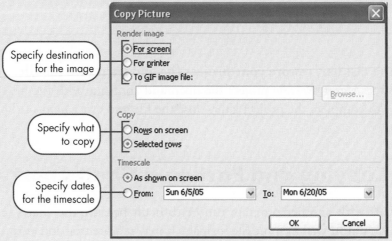

FIGURE 8.19

5 Under *Copy*, choose *Selected rows*, if necessary.

6 Under *Timescale*, choose the *From* option button.

7 Click the calendar drop-down arrow for the *From* date, and choose *Tue 6/28/05*.

8 Choose *Mon 9/12/05* as the *To* date.
Now the start and finish dates are selected for the Gantt chart to be copied to Excel (see Figure 8.20).

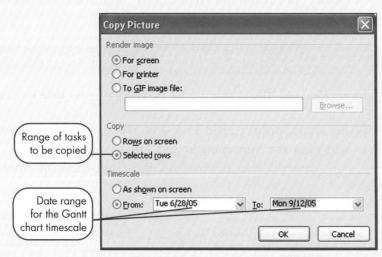

FIGURE 8.20

9 Click OK.

10 From the taskbar, maximize Microsoft Excel, choose File, New, and then double-click *Blank workbook*.
A blank workbook opens in Excel.

11 On the *Home* tab, in the *Clipboard* group, click *Paste*.
The entire Gantt chart along with a portion of the task sheet is pasted as an image into Excel (see Figure 8.21).

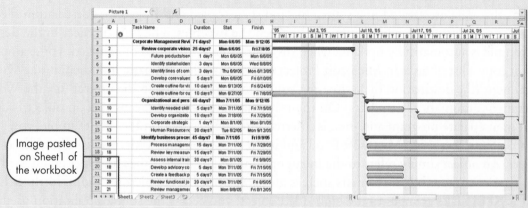

Image pasted on Sheet1 of the workbook

FIGURE 8.21

12 Choose File, Save As, and navigate to the location where your solution files are saved.

13 Click in the *File name* text box, and type `Gantt_Chart`.

14 Click **S**ave.

15 Close the Excel workbook and exit Microsoft Excel, and then restore Microsoft Project from the taskbar, if necessary.
Keep the *Mgmt_Review* project file open and continue with the next lesson. If you prefer to complete the project later, close the file and exit Microsoft Project.

LESSON 4: Linking and Embedding Project Data into Word and Excel

At times it is helpful to share data between files or even between programs called the source and destination files. The **source file** is where the data originate, and the **destination file** is where the data are pasted. Most commonly, people copy and paste data to share information. This method works fine unless the data have the potential to change.

Two other methods are available for sharing data: linking and embedding. To **paste link** means that data are created in a source file and then copied and linked in a destination file; a connection is automatically maintained between the two files. The linked object in the destination file is automatically updated when the source file is modified or changed. For example, if you copy a list of tasks in Microsoft Project (the source file) and paste link them into a Word document (the destination file), any time you change the task list in the project file, the Word document automatically updates. On the other hand, to **embed** means that an object is created in a separate program and then is inserted into the destination file. For example, you can create a bar graph using Microsoft Excel and insert the graph into a Microsoft Project file as an object. An **object** simply refers to the menu option used to insert other file types and describes any type of compatible file formats such as an Excel worksheet, a picture, and so forth. When you need to make changes to the embedded object, you access the source application used to create the object by double-clicking the object in the destination file. In doing so, you can access commands from the source application from within the destination file and make changes. Any changes you make to the embedded object are automatically reflected in the destination file.

Together, these sharing methods are called **Object Linking and Embedding (OLE),** which is a program-integration technology that you can use to share information between programs. All Microsoft Office programs support OLE, so you can share information through linked and embedded objects. Including objects such as pictures, charts, and other graphical images can give views or reports a finished look. They can clarify or enhance information as well as draw attention to a particular item you want to highlight. An obvious question is when to use linking and when to use embedding. Because a linked object changes each time its source changes, you would use linking for volatile information. For example, you might maintain monthly sales data in an Excel worksheet. You could then communicate that data to certain personnel through a memo or letter, including an excerpt of the worksheet. Obviously, the sales data change each month and those changes must be reflected in the monthly communication. On the other hand, you would use embedding if the data are not likely to change. For example, you might include a chart from Excel in an annual report created in Word. Data contained in an annual report are constant and not likely to change, so embedding is a good choice. Embedding is also the best choice when you want to include an object from another application, such as a graph, a sound file, or a video.

In this lesson, you link the task sheet data with a Microsoft Word document and view how the data automatically update in Word when you change information in the project file. You also embed a pie chart that was created in Microsoft Excel in the Milestone Date Rollup view in Microsoft Project. Then, you double-click the graph to launch the Microsoft Excel program and make a change to the color of the area surrounding the pie graph.

To Link Project Data with Word

1 | Open *Mgmt_Review*, if necessary, and close any open side panes.
The *Mgmt_Review* file is the source file in this linking scenario.

2 | Move the mouse to the Task Name column header and when it appears as a small, black down-pointing arrow, click and drag right to select the Duration, Start, and Finish columns.
The four columns are selected (see Figure 8.22).

FIGURE 8.22

3 | Choose Edit, Copy Cell.

4 | Click Start on the taskbar; point to All Programs, Microsoft Office; and then click Microsoft Word 2010.
Microsoft Word opens with a blank document, which serves as the destination file for this exercise.

5 | On the *Home* tab, in the *Clipboard* group, click the *Paste* down-arrow and then click *Paste Special*.
The Paste Special dialog box opens (see Figure 8.23).

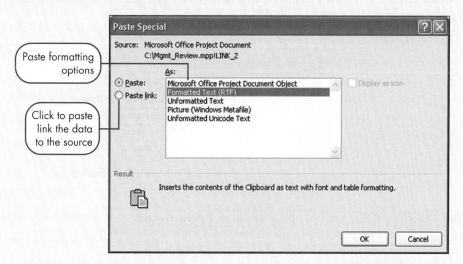

FIGURE 8.23

6 | Click the *Paste link* option button, and verify that *Formatted Text (RTF)* is selected in the *As* list box.

7 | Click OK.

The contents of the project file are paste linked and pasted into Microsoft Word, using the ***rich text format (RTF)*** format, a file type used to transfer formatted text documents between applications. Your document should look like Figure 8.24.

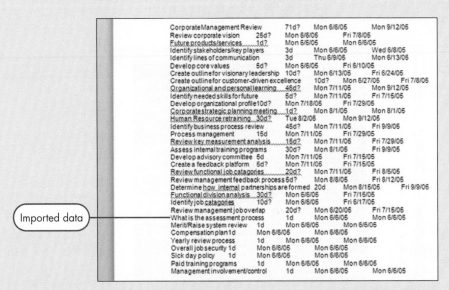

Imported data

FIGURE 8.24

8 | Choose File, Save As; then navigate to the location of your solution files, name the Word file `Linked_Mgmt_Review`, and then click Save.

9 | Minimize Word; then restore the *Mgmt_Review* project file from the taskbar, if necessary.

10 | Click Task 2 (*Review corporate vision*).

The Task 2 text now appears in the Edit bar above the column headings.

11 | Double-click the word *vision* in the Edit bar, type `plan`, and then click Enter

The change is made (see Figure 8.25).

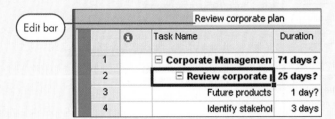

Edit bar

FIGURE 8.25

12 | Save the *Mgmt_Review* project file and minimize it.

13 **From the taskbar, restore Microsoft Word and look at the** *Linked_Mgmt_Review* **document.**

Task 2 was automatically updated in the document (see Figure 8.26). Changes in the source file are reflected in the destination file when a paste link exists between them.

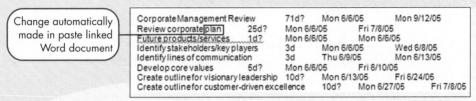

Change automatically
made in paste linked
Word document

Corporate Management Review	71d?	Mon 6/6/05	Mon 9/12/05
Review corporate plan	25d?	Mon 6/6/05	Fri 7/8/05
Future products/services	1d?	Mon 6/6/05	Mon 6/6/05
Identify stakeholders/key players	3d	Mon 6/6/05	Wed 6/8/05
Identify lines of communication	3d	Thu 6/9/05	Mon 6/13/05
Develop core values	5d?	Mon 6/6/05	Fri 6/10/05
Create outline for visionary leadership	10d?	Mon 6/13/05	Fri 6/24/05
Create outline for customer-driven excellence	10d?	Mon 6/27/05	Fri 7/8/05

FIGURE 8.26

14 **Choose File, Exit, and save the** *Linked_Mgmt_Review* **Word document.**

Microsoft Word closes along with the *Linked_Mgmt_Review* Word document.

15 **From the taskbar, restore the** *Mgmt_Review* **project file.**

You have learned how to paste link information from Microsoft Project to Microsoft Word. In the next set of steps, you embed a Microsoft Excel graph into the project file.

To Embed Excel Data in Microsoft Project

1 **Choose** <u>V</u>**iew,** <u>M</u>**ore Views, Milestone Date Rollup, and then click Apply.**

2 **Slide the horizontal scroll button in the Gantt Chart all the way to the left.**

The screen quickly moves to the status date of June 6, '05.

3 **Choose Insert,** <u>O</u>**bject.**

The Insert Object dialog box opens (see Figure 8.27).

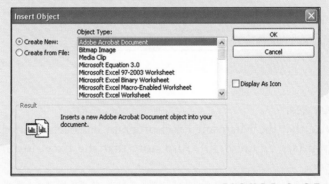

FIGURE 8.27

4 Click the *Create from File* option button.

5 Click the Browse button and navigate to the location where your student files are saved.

6 Select the *EPr1_0803* file, and click Insert.

7 Click OK in the Insert Object dialog box.

The worksheet with the pie graph is inserted into the Gantt chart area of the Milestone Date Rollup view (see Figure 8.28). The *Mgmt_Review* file is the destination file, and the *EPr1_0803* Excel file is the source file in this embedding scenario.

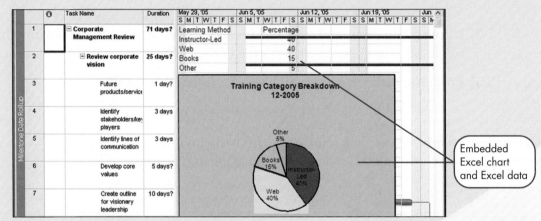

FIGURE 8.28

8 Click Save.

9 Double-click the embedded pie graph.

A message displays warning that you are about to activate an OLE object (see Figure 8.29).

FIGURE 8.29

10 Click Yes.

Notice that the Microsoft Excel program has been opened, as indicated by the Excel ribbon (see Figure 8.30). Also note that the Excel formula bar displays below the ribbon.

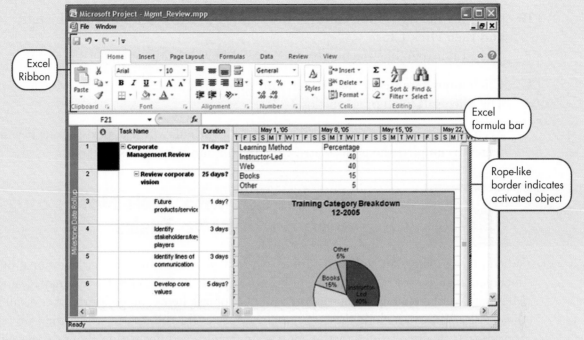

FIGURE 8.30

11 **Double-click on the gray area around the pie chart and then click on the Fill Color drop-down arrow.**

The Format Chart Area dialog box opens with the color options displayed (see Figure 8.31).

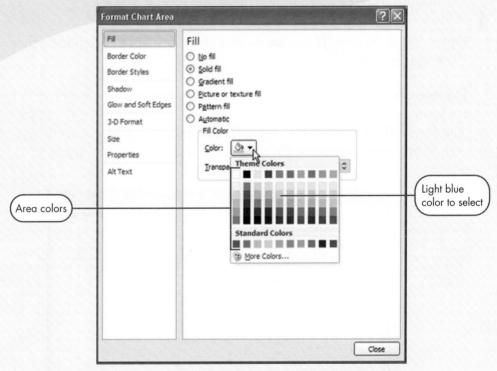

FIGURE 8.31

12 **Click on the light blue color in the third row, fifth column from the left, and then click Close.**
The area surrounding the pie chart is now light blue instead of gray.

13 **Click anywhere in the task sheet, and then click Save.**
The Microsoft Excel program closes.

Keep the *Mgmt_Review* project file open and continue with the next lesson. If you prefer to complete the project later, close the file and exit Microsoft Project.

LESSON 5: Inserting Objects into Task Notes and Adding Hyperlinks to Tasks

When project plans start to become more involved, you often find that an additional body of documentation is created around the project to support it. For example, you may have several Microsoft Word documents that support a number of task items and go into further detail about those tasks. You can include these documents as notes for the task to which they are related. Spreadsheets are often created that might have more detailed information about the overall project budget. All this information can be attached to your project file by using the Notes and Hyperlink features. A *hyperlink* is a clickable word or picture that opens another file.

In this lesson, you insert a Microsoft PowerPoint slide as a note object for a task. You also add a hyperlink to a task that opens a Microsoft Word document.

To Insert Objects into Task Notes

1 **Open *Mmgt_Review*, if necessary, and close any open side panes; then choose View, Gantt chart.**

2 **Double-click Summary Task 9 (*Organizational and personal learning*) and click the Notes tab.**
The Notes tab of the Summary Task Information dialog box contains several commands for formatting text and inserting objects into a note (see Figure 8.32).

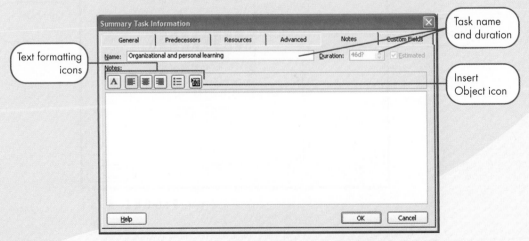

FIGURE 8.32

3 | Click the Insert Object button.
The Insert Object dialog box opens.

4 | Click the *Create from File* option button.

5 | Click Browse and navigate to the folder where your student files are located.

6 | Select the *EPr1_0804* PowerPoint file and click Insert.

7 | Click OK.
The contents of the PowerPoint file are inserted as a task note (see Figure 8.33).

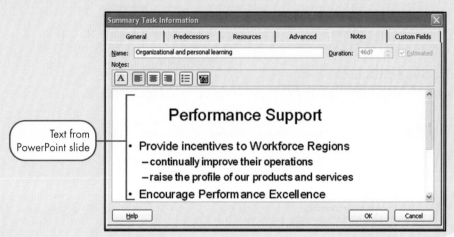

FIGURE 8.33

8 | Click OK.
A note icon appears in the Indicator column.

9 | Select Summary Task 26 (*What is the assessment process*), and then choose Insert, Hyperlink.
The Insert Hyperlink dialog box appears (see Figure 8.34).

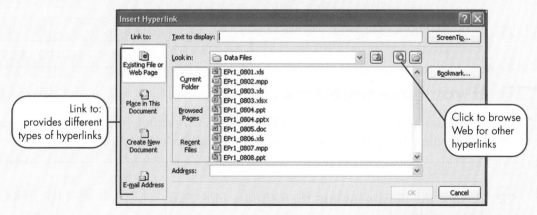

FIGURE 8.34

10 Using the Look in drop-down list, navigate to where your student files are located, select the *EPr1_0805* document, and then click OK.

A hyperlink icon appears in the Indicator column (see Figure 8.35).

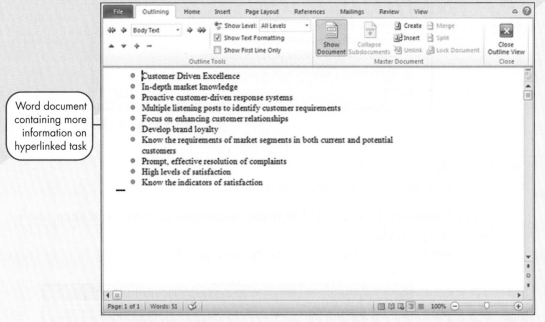

FIGURE 8.35

11 Click the hyperlink icon.

The Microsoft Word document *EPr1_0805* opens (see Figure 8.36).

FIGURE 8.36

If you have problems . . .

If you utilize security measures on the computer, a warning dialog box may appear. If the warning dialog box appears now, simply click Yes to continue.

12 Review the document and then choose File, Exit.

Microsoft Word closes.

13 Save *Mgmt_Review*.

Keep the *Mgmt_Review* project file open and continue with the next lesson. If you prefer to complete the project later, close the file and exit Microsoft Project.

LESSON 6: Using the Outlook Address Book to Add Resources

Most of us utilize an e-mail program to process a good percentage of our day-to-day work. We send and receive e-mails. We maintain names, addresses, e-mail addresses, and phone numbers in our Outlook contacts file. Some of us use the Appointment feature to keep track of meetings and other events. If you have Microsoft Outlook, Microsoft Outlook Express, or Microsoft Outlook Exchange installed on your company server, you can add resources to your project plan from the e-mail address book. Doing so saves you time because you do not need to retype information in the resource sheet. However, the only address book that Microsoft Project can utilize is the Outlook address book.

In this lesson, you add the Email Address column to the Resource Sheet view. Then, you add resources from Microsoft Outlook to the resource sheet.

To Add Resources from Microsoft Outlook

1 Open *Mmgt_Review*, if necessary, and close any open side panes; then choose **V̲iew, Resource S̲heet.**
The Resource Sheet view displays.

2 Right-click the Type column header and choose Insert C̲olumn.
The Column Definition dialog box opens.

3 Select *Email Address* from the *Field n̲ame* drop-down list, and then click OK.
The Email Address column is inserted to the left of the Type column (see Figure 8.37).

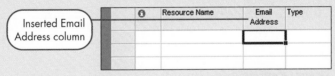

FIGURE 8.37

4 Choose I̲nsert, New Resource Fro̲m, Address B̲ook.
The Select Resources dialog box appears (see Figure 8.38).

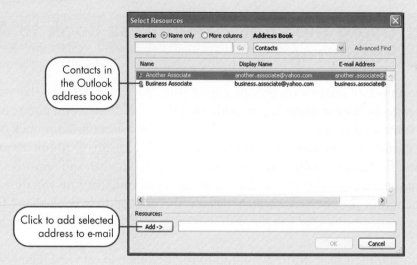

Contacts in the Outlook address book

Click to add selected address to e-mail

FIGURE 8.38

5 From the *Name* list, click the first resource you want to add and then click the Add button.

6 Click the second resource you want to add in the *Name* list box, and then click Add.
Repeat as needed until all the resources you need have been added.

7 Click OK.
The resources you added along with their e-mail addresses are be inserted into the Resource sheet, similar to Figure 8.39.

Imported resources

	ⓘ	Resource Name	Email Address	Type	Material Label	Initials	Group	Max. Units	Std. Rate	Ovt. Rate	
		Another Associate (a yahoo.com)		Work		A		100%	$0.00/hr	$0.00/hr	
2		Business Associate (yahoo.com)		Work		B		100%	$0.00/hr	$0.00/hr	

FIGURE 8.38

8 Save *Mmgt_Review* and close it.

SUMMARY

In this project, you learned how Microsoft Project shares information with other software programs. A task list was imported from Excel and appended to an already existing file. From the default Gantt Chart view, the task sheet was exported from Microsoft Project into an Excel worksheet. You linked task sheet data with a Microsoft Word document and saw how the data automatically update when changes are made in the original file. A pie chart created in an Excel worksheet was incorporated into the Milestone Data Rollup view in Project. The Insert Object button in the Notes tab of the Task Information dialog box was investigated. You learned how to add objects into a note and how to add a hyperlink to a task. Finally, you learned how to import resources from Microsoft Outlook into the resource sheet.

You can extend your learning by reviewing concepts and terms and by practicing variations of skills presented in the lessons. Use the following table as a guide to the numbered questions and exercises in the end-of-project learning opportunities.

LESSON	MULTIPLE CHOICE	DISCUSSION	SKILL DRILL	CHALLENGE	DISCOVERY ZONE
Importing a Task List from Excel	1, 4, 9	3	1	1	1
Exporting Task Sheet Information into an Excel Worksheet	8, 10	3	2	2	
Copying and Pasting a Gantt Chart	7	1		3	
Linking and Embedding Project Data into Word and Excel	2, 5	1, 2		4	
Inserting Objects into Task Notes and Adding Hyperlinks to Tasks	6	1	3		
Using the Outlook Address Book to Add Resources	3		4		2

KEY TERMS

append

Comma Separated Values (CSV)

destination file

embed

export

Extensible Markup Language (XML)

Graphics Interchange Format (GIF)

hyperlink

import

map

mapping grid

merge

object

Object Linking and Embedding (OLE)

Open Database Connectivity (ODBC)

paste link

primary key

render

rich text format (RTF)

source file

CHECKING CONCEPTS AND TERMS

MULTIPLE CHOICE

Circle the letter of the correct answer for each of the following.

1. Which of the following is not specified when creating a map to append Excel data to a project file? [L1]

   a. To and From fields

   b. Worksheet name

   c. Filters

   d. Primary key

2. Which method would you use if you need two programs to create a file but only want one file to maintain? [L4]

   a. Copy and paste

   b. Embed

   c. Link

   d. Merge

3. What project data can be imported from an address book? [L6]

   a. Tasks

   b. Resources

   c. Work

   d. Schedules

4. What specification is necessary to import data into Project? [L1]

   a. Module

   b. Macro

   c. Merge code

   d. Map

5. Which method of sharing data does not allow changes made in the source file to be reflected in the destination file? [L4]

   a. Copy and paste

   b. Embed

   c. Link

   d. Merge

6. What do you use to access an outside data source within Microsoft Project? [L5]

   a. Hyperlink

   b. Map

   c. Network diagram

   d. Macro

7. Which of the following is not an allowable rendering method when copying a chart in Microsoft Project? [L3]

   a. Screen

   b. HTML

   c. Printer

   d. GIF

8. Which program supports exported project data? [L2]

   a. Word

   b. Access

   c. Excel

   d. All of the above

9. To import additional resources to a project file without using a primary key, which method would you use? [L1]

   a. New file

   b. Append

   c. Merge

   d. Map

10. What format contains fields separated by commas or semicolons? [L2]

    a. HTML

    b. XML

    c. ODBC

    d. CSV

DISCUSSION

1. In the previous project you learned how to e-mail project files; in this project you learned about different copy, paste, link, and embed options. How do these features complement each other? How are they different? [L3–L5]

2. Explain the differences between linked data and embedded data, and describe a scenario where each option could apply. [L4]

3. Describe what a map is and how it is utilized when importing and exporting data to and from Microsoft Project. What are the two mapping options? [L1, L2]

SKILL DRILL

Skill Drill exercises reinforce project skills. Each skill reinforced is the same, or nearly the same, as a skill presented in the project. Detailed instructions are provided in a step-by-step format.

You should complete all of the Skill Drill exercises in sequence.

1. Importing a Task List from Excel

You have been assigned by your supervisor to conduct a critical business analysis of the Purchasing department of your corporation. Your supervisor hopes that this analysis will flush out any duplication in processes, identify outdated technologies, and isolate steps to improve the processing of internal purchasing orders. Your job in this project is to help the lead project manager create the initial project plan to submit to your supervisor for approval. Because some tasks already reside in an Excel workbook, you decide to import them rather than type them from scratch.

To import a task list from Excel, follow these steps:

1. Click Start from the taskbar and click on Microsoft Excel 2010 from the Microsoft Office Folder.

2. Choose File, Open.

3. Click the down arrow at the right end of the *Look in* box, and select the drive and folder containing the student files for this text.

4. Click the *EPr1_0806* filename, and then click Open.

5. Choose File, Save As and name the file **Options_Analysis**.

6. View the data contained in the Excel spreadsheet.

7. Choose File, Close; and then minimize the Excel program.

8. Start Microsoft Project, open the *EPr1_0807* file, save it as **Business_Definition**, and then close any open side panes.

9. Choose File, Open.

10. Click the *Files of type* drop-down arrow, select *Microsoft Excel Workbooks*, and then navigate to the folder where your student files are located.

11. Select the *Options_Analysis* Excel file, and then click <u>O</u>pen.

12. From the Import Wizard dialog box, click <u>N</u>ext.

13. Click the *Ne<u>w</u> map* option, if necessary, and then click <u>N</u>ext.

14. Click the *<u>A</u>ppend the data to the active project* option, and then click <u>N</u>ext.

15. Check the *<u>T</u>asks* check box, verify that *I<u>m</u>port includes headers* is also selected, and then click <u>N</u>ext.

16. Click the *Source <u>w</u>orksheet name* drop-down arrow and choose *Sheet1*.

17. In the mapping grid, click the Task Name field under *To: Microsoft Office Project Field*. Click the drop-down arrow and choose *Name*.

18. Click <u>N</u>ext and then click <u>F</u>inish.

19. Use the vertical scroll button to scroll to row 25 to view the imported data.

20. Select Task 25 (*Options Analysis*) through Task 32 (*Issues*) and click Outdent on the Formatting toolbar.

21. Select Task 26 (*Financial costs*) through Task 32 (*Issues*) and click Indent on the Formatting toolbar.

22. Save the *Business_Definition* project file and leave it open for the next exercise.

2. Exporting the Task Sheet as an Excel File

The project manager informs you that now that you have a good start on creating the project file, your supervisor wants to take a look at the file and then schedule a meeting with you to discuss changes that you might need to make. However, your supervisor does not have Microsoft Project on her system. To facilitate her request, you export the file as an Excel spreadsheet so she can review the task list at her convenience.

To export the task sheet to Excel, follow these steps:

1. Open *Business_Definition*, if necessary, and close any open side panes.

2. Choose <u>F</u>ile, Save <u>A</u>s.

3. Click the *Save as <u>t</u>ype* drop-down arrow and choose *Microsoft Excel Workbook (*.xls)*.

4. In the *File na<u>m</u>e* text box, click after the *n* in *Definition* and type **_Export**, and then click <u>S</u>ave.

5. From the Export Wizard dialog box, click <u>N</u>ext.

6. Click the *Selected Data* option and click <u>N</u>ext.

7. Click the *Ne<u>w</u> map* option button and then click <u>N</u>ext.

8. Check the *<u>T</u>asks* check box, verify that *Export includes headers* is also selected, and then click <u>N</u>ext.

9. Under *Verify or edit how you want to map the data*, click in the first cell under *From: Microsoft Office Project Field*, select *Name* in the list, and then press ⏎Enter.

10. Then, select *Duration* and press ⏎Enter.

11. Click Next and then click Finish.

12. Minimize Microsoft Project, and maximize Excel.

13. Choose File, Open; select *Business_Definition_Export*; and then click Open.

14. Verify that the data are accurate; then choose File, Exit to close the Excel file and exit the Excel program.

15. Click the *Business_Definition* Project file from the taskbar, if necessary, and save it, leaving it open for the next exercise.

3. Inserting a PowerPoint Slide into a Note

After your supervisor reviews the project file, she wants you to attach a PowerPoint file to the task where business data problems are listed. This process ensures that the standard corporate form is utilized.

To attach a PowerPoint slide to a note, follow these steps:

1. Open *Business_Definition*, if necessary, and then close any open side panes.

2. Double-click Task 12 (*List problems with business data*) and click the Notes tab.

3. Click the Insert Object button.

4. From the Insert Object dialog box, click the *Create from File* option button.

5. Click Browse and navigate to the folder where your student files are located. Select the *EPr1_0808* PowerPoint file and click Insert.

6. Click OK.

7. Save *Business_Definition* and leave it open for the next exercise.

4. Adding Resources from Microsoft Outlook

Your supervisor has given you and the project manager the go-ahead to begin adding resources to the project plan and assigning work to the team who will be conducting the critical business analysis. However, she wants to ensure that you include everyone's e-mail address. The project manager provided the list of resources and informs you that most of them can be found in the corporate address book and that you can import them from Outlook.

To import e-mail addresses from Microsoft Outlook, follow these steps:

1. Open *Business_Definition*, if necessary, and close any open side panes; then choose View, Resource Sheet.

2. Right-click the Type column header and choose Insert Column.

3. Select *Email Address* from the *Field name* drop-down list, and then click OK.

4. Choose Insert, New Resource From, Address Book.

5. From the *Name* list, click the first resource you want to add and then click the Add button.

6. Click the second resource you want to add in the *Name* list box and then click Add.

7. Click OK, then click OK again.

8. Save *Business_Definition* and close it.

CHALLENGE

Challenge exercises expand on or are somewhat related to skills presented in the lessons. Each exercise provides a brief narrative introduction, followed by instructions in a numbered-step format that are not as detailed as those in the Skill Drill section. The exercises relate to a single file, and you should work the exercises in order.

1. Importing Resource Lists

As the technical editor for a large firm, you are creating a handbook to accompany a customized in-house computer program. This handbook requires a group effort with many departments involved. You have an Excel workbook that lists each employee assigned to the handbook project. Each department has a worksheet within the workbook, including employee names, hourly cost, and availability. You must import this workbook of data into your project file to supplement the resource sheet.

To import a resource list, follow these steps:

1. Start Excel; open *EPr1_0809* and save it as **Resources.xls**.

2. View the Programmers and Software Testers worksheets, and then exit Excel.

3. Open *EPr1_0810*, save it as **Handbook**, and then switch to Resource Sheet view.

4. Open the *Resources* workbook within Microsoft Project, and begin the importing process, using a new map.

5. Choose to append the data to the open project file; select to import *Resources* and include headers in the import.

6. In the Import Wizard – Resource Mapping dialog box, choose to import the Programmers worksheet; then map the Excel Employee field to the Project Name field, the Excel Hourly Rate field to the Project Standard Rate field, and the Excel Available Time field to the Project Max Units field.

7. Import the resources on the Software Testers worksheet, using the same procedures.

8. Save *Handbook* and leave it open for the next exercise.

2. Copying a Portion of a Network Diagram to an Excel Workbook

You need to send an Excel workbook to the department head to inform her of the tasks involving the technical writers. You have a worksheet listing those tasks, but you think a diagram would be beneficial as well. So you copy a picture of the network diagram in the project file and paste it in the worksheet.

To copy part of a network diagram to a workbook, follow these steps:

1. Open *Handbook* and close any side panes, if necessary.

2. Switch to Network Diagram view, and then change the zoom to 85% (Hint: Use View, Zoom).

3. Use the Copy Picture option to copy the screen.

4. Open Microsoft Excel, open *EPr1_0811*, and then select cell A7.

5. Paste the picture; then drag the bottom-right corner handle to adjust the size of the image, filling the range A7 to J31.

6. Save the workbook as **Writers** and close it.

7. Save *Handbook* and leave it open for the next exercise.

3. Embedding a Calendar from a Project File into a Word Document

Each week, you plan to distribute a memo to all stakeholders to inform them of the next few weeks' activities concerning the handbook creation. You have decided to embed a copy of the calendar from your project file into the memo.

To embed a calendar, follow these steps:

1. Open *Handbook* and close any side panes, if necessary.

2. Display the View Bar and switch to Calendar view.

3. Save the project file and minimize Microsoft Project.

4. Start Word and open *EPr1_0812*.

5. Use the Insert Object menu option to embed the *Handbook* project file after the first paragraph.

6. Resize the embedded calendar to 3.48″ (height) by 6.13″ (width). Use Help to learn how to resize an object in a Word document if it is unfamiliar to you.

7. Save the Word document as **Schedule**.

8. Double-click the calendar and note the changes to the application window.

9. Click outside of the calendar, save the document again and close Word.

10. Close *Handbook*.

DISCOVERY ZONE

Discovery Zone exercises require advanced knowledge of topics presented in *Essentials* lessons, application of skills from multiple lessons, or self-directed learning of new skills. The exercises are independent of each other, so you may complete them in any order.

1. Using the Excel Task List Template

Microsoft Office provides continuity between programs as well as collaborative features. Data can be shared between Microsoft Project and Excel easily. In fact, Microsoft Excel contains a template designed to make importing Excel data into Microsoft Project simple.

Start Microsoft Excel and choose File, New. Select *Sample templates* and select Microsoft Project Plan Import Export Template. Look through the workbook, particularly the Info Tab. Then, create some records on each worksheet. Save the workbook as type *Excel 2010 Workbook*, name it **Template_Data**, and then close it.

In Microsoft Project, import the *Template_Data* workbook. Use the wizard to include all the worksheets. Save the new project file as **Template_Data**. Close the project file.

2. Using Resource Pools

In Project 4, you learned about resources and how to assign them to specific tasks. There are times when resources are used within multiple projects. A resource pool is a set of resources that are available for assignment to project tasks and can be used exclusively by one project or can be shared by several projects. When resources are used repeatedly, a resource pool saves a great deal of time.

Use Help to research the topic "Use another project's resources in your project." Then, create a new project file and name it **Resource_Pool**. In the resource sheet, create a list of resources to be shared with other projects. Open any existing project file and save it as **Shared_Resources**. Share the resources from the *Resource_Pool* project file with the *Shared_Resources* project file. Save and close both files once you have verified that the resources were shared correctly.

INTEGRATING PROJECTS

Essentials 2007: Microsoft Project

The Integrating Projects exercises provide additional hands-on practice working with Microsoft Project. Each exercise requires the application of skills from multiple projects; a cross-reference accompanying each exercise title tells you which projects introduced the skills applied in the exercise. The exercises are independent of each other and can be worked in any order.

You follow a checklist as you create and enhance each complete product. Many of the exercises include opportunities to make decisions about the best approach and features to use in a particular situation.

1 CREATING A SOFTWARE DEPLOYMENT PROJECT PLAN

Based on Projects 1, 2, 3, and 8

Roddenberry's and Associates has recently decided to create an internal information management systems team to handle training, computer end-user support, e-mail administration, and virus protection and recovery. You work in the Human Resources division of this company and are responsible for processing new hires. You must create a project plan to manage the job creation portion of this newly developed information systems department. The purpose of this project plan is to determine the job types needed in this new department, to develop an overall department structure or hierarchy, and to track operating expenses associated with creating this new team. Figure PrIP.1 illustrates the final project plan.

	ⓘ	Task Name	Duration	Start	Finish	Predecessors
1		**Business Analysis**	**6 days?**	**Mon 4/3/06**	**Mon 4/10/06**	
2		Determine use and function of dept. for firm	1 day?	Mon 4/3/06	Mon 4/3/06	
3		Review business goals/vision/mission statement	1 day?	Mon 4/3/06	Mon 4/3/06	
4		Determine department structure/hierarchy	1 day?	Mon 4/3/06	Mon 4/3/06	
5		Determine job types	1 day?	Mon 4/3/06	Mon 4/3/06	
6		Verify job types with human resources	1 day?	Mon 4/3/06	Mon 4/3/06	
7		**Phase II**	**6 days?**	**Mon 4/3/06**	**Mon 4/10/06**	
8		Create Information Systems analysis plan	2 days	Mon 4/3/06	Tue 4/4/06	
9		Implement plan	5 days	Tue 4/4/06	Mon 4/10/06	3
10		Identify support infrastructure	2 days	Tue 4/4/06	Wed 4/5/06	4
11		Summarize business needs	2 days	Tue 4/4/06	Wed 4/5/06	5
12		Identify market needs	1 day	Tue 4/4/06	Tue 4/4/06	6
13		Summarize operating expenses	1 day?	Mon 4/3/06	Mon 4/3/06	

	ⓘ	Resource Name	Email Address	Type	Material Label	Initials	Group	Max. Units	Std. Rate
1		Manager	mgr@emailaddress.com	Work		Mgr	Sr. Mgmt	100%	$75.00/hr
2		Computer Training	training@emailaddress.com	Work		CT	Train	300%	$150.00/hr
3		Director	direct@emailaddress.com	Work		Dir	Sr. Mgmt	100%	$150.00/hr
4		Human Resources	hr@emailaddress.com	Work		HR	HR	100%	$50.00/hr
5		Marketing	market@emailaddress.com	Work		Mrk	Mrk	200%	$100.00/hr
6		Accounting	ap@emailaddress.com	Work		AP	AP	300%	$300.00/hr
7		FedEx		Material		FedEx			$0.00

FIGURE PrIP.1

IP Exercise Checklist

❑ Open a new project file and save it as **IS_Deploy**.

❑ Set the start date as *4/3/2006*.

❑ Define the Project Working Times using the Standard calendar with the default work week of Monday–Friday, with the default 8-hour work day, 40-hour work week.

❑ Enter the following tasks:

Business Analysis

Determine use and function of dept. for firm

Review business goals/vision/mission statement

Determine department structure/hierarchy

Determine job types

Verify job types with human resources

❑ Indent Task 2 (*Determine use and function of dept. for firm*) through Task 6 (*Verify job types with human resources*) below Task 1 (*Business Analysis*) to make Task 1 a summary task.

❑ Import the next set of tasks from the *EPr1_IP01* Excel workbook. Use a new map and append the data to the existing project plan. Map only the task information on Sheet1. In the mapping grid, review the map assignments to verify that all fields are mapped to the correct and corresponding column in the task sheet.

❑ Indent Task 8 (*Create Information Systems analysis plan*) through Task 13 (*Summarize operating expenses*) below Task 7 (*Phase II*) to make Task 7 a summary task.

❑ Modify the scheduling constraint on the newly imported tasks, using the default constraint of *As Soon As Possible*.

❑ Add the Email Address column after the Resource Name column in the resource sheet and then enter the following resources:

Resource Name	Email Address	Type	Initials	Group	Max. Units	Std. Rate	Cost/Use
Manager	mgr@emailaddress.com	Work	Mgr	Sr. Mgmt	100%	$75.00/h	$0.00
Computer Training	training@emailaddress.com	Work	CT	Train	300%	$150.00/h	$0.00
Director	direct@emailaddress.com	Work	Dir	Sr. Mgmt	100%	$150.00/h	$0.00
Human Resources	hr@emailaddress.com	Work	HR	HR	100%	$50.00/h	$0.00
Marketing	market@emailaddress.com	Work	Mrk	Mrk	200%	$100.00/h	$0.00
Accounting	ap@emailaddress.com	Work	AP	AP	300%	$300.00/h	$0.00
FedEx	(blank)	Material	FedEx	(blank)	(blank)	$0.00	$5.00

❑ Preview (or print if you prefer) the Working Days report.

❑ Save and close the *IS_Deploy* project file.

2 MODIFYING TASKS AND ASSIGNING RESOURCES

You work in the Human Resources division of Roddenberry's and Associates and are managing a project file for a newly developed information systems department. Considerable work has been done on the file and you are now ready to finalize the project plan and implement a second phase so that you can begin using it to track the progress of the information systems department deployment. To complete the file, you must specify the different task predecessors to create links between tasks. You also use the outline features to better view the different phases of the project plan. You then need to assign resources to their task assignments.

IP Exercise Checklist

❑ Open *EPr1_IP02* and save it as **Final_IS_Deploy**.

❑ Use the following table to link tasks:

Task ID	Task Name	Predecessors
10	Identify dept. goals - long/short	9SS
11	Promote/Hire dept. employees	10FF
12	Complete new hire application form	11
13	Complete 941	12SS
14	Interview process with leadership	9
16	Make offers	15
17	Set start dates	16
18	Infrastructure Review	17
19	Identify standard computer workstation	9
21	Determine connectivity LAN/WAN needs	20
22	Determine server needs	21
23	Develop detailed infrastructure plan	22
26	Implement plan	3
27	Identify support infrastructure	4
28	Summarize business needs	5
29	Identify market needs	6
30	Summarize operating expenses	7

❑ Use Outdent and Indent to outline the project plan and organize the tasks as follows:

❑ Task 8 (*Staff Information Systems department*) through Task 23 (*Develop detailed infrastructure plan*) as subtasks for Task 1 (*Phase 1*)

❑ Task 9 (*Identify leadership*) through Task 13 (*Complete 941*) as subtasks for Task 8 (*Staff Information Systems department*)

❑ Task 15 (*Select candidates*) through Task 17 (*Set start dates*) as subtasks for Task 14 (*Interview process with leadership*)

❑ Task 20 (*Decide upon software package*) through Task 23 (*Develop detailed infrastructure plan*) as subtasks for Task 19 (*Identify standard computer workstation*)

❑ View the resource sheet and familiarize yourself with the resources. Then switch to Gantt Chart view and assign resources to each task as appropriate. Remember: Multiple resources may be assigned to one task.

❑ Save a copy of the baseline.

❑ View the Tracking Gantt to preview (or print if you prefer) the baseline.

❑ Save the project file, and then close *Final_IS_Deploy*.

Based on Projects 2, 4, 5, and 8

3 USING A TEMPLATE TO CREATE A NEW PROJECT FILE

You are a department administrative professional for a large manufacturing firm. Your company recently received a federal training grant. In order to be eligible for the federal money, however, all corporate employees must receive several hours of OSHA (Occupational Safety and Health Administration) training. Your supervisor has asked you to be the communications liaison between her and several employees managing this large-scale training project. Your job is to work at the direction of your supervisor as well as a group of training professionals, to create and maintain a project plan that the group will use.

To get started with creating the project plan, use an already existing template from Microsoft templates online and modify the start date. You customize this template. A hyperlink to a Word document listing the different departments to receive OSHA training is added and resources are entered in the resource sheet. You also assign these resources to the tasks listed in the project file and save a baseline.

IP Exercise Checklist

❑ Start Word, open *EPr1_IP03*, and save it as **Target_Department**.

❑ View the *Target_Department* document and then exit Word.

❑ Create a new Project file by searching the *Templates on Office Online* for **training rollout**, selecting the *Training rollout initiative and plan*, downloading the template, and saving it as **Training**.

   Note: Use the monospace typeface for **training rollout** and **Training** above.

❑ Familiarize yourself with the tasks in this template.

❑ Set the start date and the status date to *Sun 3/5/06*.

❑ Create a hyperlink from Task 6 (*Create list of target departments*) to the *Target_Department* Word document you saved.

❑ Create a list of resources in Resource Sheet view. Be sure to add at least eight work resources and two material resources. Assign the resources to the following groups:

Group

Planning

Training

Vendor Management

Marketing

Registration and Staff Support

ROI Team

❏ For each task, assign a resource or multiple resources as you see fit.

❏ Save a baseline for the project.

❏ Preview (or print if you prefer) a Who Does What report.

❏ Save and close the *Training* project file.

CREATIVE SOLUTION

4 MONITORING THE PROGRESS OF A TRAINING ROLLOUT INITIATIVE

Based on Projects 1, 3, 4, 5, 6, and 7

You are a department administrative professional for a large manufacturing firm that is implementing a large-scale OSHA (Occupational Safety and Health Administration) training program to receive a federal grant. Working at the direction of a group of training professionals and your supervisor, you update the project plan as instructed. With the project plan well under way, you start tracking how well the training program is progressing. Using a variety of values including percentage complete and remaining duration, update the task progress as communicated to you from the team. You also need to communicate the overall project status to your supervisor.

IP Exercise Checklist

❏ Open the *EPr1_IP04* project file and save it as **Training_Initiative**.

❏ View the Tracking table and display the Tracking toolbar.

❏ Mark the following tasks as complete:

Task 3 (*Define project objectives and describe mission statement*)

Task 4 (*Ensure total participation by training team support staff*)

Task 6 (*Create list of target departments*)

Task 13 (*Define vendor deliverables - can they meet our needs?*)

Task 29 (*Reserve training rooms*)

Task 31 (*Order training manuals and necessary material*)

Task 52 (*Call 1*)

Task 53 (*Call 2*)

Task 54 (*Call 3*)

❏ Mark the following tasks as 75% complete:

Task 7 (*Perform departmental training needs analysis*)

Task 14 (*Obtain vendor commitment to training rollout schedule*)

Task 43 (*In-house instructors*)

Task 44 (*Outsourced instructors*)

❏ Mark the following tasks as 50% complete:

Task 16 (*Obtain approval for purchase orders to cover vendor invoices*)

Task 18 (*Create a list of training recipients by department*)

Task 26 (*Determine course dates, start and end times, and locations*)

❑ Mark the following tasks as 25% complete:

Task 8 (*Compile results and present findings to training coordinator*)

Task 9 (*Prioritize training delivery according to critical need*)

Task 33 (*Order promotional material*)

❑ Modify the Actual Finish date for Task 3 (*Define project objectives and describe mission statement*) to *Tue 3/7/06*.

❑ Modify the Remaining Duration for Task 7 (*Perform departmental training needs analysis*) and Task 8 (*Compile results and present findings to training coordinator*) to display *3 days*.

❑ View the Entry Table and remove the lag time between Task 21 (*Initiate end-user placement matrix*) and Task 22 (*Finalize project budget*).

❑ Split Task 7 (*Perform departmental training needs analysis*) at *Tue 3/14/06*.

❑ View the Project Statistics and then preview (or print if you prefer) the Project Summary report.

❑ Save and close the *Training_Initiative* project file.

5 COMPLETING AND E-MAILING A MAINTENANCE SCHEDULE PROJECT FILE

Based on Projects 3, 4, 5, 7, and 8

You have recently been hired as a property manager by a large property management company. The community you are responsible for is very exclusive and is in a large metropolitan area. The property was recently purchased by the company that hired you and several maintenance issues have been identified. Your first job is to work with your maintenance staff to identify those items that require immediate maintenance. You also utilize this list as a quarterly maintenance tool to check everything on a more regular basis. In addition, because so many items are expected to be repaired, this schedule needs to be approved by the vice president of leasing.

Complete the task table by adding durations and specifying predecessors. Import resources from an Excel spreadsheet, modify task information, and create a custom view to apply when sending the project plan as an attachment for review. Figure PrIP.2 illustrates your plans for the completed project plan. Save your work periodically as you make your changes.

FIGURE PrIP.2

IP Exercise Checklist

❑ Open the *EPr1_IP05* project file and save it as **Repair_Schedule**.

❑ Review the current list of tasks to familiarize yourself with the project plan.

❑ Using the table below, complete the task durations and predecessors.

ID	Task Name	Duration	Predecessors
3	Check faucets for leaks, corrosion	20d?	
4	Check drains for clogs	20d?	3SS
5	Check toilets for stability and leaks	20d?	4SS
6	Drain water heaters, check for leaks	60d?	5SS
7	Complete maintenance checklist for each unit	2d?	
8	Submit copy to property manager and resident	1d?	7
9	Develop repair schedule	5d?	8
10	Notify residents	5d?	9
11	Complete repairs	60d?	10
13	Clean and replace HVAC filters	25d?	
14	Clean all kitchen exhaust fans	25d?	13SS
15	Empty and clean fridge drain pans	15d?	14SS
16	Check dishwashers for leaks	20d?	15SS
17	Check outlets for wear	30d?	
18	Test all smoke detectors	30d?	17SS
19	Complete maintenance checklist for each unit	5d?	
20	Submit copy to property manager and resident	1d?	19
21	Develop repair schedule	5d?	20
22	Notify residents	5d?	21
23	Complete repairs	25d?	22
25	Inspect foundation of each building	10d?	
26	Inspect all ducts and vents for clogs	10d?	25SS
27	Check sprinkler system	1d?	
28	Inspect for proper drainage	1d?	27
29	Submit repair list to property manager	1d?	
30	Hire repair crews	5d?	29
31	Develop schedule of repairs	1d?	30
32	Complete repairs	15d?	31

❑ Insert a recurring meeting task with the name *Telephone conference with corporate* above Task 2 (*Plumbing*) that meets every other week on Tuesday. Make the end date for the recurring task *Mon 8/22/05*.

❑ Check the spelling and correct any spelling mistakes that exist in the file.

❑ Switch to Resource Sheet view and import the *EPr1_IP06* Excel file, using a new map and appending the data to the existing project plan. Map only the resources on Sheet1. In the mapping grid, review the map assignments to verify that all fields are mapped to the correct and corresponding column in the resource sheet.

❑ Complete the resource sheet by adding the following material resources:

Resource	Type	Cost/Use
Heating/AC filter	Material	2.50
Smoke alarm	Material	15.75
Toilet kit	Material	5.25

❑ Create a custom view with the following attributes:

Attribute	Selection
View Type:	Combination View
Name:	Task Detail for Supervisor
Top:	Resource Usage
Bottom:	Task Details Form

❑ Apply the Task Detail for Supervisor view.

❑ E-mail the project file as an attachment to one individual. Rather than sending the e-mail, save the file. From the Save as type: drop-down, choose Outlook Message Format (*.msg) and save the file where your solution files are located. Close the e-mail form without sending it.

❑ Save the *Repair_Schedule* project file and close it.

6   USING A ROUTED PROJECT FILE

You are a property manager at a large, upscale urban rental community. You have created a project plan to track and regularly check items in the rental units and the overall property that require regular maintenance. The project file you created was routed to several people in the leasing division of the property management company for which you work. The last recipient has sent the routed file back to you, and you need to review the changes that have been made to it.

Based on Projects 4, 7, and 8

In the following steps, you open the project file, save it with a new name, and review the changes. In addition, the task items you created should be paste linked into a Microsoft Word document. The company you work for wants this information shared with other community managers so they can develop their own maintenance plans.

IP Exercise Checklist

❑ Open the *EPr1_IP07* project file and save it as **Repair_Schedule_Routed**.

❑ Switch to Gantt Chart view and close the lower pane in the view by double-clicking the split line.

❑ Review the project file and the resources.

❑ Switch to Resource Usage view and review the task assignments for the Maintenance Staff resource. Notice that this resource is overallocated and needs to be leveled.

❑ Modify the Maintenance Staff resource so that it now has Max. Units of 500%—which reflects that the staff will have five full-time employees during the project time frame.

❑ Remove the Maintenance Staff from the following tasks, and apply the Leasing Assistant instead, accepting the default SmartTag options as prompted.

Task ID	Task Name
24	Develop repair schedule
25	Notify residents
36	Develop repair schedule
37	Notify residents

❑ Switch to Gantt Chart view and save the project baseline.

❑ Select the Task Name, Duration, Start, and Finish columns in the task sheet and copy these columns.

❑ Save *Repair_Schedule_Routed* and minimize it.

❑ In a new blank Word document, link the columns that you copied in the *Repair_Schedule_Routed* project file as Formatted Text (RTF). Save the file in the same directory where your other solution files are located, and name it **Paste_Link_Repair_Schedule**. Exit Microsoft Word.

❑ In the *Repair_Schedule_Routed* project file, double-click Task 25 (*Notify residents*) and insert a Note object created from a file. Use the *EPr1_IP08* Excel file as the linked file.

❑ Insert the same *EPr1_IP08* Excel file as a Note object for Task 37 (*Notify residents*).

❑ Preview (or print if you prefer) a Who Does What report.

❑ Save the *Repair_Schedule_Routed* project file and close it.

FILE GUIDE

Guide to Files in Essentials: Microsoft Project 2007

P#-L# or P#-ex type	Original Student File	Student File Saved As	Related Solution Notes
Project 1			
P1-L1 thru L7	EPr1_0101.mpp	Apartment_Brochure.mpp	
P1-SD1 thru SD4	EPr1_0102.mpp	Software_Deployment.mpp	
P1-SD5			No files; explore Help topics
P1-CH1 thru CH3	New project (template)	New_Business.mpp	
P1-CH4	EPr1_0103.mpp	Software.mpp	
P1-DZ1			Creative Solution exercise (explore Help topics); solution not provided
P1-DZ2			Creative Solution exercise (Web research on project management); solution not provided
Project 2			
P2-L1	New project	New_Hires.mpp	
P2-L2 thru L5	EPr1_0201.mpp	New_Hire_Orientation.mpp	
P2-L6	New project (template)	Office Move.mpp	
P2-SD1 thru SD2	New project	Board_New_Member.mpp	
P2-SD3	EPr1_0202.mpp	Forms_Procedures.mpp	
P2-SD4	EPr1_0203.mpp	PO_Routing.mpp	
P2-CH1 and CH2	EPr1_0204.mpp	Manual_Schedule.mpp	
P2-CH3	EPr1_0205.mpp	Magazine_Article.mpp	
P2-CH4	New project (template)	Building_Plan.mpp	
P2-DZ1	New project	Production.mpp	Creative Solution exercise (project calendars); solution not provided

P = Project   L = Lesson   SD = Skill Drill   CH = Challenge   DZ = Discovery Zone   IP = Integrating Projects

Creative Solution exercises permit individual choices that produce unique solutions

P#-L# or P#-ex type	Original Student File	Student File Saved As	Related Solution Notes
P2-DZ2			Creative Solution exercise (create a template from project of choice); solution not provided

Project 3

P#-L# or P#-ex type	Original Student File	Student File Saved As	Related Solution Notes
P3-L1	New project	Conference_Preplanning.mpp	
P3-L2 thru L7	EPr1_0301.mpp	Conference_Plan.mpp	
P3-SD1	New project	Cruise_Planning.mpp	
P3-SD2 thru SD5	EPr1_0302.mpp	Club_Cruise.mpp	
P3-CH1	New project	Signs_Graphics.mpp	
P3-CH2 and CH3	EPr1_0303.mpp	Apartment_Artwork.mpp	
P3-CH4	EPr1_0304.mpp	Training_Portal.mpp	
P3-DZ1	New project	Accounting_Software.mpp	Creative Solution exercise (project templates); solution not provided
P3-DZ2	New project	Constraint.mpp	Creative Solution exercise (task constraints); solution not provided

Project 4

P#-L# or P#-ex type	Original Student File	Student File Saved As	Related Solution Notes
P4-L1 thru L6	EPr1_0401.mpp	Business_Model.mpp	
P4-SD1 thru SD5	EPr1_0402.mpp	Virus_Recovery.mpp	
P4-CH1 thru CH5	EPr1_0403.mpp	Temps_Hiring_Plan.mpp	CH4 is a Creative Solution exercise (level resources); solution file is a representative solution and will vary depending upon CH4
P4-DZ1			Creative Solution exercise (template); solution not provided
P4-DZ2			Creative Solution exercise (costs); solution not provided

Project 5

P#-L# or P#-ex type	Original Student File	Student File Saved As	Related Solution Notes
P5-L1 thru L6	EPr1_0501.mpp	Fundraiser.mpp	
P5-L7	EPr1_0502.mpp	Programming.mpp	
P5-SD1 thru SD6	EPr1_0503.mpp	Software_Manual.mpp	

P = Project   L = Lesson   SD = Skill Drill   CH = Challenge   DZ = Discovery Zone   IP = Integrating Projects

Creative Solution exercises permit individual choices that produce unique solutions

P#-L# or P#-ex type	Original Student File	Student File Saved As	Related Solution Notes
P5-CH1 thru CH4	EPr1_0504.mpp	Direct_Market.mpp	Creative Solution exercise (project tracking); solution not provided
P5-DZ1			Creative Solution exercise (using Help); solution not provided
P5-DZ2			Creative Solution exercise (create views using a template); solution not provided

Project 6

P#-L# or P#-ex type	Original Student File	Student File Saved As	Related Solution Notes
P6-L1 thru L6	EPr1_0601.mpp	Ad_Campaign.mpp	
P6-SD1 thru SD4	EPr1_0602.mpp	Request_For_Proposal.mpp	
P6-CH1 thru CH4	EPr1_0603.mpp	Orientation.mpp	
P6-DZ1			Creative Solution exercise (multiple progress lines); solution not provided
P6-DZ2			Creative Solution exercise (reports); solution not provided

Project 7

P#-L# or P#-ex type	Original Student File	Student File Saved As	Related Solution Notes
P7-L1 thru L8	EPr1_0701.mpp	Restaurant.mpp	
P7-SD1 thru SD5	EPr1_0702.mpp	Fundraiser_Auction.mpp	
P7-CH1 thru CH5	EPr1_0703.mpp	PIMS.mpp	
P7-DZ1			Creative Solution exercise (Help, views); solution not provided
P7-DZ2	EPr1_0702.mpp	PERT.mpp	Creative Solution exercise (Help, PERT analysis); solution not provided

Project 8

P#-L# or P#-ex type	Original Student File	Student File Saved As	Related Solution Notes
P8-L1 thru L6	EPr1_0802.mpp	Mgmt_Review.mpp	
P8-L1	EPr1_0801.xls	Assessment.xls	Import Excel data into Mgmt_Review
P8-L2		Mgmt_Review_Export.xls	Export Mgmt_Review data to Excel
P8-L3		Gantt_Chart.xls	Copy Gantt chart from Mgmt_Review to a new Excel workbook

P = Project   L = Lesson   SD = Skill Drill   CH = Challenge   DZ = Discovery Zone   IP = Integrating Projects

Creative Solution exercises permit individual choices that produce unique solutions

P#-L# or P#-ex type	Original Student File	Student File Saved As	Related Solution Notes
P8-L4 (part 1)		Linked_Mgmt_Review.doc	Link Mgmt_Review data to a new Word document
P8-L4 (part 2)	EPr1_0803.xlxs		Embed an Excel chart and data in Mgmt_Review
P8-L5	EPr1_0804.pptx EPr1_0805.docx		Insert a slide (EPr1_0804.pptx) into Mgmt_Review; then add a hyperlink that opens the Word file EPr1_0805
P8-L6			Import resources from Microsoft Outlook to Mgmt_Review
P8-SD1 thru SD4	EPr1_0807.mpp	Business_Definition.mpp	
P8-SD1	EPr1_0806.xls	Options_Analysis.xls	Import Excel data into Business_Definition
P8-SD2		Business_Definition_Export.xls	Export Business_Definition data to Excel
P8-SD3	EPr1_0808.pptx		Insert slide (EP1_0808.pptx) into Business_Definition
P8-CH1 thru CH4	EPr1_0810.mpp	Handbook.mpp	
P8-CH1	EPr1_0809.xls	Resources.xls	Import Excel data (Resources.xls) into Handbook
P8-CH2	EPr1_0811.xlsx	Writers.xlsx	Copy part of a network diagram in Handbook to Excel (Writers.xlsx)
P8-CH3	EPr1_0812.docx	Schedule.docx	Embed a calendar from Handbook into a Word document (Schedule.docx)
P8-DZ1	New Excel workbook from template; New project file	Template_Data.xls Template_Data.mpp	Creative Solution exercise; add data of choice to Excel template and save as Template_Data.xls; then import those data into a new project file Template_Data.mpp; solution not provided
P8-DZ2	New project Choice of any existing project file	Resource_Pool.mpp Shared_Resources.mpp	Creative Solution exercise; get Help on sharing resources; then share resources from Resource_Pool with Shared_Resources; solution not provided

Integrating Projects

IP1	New project EPr1_IP01.xls	IS_Deploy.mpp	Create new project IS_Deploy; includes importing Excel data (EPr1_IP01.xls)
IP2	EPr1_IP02.mpp	Final_IS_Deploy.mpp	Creative Solution exercise; assign resources and save/view a baseline

P = Project   L = Lesson   SD = Skill Drill   CH = Challenge   DZ = Discovery Zone   IP = Integrating Projects

Creative Solution exercises permit individual choices that produce unique solutions

P#-L# or P#-ex type	Original Student File	Student File Saved As	Related Solution Notes
IP3	EPr1_IP03.docx New from template	Target_Department.docx Training.mpp	Creative Solution exercise; use online template to create Training.mpp; set up project file; create hyperlink to a Word document; add and assign resources to tasks; save a baseline; and view a report
IP4	EPr1_IP04.mpp	Training_Initiative.mpp	Track progress and enter actuals; create lag time for one task; split a task; and view Project Statistics
IP5	EPr1_IP05.mpp EPr1_IP06.xls	Repair_Schedule.mpp	Enter durations and predecessors for select tasks; insert a recurring task; check spelling; import an Excel worksheet (EPr1_IP06.xls); add material resources; create a custom view; and e-mail the project file as an attachment
IP6	EPr1_IP07.mpp EPr1_IP08.xlsx New Word document	Repair_Schedule_Routed.mpp Paste_Link_Repair_Schedule.docx	Level resources; create a baseline; link the project file to the Paste_Link_Repair_Schedule.docx file; insert the EPr1_IP08.xlsx file as a note in the Task Information for two tasks; and view a report

P = Project   L = Lesson   SD = Skill Drill   CH = Challenge   DZ = Discovery Zone   IP = Integrating Projects

Creative Solution exercises permit individual choices that produce unique solutions

MICROSOFT PROJECT 2007 TASK GUIDE

A book in the *Essentials* series can serve as a handy reference beside your computer even after you complete all the projects and exercises. When you need a refresher for the sequence of steps or a shortcut to achieve a result, look up the task category in the alphabetized listing that follows. Then turn to the page number listed in the second column to locate the step-by-step exercise or other detailed description. Entries without page numbers describe tasks that are closely related to those presented in the projects.

Project Task	Page	Mouse	Menu Bar	Shortcut Menu	Shortcut Keys
Baseline, save	142	Click **Track** ▾ on Project Guide toolbar, click *Save a baseline plan to compare with later versions* link, and click Save Baseline	Tools | Tracking | Set Baseline		
Baseline, view data	143		View | Tracking Gantt		
Calendar, apply to a task	81	Click 🗐 on Standard toolbar and the Advanced tab and click the Calendar drop-down	Project | Task Information | Advanced tab | Calendar drop-down		
Calendar, creating a new custom	40		Tools | Change Working Time | Create New Calendar | complete dialog box		
Calendar, modify Project Working Times	45	Click *Define general working times* on the Tasks side pane	Tools | Change Working Time | Complete dialog box		
Calendar, modify work week	45		Tools | Options | Calendar tab | enter number in *Hours per week* box		
Calendar, set start date	40	Click *Set a date to schedule from* on the Tasks side pane	Project | Project Information		
Column, hide a column in the Task Table	14		Select column | Edit | Hide Column	Right-click column heading | Hide Column	
Column, view Indicator column icon ScreenTip	12	Point and pause on the icon in the Indicator column			

Project Task	Page	Mouse	Menu Bar	Shortcut Menu	Shortcut Keys
Constraint, set	84	Click [icon] on Standard toolbar and the Advanced tab and click the *Constraint type* drop-down	Project	Task Information	Advanced tab	Constraint type		
Copy a Gantt chart (from Gantt Chart view)	257		Report	Copy Picture	complete dialog box	switch to destination file	Edit	Paste		
Costs, enter fixed costs	108	In Cost table, click in Fixed Cost field and type data	View	Table: Entry	Cost; click in Fixed Cost field and type data		
Critical path, view the critical path	188		View	Tracking Gantt		
Current Date, Modify	44		Project	Project Information		
Custom field, create using a value list	213		Tools	Customize	Fields; name field; Lookup; enter list		
Custom report, create	219		Report	Reports	Custom	New	Complete dialog box		
Custom view, create	217		View	More Views	New	Complete dialog box		
Duration, change default	66		Tools	Options	Schedule tab; enter number in *Duration is entered in* box		
E-mail a project file	227		File	Send To	Mail Recipient (as Attachment)		
Embed Excel data in Project	263		Insert	Object	Create from file; select file	OK		
Exit Microsoft Project	25	[X icon] in upper-right corner	File	Exit		Alt + F4
Export, data into an Excel Worksheet	253		File	Save As	change *Save as type* to *Microsoft Excel Workbook*	Save	complete wizard		

Project Task	Page	Mouse	Menu Bar	Shortcut Menu	Shortcut Keys
Finish Date, set	40		Project	Project Information		
Format, view details (from Resource Usage view)	207		Format	Detail Styles		
Getting Started task pane, Close	37	✕ in upper-right corner of the pane			
Gridlines, adding to Gantt chart	18	Right-click the Gantt chart and choose Gridlines	Format	Gridlines		
Help, accessing web-based	23		Help	Microsoft Office Online		
Help, display Microsoft Help task pane	23	Click 🔘 on the Standard toolbar	Help	Microsoft Office Project Help		F1 or Alt+H
Help, *Type a question for help* box	21	Click *Type a question for help* box, type term or question, press ↵Enter			
Help, version of Project	24		Help	About Microsoft Project		Alt+H and A
Hyperlink, insert	267		Insert	Hyperlink	complete dialog box		
Import, from Excel	246		File	Open	change *Files of type* to *Microsoft Excel Workbooks*	complete wizard		
Insert, recurring task	70		Insert	Recurring Task	Complete dialog box		
Task link line, view the ScreenTip	15	Point and pause on the task link line			
Link, create	75	Click 🗎 and click the Predecessors tab and choose predecessor task name from the drop-down in the Task Name column.	Project	Task Information	Predecessors tab	Complete dialog box	Click in the Predecessors field in the task table for the successor task and type the Task ID for the link task followed by FF, SS, FS, or SF	
Link, project data with Word (with selected data)	261	Click 🗎 on the Standard toolbar, switch to Word document, Past Special from the Home tab, and select the Paste link button	Edit	Copy Cell	switch to Word document	Home	Paste Special	Paste link button		Select data, Ctrl+C, switch to Word document, Home, Paste Special, Paste link button

Project Task	Page	Mouse	Menu Bar	Shortcut Menu	Shortcut Keys
Link, remove	180	Click [icon] on the Standard toolbar or double-click task link line on Gantt chart and choose *(None)* using the Type down-arrow	Project | Task Information | Predecessors tab; select link and press Del.		Click in the Predecessors field in the task table for the successor task and press Del
Link, tasks	75	Select tasks to link and click [icon] on the Standard toolbar or Click in the Predecessors field in the task table for the successor task and type the Task ID for the link task	Project | Task Information | Complete dialog box		
Milestone task, create	70	Click in the Duration cell for the task and type 0			
Milestone, view the ScreenTip	16	Point and pause on the black diamond			
Modify the timescale	207		Format | Timescale | Complete dialog box		
Move, to beginning of the task table	10				Ctrl + Home
Organizer, copy a custom item	223		Tools | Organizer | appropriate tab | select item | Copy		
Organizer, remove item from global file	225		Tools | Organizer | appropriate tab | select item | Delete		
Organizer, rename an item	226		Tools | Organizer | appropriate tab | select item | Rename		
Outlining, create subtask	78	Select tasks and click [icon] on the Formatting toolbar			
Outlining, create summary task	78	Select tasks and click [icon] on the Formatting toolbar			

Project Task	Page	Mouse	Menu Bar	Shortcut Menu	Shortcut Keys
Outlining, show outline by levels	79	Click `Show ▾` on Formatting toolbar and choose the outline level to display	Click expand (+) or collapse (-) buttons		
Print, current view	19	Click 🖨 on the Standard Toolbar	File | Print		Alt + F and P
Print Preview, current view	19	Click 🔍 on the Standard Toolbar	File | Print Preview		Alt + F and V
Progress line, add to Gantt chart	178	▧ on the Tracking toolbar	Tools | Tracking | Progress Lines | Dates and Intervals tab | Complete dialog box		
Progress lines, remove	178		Tools | Tracking | Progress Lines | Dates and Intervals tab; deselect *Always display current progress line*		
Progress, tracking by adding Status column to task table	178		Insert | Column | Choose Status from Field name drop-down	Right-click column heading, Insert Column, Choose Status from Field name drop-down	
Project file, close	25	Click ✕ (to right of *Type a question for help* box)	File | Close		Ctrl + F4 or Ctrl + W
Project file, create from a template	50		File | New | click *On computer;* or File | New | click *Templates on Office Online*		
Project file, open	5	Click 📂 on the Standard toolbar	File | Open		Alt + F and O or Ctrl + O
Project Guide side pane, Show/Hide	10	Click ▦ on the Project Guide toolbar			
Project Guide Toolbar, show	38	Right-click on a toolbar and choose *Project Guide*	View | Toolbars | Project Guide		
Project, Save As, (copy)	8		File | Save As		Alt + F and A or Alt + F2

Project Task	Page	Mouse	Menu Bar	Shortcut Menu	Shortcut Keys
Report, preview	All		Report | Reports | select Category and click Select and then choose report		
Report, print	All		Report | Reports | select Category and click Select and then choose report | Print		
Resources, add using Outlook Address Book (from Resource Sheet view)	269		Insert | New Resource From | Address Book		
Resources, assign to a task (from Gantt Chart view)	109	Type resource name in the Resources Name field of desired task in the task table or Click [icon] on the Standard toolbar and choose the Resources tab or Click [icon] on the Standard toolbar, choose the resource name, and assign to the task	Tools | Assign Resources; click the resource name and click Assign		Alt + F10
Resources, change assignment units (from Gantt Chart view)	111, 116, 138	Double-click task, select Resources tab, and use spinner to change Units amount. Respond to smart tags appropriately, or Click [icon], select Resources tab, and use spinner to change Units amount	Project | Task Information	Right-click task and choose Task Information	
Resources, edit resource (from Resource Sheet view)	105	Double-click resource and make modifications, or click [icon]	Project | Resource Information	Right-click resource and choose Resource Information	

Project Task	Page	Mouse	Menu Bar	Shortcut Menu	Shortcut Keys
Resources, insert resource (from Resource Sheet View)	103	In Resource Sheet view, click in blank row, type resource name, press Tab⇄ to move to each successive field	Insert | New Resource		Insert
Resources, sort resources (from Resource Sheet view)	103		Project | Sort | click sorting preference		
Resources, unassign resource from task (from Gantt Chart view)	116	Select task, click ⬛ on the Standard toolbar, click resource name, and click Remove			Click in the Resource Names field for the task and press Del
Resources, view initials (from Gantt Chart view)	113		Select task(s) | Format | Bar | Bar Text tab; select Resource Initials in the Right position		
Route a project file	228		File | Send To | Routing Recipient | Address | Complete dialog box		
Routing slip, view (from e-mail program)	230	Double-click attachment to e-mail from e-mail program			
ScreenTip, view the summary task	12	Point and pause on the black Gantt bar			
ScreenTip, view the task relationships	16	Point and pause on the blue Gantt bar			
Send project to next routing recipient (assumes *One after another* option used)	230		File | Send To | Next Routing Recipient		
Send scheduled note message	231		File | Send To | Mail Recipient (as Schedule Note)		
Spell check	139	⬛	Tools | Spelling		F7
Split a task	183	Click ⬛ on the Standard toolbar		Right-click task and choose Split task	
Split bar, move	15	Click the bar and drag left or right			

Project Task	Page	Mouse	Menu Bar	Shortcut Menu	Shortcut Keys
Split, modify duration	187	Drag the right edge of the second Gantt bar to adjust the duration of the unfinished portion of task			
Split, modify resume date	187	Drag the second Gantt bar to adjust the resume date			
Split, remove	187	Drag one Gantt bar to touch the other			
Status Date, modify	44	Click *Set a date to schedule from* on the Tasks side pane	Project | Project Information		
Task Bar, view ScreenTip	12	Point and pause on the progress bar			
Task Information dialog box, view	13	Double-click on the task or Select task and click ⬛ on the Standard toolbar	Project | Task Information		⬆Shift + F2
Task notes, insert objects into	266	Double-click task, click Notes tab, click ⬛			
Task, create lag time	155	Click ⬛, Predecessors tab, type positive number (or '+' and a number) after the Predecessor listed in Lag column			

Project Task	Page	Mouse	Menu Bar	Shortcut Menu	Shortcut Keys
Task, create lead time	155	Click ▣, Predecessors tab, type negative number (or '-' and a number) after the Predecessor listed in Lag column			
Task, cut (with item selected)	69	Click ✂ on the Standard toolbar	**E**dit | Cu**t** Task	**Right-click task to cut | Cut Task**	Ctrl + X
Task, paste (with item cut or copied)	70	Click 📋 on the Standard toolbar	**E**dit | **P**aste	**Right-click task row where you want the task | Paste**	Ctrl + V
Task, specify duration	65	Click in the Duration column and type a number and the letter *D* for Day, *M* for Minute, *H* for Hour, or *W* for Week			
Task, view constraint dates	158		**V**iew | Ta**b**le: Entry | **M**ore Tables | select Constraint Dates | App**l**y		
Tasks side pane, view	11, 38	Click [Tasks ▾] on the Project Guide toolbar			
Tasks, collapsing	15	Click ▭ on Formatting toolbar, or click [-] beside summary task in the task table			
Tasks, enter actuals	151		**V**iew | **M**ore Views | select Task Sheet | App**l**y | **V**iew | Ta**b**le | **T**racking		
Tasks, enter new	68	Click *List the tasks in the project* on the Tasks side pane and begin typing in the Task Name column in row 1 or Click in the Task Name column from Gantt chart view in row 1 and begin typing	**I**nsert | **N**ew task	**Right-click any row selector and choose New Task**	Insert

Project Task	Page	Mouse	Menu Bar	Shortcut Menu	Shortcut Keys
Tasks, enter percent complete	147	Double-click task or click [icon], click General tab, use spinner to change Percent complete field	View | Toolbars | Tracking | use any percentage complete button		
Tasks, expanding	12	Click [+ icon] on Formatting toolbar, or click [+] beside task in the task table			
Tasks, set constraint date	158	Click [icon], click Advanced tab, click Constraint date drop-down arrow and choose constraint date	Project | Task Information | Advanced tab		
Tasks, set constraint type	158	Click [icon], click Advanced tab, click Constraint type drop-down arrow and choose constraint type	Project | Task Information | Advanced tab		
Tasks, set deadline	160	Click [icon], click Advanced tab, click Deadline drop-down arrow and select date	Project | Task Information | Advanced tab		
Tasks, view percent complete in task table (from Gantt chart view)	148	Point and pause on progress bar in Gantt chart to view ScreenTip	Insert | Column | % Complete	Right-click column heading, Insert Column, % Complete	
Tasks, view Task Usage	138	Click [Task Usage icon] on the View Bar	View | Task Usage		
Toolbars, show Formatting and Standard toolbars on two rows	5		Tools | Customize | Toolbars | Options tab; check *Show Standard and Formatting toolbars on two rows*	Right-click any toolbar | Customize | Options tab | Check *Show Standard and Formatting toolbars on two rows*	
View project statistics	192	Click [icon]			
View variance data (from Gantt Chart view)	143		View | Table: Entry | Variance		

Project Task	Page	Mouse	Menu Bar	Shortcut Menu	Shortcut Keys
View, change	All	Click desired view on View Bar	View	select desired view or More Views		
View, project progress	151		View	Tracking Gantt		
View Bar, turn it on	18		View	View Bar		
WBS code, define	81		Project	WBS	Define code		
WBS code, view	81	Double-click task and click the Advanced tab or Click on Standard toolbar and click the Advanced tab	Project	Task Information	Advanced tab		
Work, reschedule	185	Click on the Tracking toolbar			

GLOSSARY

All key terms appearing in this book (in bold italic) are listed alphabetically in this Glossary for easy reference. If you want to learn more about a feature or concept, use the Index to find the term's other significant occurrences.

Accrue At field   A field in the resource information that defines when a cost for a resource is incurred and when actual costs are charged to the project (start, end, or prorated).

actual duration   The field that shows the span of actual working time for a task so far, based on the scheduled duration and current remaining work or percent complete.

actual finish   The date when a task actually ends.

actual start   The date when a task actually begins.

actual work   The amount of work that has been performed on a task or assignment; also called *actuals*.

actuals   The amount of work that has been performed on a task or assignment; also called *actual work*.

append   A method of importing data into Microsoft Project that adds the data to the end of the active project file without the use of a primary key.

As Late As Possible (ALAP)   A constraint that allows you to start a task as near as possible to the scheduled project finish date.

As Soon As Possible (ASAP)   A constraint that allows you to start a task as soon as possible in relation to the scheduled start date.

assignment units   The percentage of a work resource's time, or units, that is allocated to a task.

attachment   A file that is included with an e-mail but is not part of the e-mail message.

base calendar   A calendar that can be used as a project and task calendar that specifies default working and nonworking time for a set of resources.

baseline   The original project plan (up to 11 per project) used to track the project's progress. It represents a "snapshot" of the schedule at the time that you save the baseline and includes information about tasks, resources, and assignments.

bottom tier   The bottom level of the timescale.

budget   The amount of money slated for the completion of a project plan.

Budget report   A report that lists all project tasks and costs.

Code field   A field in the Resource Sheet view that can be used to contain any type of custom data about a resource.

combination view   A view containing two views; the bottom pane view shows detailed information about the tasks or resources in the top pane view.

Comma Separated Values (CSV)   A file format in which each field is separated by a comma or semicolon.

consolidated resources   Multiple interchangeable resources with the same knowledge and skills concerning a project, such as a group of engineers; also called *group resources*.

constraint   A restriction set on the start or finish date of a task. For instance, you can specify that a task must start on or finish no later than a particular date. Constraints can be flexible (not tied to a specific date) or inflexible (tied to a specific date).

constraint icon   An icon that appears in the Indicator column if a task has a scheduling constraint.

constraint triangle   The three critical components of a project: budget, time, and scope.

controls   The various elements that comprise a view.

cost resource   Any resource that does not depend on the amount of work on a task or the duration of a task, such as travel expenses.

Cost/Use field   Resource field that assigns a flat rate or fee for the use of a resource that can be in place of, or in addition to, other cost variables. For work resources, a per-use cost accrues each time the resource is used. For material resources, a per-use cost is accrued only once.

count   The unit of time that appears between labels in the timescale.

critical path   The series of tasks that must be completed on time for a project to finish on schedule. Each task on the critical path is a *critical task*.

critical task   A task that, along with its predecessors, drives the overall finish date of the project.

crosstab report   A report in which the data are presented in column and row format with totals that can be applied to the column, the row, or both, like a spreadsheet.

current date   The system date that can be used as an optional start date for new tasks rather than the project start date and is the Microsoft Project 2007 default setting.

custom field   A field used to store unique data that can be any number, cost, text string, date, or even formula. Custom fields are used to track information that Microsoft Project, by default, does not monitor.

deadline   A target date indicating when you want a task to be completed.

default   A setting that a program uses automatically unless you specify a different setting.

default working time   The hours a resource normally works on a project.

deliverables   Tangible and measurable results, outcomes, or items that must be produced to complete a task or series of tasks.

destination file   The file where linked or embedded data are pasted.

duration   The total span of active working time that is required to complete a task—generally the amount of working time from the start to finish of a task, as defined by the project and resource calendars. The default duration is days, but you can change it to minutes, hours, weeks, or months.

earned value   The cost of work up to the status date.

effort-driven scheduling   The adjustments that Microsoft Project makes to lengthen or shorten the duration of a task based on the amount of resource units assigned to it, but without changing the total amount of work for the task.

embed   To create an object in a separate program and then insert it into a destination file; once embedded, the inserted object becomes part of the destination file.

entry bar   A toolbar that displays the contents of the current field.

entry table   The default task table used to enter and edit tasks.

export   To copy data from Microsoft Project to another software program.

field   A column of data that represents a category of information.

filter control   A control that limits or highlights those tasks for a view that fit the criteria.

Finish field   The date that a task is scheduled to be complete.

Finish No Earlier Than (FNET)   A constraint that requires a task to finish on or after a specific date.

Finish No Later Than (FNLT)   A constraint that requires a task to finish on or before a specific date.

Finish-to-Finish (FF)   A link in which a predecessor task finishes and the successor task also finishes.

Finish-to-Start (FS)   A link in which the successor cannot begin until the previous task or predecessor is complete.

fixed cost   A set cost for a task that remains constant regardless of the task duration or the work performed by a resource.

flexible constraint   A constraint that is not tied to a task on a specific date but rather takes into account other task dependencies and constraints.

Formatting toolbar   A toolbar that provides shortcuts to frequently used commands for changing the appearance of field contents.

Gantt bar   A horizontal bar within a Gantt chart showing task information, due date, and task dependencies.

Gantt chart   A project management tool that can be used to represent the timing of tasks required to finish a project and to measure the progress toward completing the tasks.

Gantt Chart view   The default view for a project; includes the task table and the Gantt chart.

global template (global file)   A collection of default settings controlling everything from startup view options to how Microsoft Project calculates formulas; the default global template for Microsoft Project is *global.mpt*.

Graphics Interchange Format (GIF)   A bitmapped graphics file format used by the World Wide Web.

group control   A control used to combine or rearrange tasks or resources in a project according to specific criteria, such as task duration, priority, resource overallocation, or finish date.

Group field   A resource field that provides a keyword to be used in sorting, grouping, and filtering resources.

group resources   Multiple interchangeable human resources with the same knowledge and skills concerning a project, such as a group of engineers; also called *consolidated resources*.

hyperlink   A clickable word or object that opens another file, e-mail message, or Web site.

hyperlink icon   An icon in the Indicator column that associates the resource or task to a Web page or document.

ID field   A field in the task information or resource information that contains an automatically supplied number used to identify a task or resource.

import   To copy data from another program into Microsoft Project.

Indicator column   A field in the task information or resource information that provides information about the state of a task or resource.

individual resource   An individual person or asset used as a resource.

inflexible constraint   A constraint that ties a task to a specific date.

Initials field   A field that provides a brief name for a resource in the Gantt Chart or Network Diagram views.

lag time   A delay between tasks that have a dependency.

lead time   An overlap between tasks that have a dependency.

leveling   An automatic Microsoft Project feature used to balance the workload for a resource by adding delays and splits in the project plan.

map   A set of instructions that defines the data you import or export, the order, and the destination fields in Microsoft Project into which the data will be imported or exported.

MAPI   Acronym for *Messaging Application Programming Interface,* the standard programming interface supported by Microsoft for accessing electronic messaging.

mapping grid   The columns of data that are to be imported or exported, along with the corresponding Microsoft Project field to which they will be mapped in the Export Wizard or Import Wizard dialog boxes.

Material Label field   A field in Resource Sheet view that defines the unit of measure (quarts, boxes, gallons, and so on) for material resources.

material resource   Any resource that is used up through the work involved in a task, such as gasoline.

Max. Units field   A field in Resource Sheet view that defines the maximum percentage, or units, that a resource is available to be scheduled for any tasks. The maximum units value indicates the highest capacity at which the resource is available for work; the default value is 100%.

menu bar   A toolbar that contains common menu items that, when activated, display a list of related commands.

merge   A method of importing data to the end of the active project file; requires a primary key.

middle tier   The middle level of the timescale.

milestone   A task that marks the completion of one or more tasks yet has no duration of its own. A milestone is a reference point marking a major event in a project and is used to monitor the project's progress.

module   Programming code that performs an action.

Must Finish On (MFO)   A task with an associated date that controls when the task finishes.

Must Start On (MSO)   A task with an associated date that controls when the task starts.

noncontiguous link   A join between tasks that are not adjacent.

nondefault working time   Work day hours that are not available for the project plan.

nonworking time   Any time that work is not being completed, such as holidays or vacation time.

note icon   An icon in the Indicator column that provides text about the resource that the user added.

object   In OLE, shared information that is compatible in format and can be used among different files and programs such as a Microsoft Graph chart or an Excel spreadsheet. The program used to create the object and the object type determines the programs that can be used to edit the object, as well as how it can be edited.

Object Linking and Embedding (OLE) A program-integration technology that you can use to share information between programs.

ODBC   Acronym for *Open Database Connectivity,* a compliant database format that Microsoft supports.

Organizer   A tool that allows you to copy Microsoft Project elements such as views, reports, and project base calendars between the open file and the global file.

overallocation icon   An icon in the Indicator column that reveals that a resource has too much work assigned to it for the time frame involved or has been assigned to two tasks at the same time.

overflow markers   Crosshatch characters (###) that indicate the entry in a field is too wide to fit in the column.

Overtime Rate (Ovt. Rate) field   A field in Resource Sheet view that assigns charges per unit of overtime work for a work resource.

paste link   An object or data created in a source file and inserted into a destination file; objects in the destination file are automatically updated to reflect changes in the source object.

percent complete   Term to denote how much of a task has been completed; expressed as a percentage.

phases   The major steps for a group of related tasks that are present throughout the project life cycle.

predecessor task   A task that must start or finish before another task can start or finish.

Predecessors field   A field that shows any tasks that must be considered before

calculating the start or finish date of the current task.

primary key   A field that uniquely identifies each task.

progress bar   A visual representation in a Gantt bar that depicts the progress of work on a task.

progress date   The date used to set a progress line. It can be the current date (computer clock) or the status date, which is user-specified in the Progress Information dialog box.

progress line   A vertical line added to the Gantt chart on a particular date of interest, including peaks to the left for tasks behind schedule and peaks to the right for tasks ahead of schedule.

project   A self-contained group of tasks performed to achieve a specific objective.

project calendar   The working days and hours, the number of hours in a given week, and any nonworking time such as holidays or vacation time used in a project.

project finish date   The date when a project is scheduled to be completed.

Project Guide   A side pane that is accessed from the Project Guide toolbar that provides step-by-step instruction to guide you through the process of creating and managing a project.

project manager   The individual who oversees all aspects of a project, including the assignment of tasks, resources, and budgeting.

project start date   The date when a project begins. By default, projects are scheduled from the project start date.

project statistics   Project data displayed in the Project Statistics dialog box—including the current project start date, project baseline data, the project finish date, the duration, work, and cost of the overall project.

Project Summary report   A report that outlines actual and baseline data for the overall project plan.

recipient   The person to whom you are addressing an e-mail message.

recurring task   A task that repeats with some pattern, such as weekly, monthly, or biweekly.

remaining duration   The amount of time left to work on a task before the task is completed.

remaining work   The amount of hours still required to complete a task.

render   To capture a picture of data.

resource   Anything needed to complete a task, such as an employee, a vendor, a conference room, a building, or equipment. Each task has at least one resource.

Resource calendar   A calendar assigned to each resource to reflect unique scheduling considerations such as the type of work day and vacation schedules.

resource cost   The costs incurred due to the expense of using a resource.

Resource Names field   A field that shows the resources assigned to work on the task.

resource pool   A set of resources available for assignment to project tasks. A resource pool can be used exclusively by one project or can be shared by several projects.

Resource Usage report   A report designed to provide assignment hours for each resource by week.

response pending icon   An icon in the Indicator column that shows a resource has not responded to an e-mail notification about task assignment.

resume date   The new start date for the rescheduled portion of a task.

Rich Text Format (RTF)   A file type used to transfer formatted text documents between applications.

routing   A way to send the project file to one or more individuals for comments and modifications and have the file returned to the originator after the routing recipients have reviewed the project.

routing slip   A project file that contains e-mail address information along with instructions and message text for the e-mail recipients.

schedule calculations   Values that Microsoft Project calculates, such as work hours. Schedule calculations are automatic by default but can be made manually, if necessary.

scheduled note message   Either a picture of selected tasks or an attached project file that is automatically addressed to members of the project team and sent as an e-mail message.

scheduling formula   The formula that Microsoft Project uses to schedule a task (*Duration = Work / Units*).

scope   The performance expectations (quality) of a project plan.

screen control   The underlying structure for an entire onscreen view.

scrollbar   A horizontal or vertical bar that enables you to move the project window vertically and horizontally so that you can see other parts of the work area.

scrollbox   A square object within a horizontal or vertical scrollbar that you can drag to move quickly within the window.

sheet view   The spreadsheet-like presentation of data, such as a task table.

side pane   A pane displayed on the left side of the Microsoft Project window. The side pane contains Project Guide information.

single view   A view such as the Gantt Chart view or Network Diagram view.

source file   The file where linked or embedded data originate.

split task   To divide a task by inserting a time delay, thereby creating two or more segments.

stakeholders   Individuals who have an interest in the success of the project plan.

Standard Rate (Std. Rate) field   A field in Resource Sheet view that assigns a charge per unit of normal working time for a work resource.

Standard toolbar   A toolbar that provides shortcuts to common tasks including Save, Print, Cut/Paste (Move), and Copy/Paste.

Start field   A field that specifies when the task is scheduled to begin.

Start No Earlier Than (SNET)   A constraint that schedules the task to start on or after a specified date.

Start No Later Than (SNLT)   A constraint that schedules the task to start on or before a specified date.

Start-to-Finish (SF)   A dependency in which, as soon as a predecessor task starts, the successor task can finish.

Start-to-Start (SS)   A dependency in which both the predecessor and successor task start at the same time.

status bar   The bar at the bottom of the Microsoft Project window that provides information about the current actions or settings.

status date   A date you specify when reporting progress information for a task or when calculating earned value totals.

subtask   A task that is part of a summary task.

successor task   A task that cannot start or finish until another task starts or finishes.

summary task   A task that is made up of subtasks and summarizes those subtasks.

table control   The list of fields you want in a view, determined by the screen that you choose.

task dependency   A dependency in which the start or finish of one task depends on the start or completion of another task; also called *task link*.

Task ID   An automatic number assigned to each task, shown on the left side of each row.

task link   A dependency in which the start or finish of one task depends on the start or completion of another task; also called *task dependency*.

Task Name field   A field that describes the task; it can contain up to 255 characters.

task pane   A window within an Office application that provides commonly used commands. Its location and small size allow you to use these commands while still working in the open file.

task table   A list of tasks displayed on the left side of the project window in Gantt Chart view.

tasks   Specific activities within a project that have a start date, duration, and completion time.

template   A model providing generic tasks and resources, which you can then modify to suit your individual project plan specifications.

time constraint   The deadline of the overall project as well as how much time each individual task requires.

timeline   The horizontal bar graph displayed on the right side of the Gantt chart.

timephased   Type of graph or chart that shows how tasks, resources, or assignments are distributed over time.

timescale   The time period legend appearing across the top of the Gantt chart.

title bar   A bar at the top of the Microsoft Project window that displays the name of the software and the name of the active project—either a default name, such as *Project1,* or a user-determined filename.

To-do List report   A report of the assigned tasks for a particular resource, including the week the task begins and the start date of the task.

toolbar   A set of buttons onscreen. Each button provides a shortcut to a frequently used command.

top tier   The top level of the timescale.

total cost   The sum of all resource costs and fixed costs.

Tracking Gantt view   A Gantt chart that displays a baseline Gantt bar beneath the current Gantt bar and highlights the critical tasks by displaying them in red.

Tracking toolbar   A toolbar used to update the percent complete for a task.

***Type a question for help* box**   A box at the right end of the menu bar in which you enter a keyword or phrase to specify a new Help topic or redisplay a previous Help topic.

Type field   A resource information field that identifies a resource as a work resource or a material resource.

unlink   To remove a task dependency.

Extensible Markup Language (XML)   Standard format used to publish Project 2007 data onto web pages.

wizard   A feature of Microsoft Office programs that guides you step-by-step through an activity.

work   The time assigned to a resource to complete a task; also represents the total labor required to complete a task.

Work Breakdown Structure (WBS) codes   The default outline numbers automatically assigned to each task that identify the task's hierarchical position within your project plan.

work resource   Any resource, such as a human resource, that contributes to the project through work and effort but is not used up by the task performed.

work unit   The amount of time it should take a resource to complete a task.

Working Days report   A report for printing a project's calendar, which displays the working days and times and any exceptions (the nonworking days).

working time   Any time that work is being completed. Working time may be the typical 8:00 A.M. to 5:00 P.M. time frame, but it can also include holidays and other nonworking times, such as evenings and weekends.

INDEX

SYMBOLS

(crosshatch) characters
 in task table columns, 66
% Complete column (task sheet)
 impact of actuals on, 154
% Complete column (task tables),
 149–150
.htm, .html file format, saving Project
 files in, 257, 276–277
.mpp files, 7
.xls (Excel) file format, saving Project
 files in, 253
24 Hours calendar, 39–40
 limits, 60

A

About Microsoft Project command, 24
Access, exporting Project files to, 253
Accountant resource
 Modifying overallocated work hours,
 116–120
Accrue At field (resource sheet), 102
actual duration calculations, 148
actual duration column (task sheet),
 152–154
actual finish date, 150
actual start date, 150
actual work column (task sheet),
 153–154
Actuals, 150–151
 comparing progress line to, 175
 entering on task sheets, 152–154, 165
 generating project statistics using, 191
 tracking progress using, 168
Add Progress Line button (Tracking
 toolbar), 178
Add Slip dialog box (Routing Slip dialog
 box), 229
Address Book dialog box (Routing Slip
 dialog box)
 selecting file recipients, 229
address books (e-mail)
 adding resources using, 269–270, 275
addresses
 e-mail
 adding to Resource Sheet, 233
 e-mail recipients, 227

routing recipients, selecting, 229
scheduled note messages, 232
adjacent tasks, selecting, 74
Advanced tab (Task Information dialog
 box)
 viewing constraints and supplemental
 information, 14
ALAP (As Late As Possible) constraint,
 45, 83
allocating resources, 100
 templates for, 133
Allow additional items to be entered into
 the field option (Custom Fields dialog
 box), 215
Always display current progress line
 option (Progress Line dialog box), 174
Analysis, expected versus actual
 costs/durations, 142
analysis tools, 172
 progress lines, 173
 *adding to Gantt charts, 174, 178,
 199*
 *comparing to baselines or actuals,
 176–178*
 display options, 174–175, 178
 spikes, 173
 summary tasks, 174–177
 project statistics, 191
 printing, 192–193, 201
 viewing, 192, 200, 203
 tracking critical tasks, 188–190, 200
 tracking progress against baseline,
 201–202
Append new entries to the value list
 option (Custom Fields dialog box), 215
Append the data to the active project
 option (Import Wizard), 249
appending data, 246
 Excel workbook example, 249
 task mapping, 249–252
As Late as Possible (ALAP) constraint,
 45, 83
As Soon As Possible (ASAP) constraint, 83
 changing constraint types to, 159
ASAP (As Soon As Possible) constraint,
 83
 changing constraint types to, 159
assets, identifying, 100

Assign people and equipment to tasks
 option (Project Guide toolbar), 113
Assign Resource dialog box
 creating resources, 113
Assign Resources button (Standard
 toolbar), 111
Assign Resources dialog box, 111
 Assign button, 112
 assigning resources, 112–113, 127
Assign Resources side pane (Project
 Guide)
 Assign resources link, 113
assigning resources
 modifying overallocated resources,
 116
 reviewing and modifying assignments,
 115–116, 127–128
 *overallocated resources, 116–120,
 128–129*
 summary tasks, 111
 using Assign Resources dialog box,
 112–113, 127
 using Project Guide, 113
 using Resource Names column, 110
Assignment Information dialog box
 adjusting work hours and durations,
 116–120
 Units option, 117
Assignment reports
 generating, 19
 previewing, 19
 printing, 19
 To Do Lists, 31
Assignment Reports dialog box, 19
 To-do List drop-down box, 31
 Who Does What option, 19
assignment units, 116
 modifying, 167
assignments
 tracking progress, 136
At project status date display option
 (Progress Line dialog box), 175
attachment (e-mail), 226
Auto Tile mode, 22–23
Auto Tile/Untile buttons (Project Help
 window), 23
AutoFit feature, 65
automatic rescheduling, 184–185